KIERKEGAARD AS A CHRISTIAN THINKER

C. Stephen Evans and Paul Martens
General Editors

The KIERKEGAARD AS A CHRISTIAN THINKER series seeks to promote and enrich an understanding of Søren Kierkegaard as a Christian thinker who, despite his many critiques of Christendom, self-consciously worked within the Christian tradition and in the service of Christianity. Volumes in the series may approach Kierkegaard's relationship to Christianity historically or topically, philosophically or theologically. Some will attempt to illuminate Kierkegaard's thought by examining his works through the lens of Christian faith; others will use Kierkegaard's Christian insights to address contemporary problems and competing non-Christian perspectives.

That Søren Kierkegaard profoundly influenced nineteenth- and twentieth-century theology and philosophy is not in doubt. The direction, extent, and value of his influence, however, have always been hotly contested. For example, in the early decades of the twentieth century, German theologians Karl Barth, Dietrich Bonhoeffer, and Emil Brunner all acknowledged deep debts to Kierkegaard, debts that would echo through the theological debates of the entire century. In spite of this, by the middle of the twentieth century, Kierkegaard was also hailed (or cursed) as a father of existentialism and nihilism because of his appropriation by Heidegger, Sartre, and others. At the same time, however, he was beginning to become the reveille for a return to true Christianity in North America through the translating efforts of Walter Lowrie and David Swenson. At the beginning of the twenty-first century, Kierkegaard's legacy is once again being seriously and rigorously debated.

While acknowledging and affirming the postmodern appreciation of elements of Kierkegaard's thought (such as irony, indirect communication, and pseudonymity), this series aims to engage Kierkegaard as a Christian thinker who self-consciously worked as a Christian in the service of Christianity. And, as the current discussion crosses the traditional boundaries of philosophy and theology, this series will necessarily do the same. What these volumes all share, however, is the task of articulating Kierkegaard's continuities with, challenges to, and resources for Christianity today. It is our hope that, in this way, this series will deepen and enrich the manifold contemporary debates concerning Kierkegaard and his legacy.

KIERKEGAARD AS A CHRISTIAN THINKER

Eros and Self-Emptying: The Intersections of Augustine and Kierkegaard
Lee C. Barrett

Kierkegaard and the Paradox of Religious Diversity
George B. Connell

Kierkegaard's Concept of Faith
Merold Westphal

KIERKEGAARD AND THE PARADOX OF RELIGIOUS DIVERSITY

George B. Connell

WILLIAM B. EERDMANS PUBLISHING COMPANY
GRAND RAPIDS, MICHIGAN / CAMBRIDGE, U.K.

Published 2016 by
Wm. B. Eerdmans Publishing Co.
2140 Oak Industrial Drive N.E., Grand Rapids, Michigan 49505 /
P.O. Box 163, Cambridge CB3 9PU U.K.

www.eerdmans.com

Printed in the United States of America

21 20 19 18 17 16   7 6 5 4 3 2 1

Library of Congress Cataloging-in-Publication Data

Connell, George, 1957-
Kierkegaard and the paradox of religious diversity / George B. Connell.
pages   cm. — (Kierkegaard as a Christian thinker)
Includes bibliographical references and index.
ISBN 978-0-8028-6804-6 (pbk. : alk. paper)
1. Kierkegaard, Søren, 1813-1855. 2. Religions. 3. Religious pluralism.
4. Cultural pluralism — Religious aspects. 5. Christianity and other religions. I. Title.

B4378.R44C66   2016
198'.9 — dc23

2015030833

Unless otherwise noted, Scripture quotations are from the New Revised Version
of the Bible, copyright © 1989 by the Division of Christian Education of the National Council of the Churches of Christ in the U.S.A., and used by permission.

To Ginny

Contents

Foreword

The group of problems related to religious pluralism certainly includes some of the major issues of our time, not just for theologians and philosophers of religion, but for any thoughtful person, especially someone committed to a particular religious tradition. How should a committed religious believer of one faith think about other faiths? How should such a person relate to those who profess a different faith or are committed to a different tradition? It is clear that the "secularization thesis," which held that religion was destined to die out and play no significant role in modern culture, has so far not panned out. Religions and religious conflicts are at the center of many of the most recalcitrant human struggles all over the world. Although the cluster of problems connected to these questions has been much discussed in recent years, a good deal of the discussion seems to have reached a stalemate. In particular, the partisans of "inclusivist" and "exclusivist" views of other faiths often seem to be talking past each other.

Few people would, I believe, immediately turn to Kierkegaard for help in thinking about religious diversity, but this is just what George Connell has done in this work. Kierkegaard was certainly a religious thinker, deeply Christian as the series title implies. However, on the surface Kierkegaard does not appear to have much to say about other religions (with the notable exception of Judaism). Rather, Kierkegaard seems to write in the context of "Christendom" and mainly address people who at least think of themselves as nominal Christians. Countering this surface impression, however, is the striking fact that people outside of Christendom have shown and continue to show deep interest in Kierkegaard's thought. It is worth noting, for example, that Kierkegaard was translated into Japanese before he was translated into English.

We think that George Connell has in this book shown that Kierkegaard can indeed shed new light and fresh air on the problems posed by religious pluralism. Connell makes no attempt to tidy Kierkegaard up and present a "theory of religions" or anything that resembles such a theory. Rather, he shows how Kierkegaard can help existing individuals wrestle with the tensions that emerge for those who see how essential genuine conviction and commitment are for religious faith, but also want to appreciate and respect the commitments of others. Kierkegaard can, for example, help us think through what we mean by "religious truth" and how such truth is related to pluralism.

In this work Connell also presents memorable readings of some important films that reflect Kierkegaardian themes, including questions about how the religious "individual" relates to the ethical ideals of a particular society. He thereby helps us rethink the role religion might play in public life, paradoxically by focusing on the religious "individual" who is willing to dissent from established ways of thinking. Connell shows us how Kierkegaard can help us rethink the very concept of a "religion," and he concludes with a suggestive cross-cultural comparison of the paths to authentic selfhood found in Kierkegaard and Confucius.

This work will not be the last word on the problems raised by the diversity of world religions. But it does, we think, show that Kierkegaard is a most helpful conversation partner for those who are thinking about these issues, especially those, like Kierkegaard himself, who are committed believers. Written in clear and engaging prose, this book will change the way its readers think not only about Kierkegaard but about religion and religions as well. It is exactly the kind of work we envisioned when we proposed this series. Readers will not only have their thinking challenged, but, if they are honest, their lives as well. And that is surely something Kierkegaard would have welcomed.

C. Stephen Evans
Paul Martens

Acknowledgments

This project began through my participation in the 2004 Lutheran Academy of Scholars Summer Seminar directed by the late Ronald Thiemann of Harvard Divinity School and DeAne Lagerquist of St. Olaf College. I gratefully acknowledge their valuable feedback on this project and more generally their roles in creating the vibrant intellectual community that characterized the Lutheran Academy of Scholars Summer Seminars year after year.

I also gratefully acknowledge Miroslav Volf of Yale Divinity School for his 2010 Summer Seminar on Religion and Globalization at Calvin College for valuable conversations and readings that enriched this project.

Thanks also to my former colleague, Matthew van Cleave, now at Lansing Community College, for thoughtful, probing comments on drafts of several chapters of this book. I benefited greatly from our conversations about philosophy of religion in general and the issue of religious diversity in particular.

I am grateful to the editors of this series, C. Stephen Evans and Paul Martens, both at Baylor University, for their feedback on drafts of this project. Their questions and comments were always constructive and challenging.

I gratefully acknowledge permission to publish modified versions of previously published essays:

"Transposing Transgression: Teaching *Fear and Trembling* through Danish Film," *Film and Philosophy* 13 (2009): 51-64.
"Kierkegaard and Confucius: The Religious Dimensions of Ethical Selfhood," *Dao* 8 (2009): 133-49.

Sigla

BA   *The Book on Adler,* trans. Howard V. Hong and Edna H. Hong. Princeton: Princeton University Press, 1998.

CA   *The Concept of Anxiety,* trans. Howard V. Hong and Edna H. Hong. Princeton: Princeton University Press, 1980.

CD   *Christian Discourses* and *The Crisis and a Crisis in the Life of an Actress,* trans. Howard V. Hong and Edna H. Hong. Princeton: Princeton University Press, 1997.

CI   *The Concept of Irony, together with "Notes on Schelling's Berlin Lectures,"* trans. Howard V. Hong and Edna H. Hong. Princeton: Princeton University Press, 1989.

CUP   *Concluding Unscientific Postscript to "Philosophical Fragments,"* 2 vols., trans. Howard V. Hong and Edna H. Hong. Princeton: Princeton University Press, 1992.

EO 1   *Either/Or,* Part One, trans. Howard V. Hong and Edna H. Hong. Princeton: Princeton University Press, 1987.

EO 2   *Either/Or,* Part Two, trans. Howard V. Hong and Edna H. Hong. Princeton: Princeton University Press, 1987.

FT   *Fear and Trembling* and *Repetition,* trans. Howard V. Hong and Edna H. Hong. Princeton: Princeton University Press, 1983.

JP   *Søren Kierkegaard's Journals and Papers,* 7 vols., trans. Howard V. Hong and Edna H. Hong. Princeton: Princeton University Press, 1967-78.

KJN   *Kierkegaard's Journals and Notebooks,* vols. 1-11, ed. Niels Jørgen Cappelørn, Alastair Hannay, David Kangas, Bruce H. Kirmmse, George Pattison, Vanessa Rumble, and K. Brian Söderquist. Princeton: Princeton University Press, 2007-.

Sigla

M   *The Moment and Late Writings,* trans. Howard V. Hong and Edna H. Hong. Princeton: Princeton University Press, 1998.

PC   *Practice in Christianity,* trans. Howard V. Hong and Edna H. Hong. Princeton: Princeton University Press, 1991.

PF   *Philosophical Fragments* and *Johannes Climacus,* trans. Howard V. Hong and Edna H. Hong. Princeton: Princeton University Press, 1985.

PV   *The Point of View,* trans. Howard V. Hong and Edna H. Hong. Princeton: Princeton University Press, 1998.

SKP   *Søren Kierkegaards Papirer,* vols. I to XI-3, ed. Peter Andreas Heiberg, Victor Kuhr, and Einer Korsting. Copenhagen: Gyldendalske Boghandel Nordisk Forlag, 1909-48. 2nd expanded ed., vols. I to XI-3, by Niels Thulstrup; vols. XII to XIII, supplementary volumes, ed. Niels Thulstrup; vols. XIV to XVI, index, by Niels Jørgen Cappelørn. Copenhagen: Gyldendal, 1968-78.

WA   *Without Authority,* trans. Howard V. Hong and Edna H. Hong. Princeton: Princeton University Press, 1997.

WL   *Works of Love,* trans. Howard V. Hong and Edna H. Hong. Princeton: Princeton University Press, 1995.

Introduction

The popular conception of Kierkegaard, bequeathed us by uncounted surveys of existentialism, frames him in the binary logic of Pascal's wager: believe or don't believe, leap or don't leap. Christian or atheist. Either/or. *Tertium non datur.*

Kierkegaard's actual writings defy this simplistic picture. His texts, instead, explore many ways of being religious. Socrates' irony, Judge William's civil religion, Johannes de Silentio's infinite resignation, Johannes Climacus's humor, the immanent religion of the Upbuilding Discourses, the transcendent religion of Anti-Climacus and the late non-pseudonymous works: all represent distinctive responses to the divine. Since Kierkegaard's authorship is itself marked by religious diversity, and since he spent the last year of his life attacking the monolithic cultural Lutheranism of Denmark, it is worth asking whether he can help us think through our own issues of religious diversity.

To reframe the question: Can Kierkegaard, that great connoisseur of anxiety, offer insight into an anxiety that pervades the contemporary spiritual landscape — anxiety over religious diversity? In a time such as our own of instant communication, mass migration, and global interconnection, the religious Other — or, rather, the many different religious Others — is pervasively and insistently present to us in ways that often evoke strong anxieties. Consciousness of religious diversity can easily overwhelm us with a sense of brute contingency: Had I been born in Mumbai or Medina rather than Macon, Georgia, presumably my religious identity would have been other than it is. Some deal with such a realization by skeptically distancing themselves from their own inherited religious identities (if they have one); others embrace one or another of the fundamentalisms on offer today in an attempt to escape the vertigo of religious uncertainty.[1] Instead of Pascal's either/or, our responses to religious pluralism seem to be framed by the options presented in William Butler Yeats's poem "The Second Coming." We seem pressed either toward a slack indifference in which religious belief is dismissed as a matter of personal preference or toward an intolerant dismissal of any whose faith differs from our own. As Yeats put it, "The best lack all conviction, while the worst/Are full of passionate intensity."[2] What can Kierkegaard say to us as we seek some better third alternative to Yeats's dire either/or?

For Kierkegaard, religious identity is, of course, appropriately an occasion for anxiety; faith, as he puts it, is to be out over 70,000 fathoms.[3] But the existence of multiple religions does not seem to have been much of an issue for Kierkegaard himself. Despite his withering critique of Christendom, Kierkegaard seems to radiate a Christian self-confidence as regards other religions that is a hallmark characteristic of that very Christendom. Within the pseudonymous authorship, the religious alternatives he explores are all permutations of the theistic framework associated with established Christianity. Both of the religious alternatives to Christianity that he seriously considers in his writings are ancient: the religion of classical Greece (which he labels paganism [hedenskab]) and the faith of biblical Judaism. While he had significant personal interactions with Denmark's small Jewish minority, Kierkegaard does not appear to have taken contemporary Judaism as a serious matter for reflection, regarding it as a faith superseded by Christianity.[4] Of Christianity's purported successor faith, Islam, Kierkegaard has little of substance to say. Where Luther's writings make significant references to Muslims (the Ottoman armies were after all before the gates of Vienna in his day), Kierkegaard's references to Muslims are most often to Oriental exotics from the pages of A Thousand and One Nights.[5] Of the great religions

1. On the idea of religious vertigo, see Maria Pia Lara, "In and Out of Terror: The Vertigo of Secularization," *Hypatia* 18, no. 1 (Winter 2003): 183-96.

2. William Butler Yeats, "The Second Coming," in *The Collected Poems of W. B. Yeats*, ed. Richard J. Finneran (New York: Simon and Schuster, 1996), p. 187.

3. This is an image used recurrently throughout Kierkegaard's writings. See, for example, *CUP* 1:140.

4. Peter Tudvad notes that, with the exception of Spinoza, writings by Jewish thinkers are absent from the Auction Protocol of Kierkegaard's library. *Stadier På Antisemetismens Vej: Søren Kierkegaard og Jøderne* (Copenhagen: Rosinante, 2010), p. 168.

5. In 1848, Kierkegaard makes a marginal comment on his notes from *A Thousand and One Nights:* "All of these stories are excellent and ought to be remembered" (*JP,* entry 4615). Quoted in *M,* 394.

of Asia, we find almost nothing in his writings, even though those religions were already part of the broader intellectual conversation of his day.[6] Kierkegaard's substantial neglect of contemporary religious diversity indicates that such faiths did not speak to him; they did not represent Jamesian "live options," and so their existence awakened no particular anxiety in him. The great critic of Christendom was nonetheless still part of Christendom and so was existentially distant from our distinctive anxieties as members of the multi-confessional world of post-Christendom.

But if we look again and look differently, we see that the question of religious diversity is always already present in Kierkegaard's thought and writings, even if in a different form than the one with which we are most familiar. For there is no single problem of religious diversity, just as there is no single problem of evil. Marilyn McCord Adams usefully distinguishes between an atheistic problem of evil, in which evil is considered as evidence against belief in the good and omnipotent God of theism, and an aporetic problem of evil, in which the theistic believer wrestles with apparent conflicts among beliefs to which she is deeply committed.[7] A parallel distinction can be drawn between fundamentally different versions of the problem of religious diversity. In his famous discussion of belief in miracles, Hume points to religious diversity as undermining the rational warrant of such belief; the conflicting reports of miracles offered by different faiths mutually discredit each other.[8] As in the case of the atheistic problem of evil, religious diversity is invoked as evidence against the truth of any and all particular religious beliefs. But, as in the case of Marilyn Adams's aporetic problem of evil, in which a believer asks how to reconcile apparently conflicting convictions, so can a believer committed to a particular faith ask within that faith how to understand the welter of different faiths so manifest in the world today.[9]

6. See, for example, discussions of Asian religion in G. W. F. Hegel, *Lectures on the Philosophy of Religion,* trans. and ed. Peter C. Hodgson (Oxford: Oxford University Press, 2006).

7. Marilyn McCord Adams, *Horrendous Evils and the Goodness of God* (Ithaca: Cornell University Press, 2000), pp. 7-8.

8. "[A]ll the prodigies of different religions are to be regarded as contrary facts, and the evidences of these prodigies, whether weak or strong, as opposite to each other." David Hume, *An Enquiry concerning Human Understanding,* 2nd ed. (Indianapolis: Hackett, 1993), p. 81.

9. Richard J. Plantinga gives a useful statement of an aporetic version of the issue of pluralism: "To focus on a group of people in the West for whom religious pluralism represents a particular challenge and conundrum, the position of dedicated adherents of the mainline, Western traditions caught in the vertigo of these modern and postmodern developments must now be considered. These believers — let us say, more particularly, Christian believers . . . — have not given up their faith and are very much committed to their religious traditions; but

For Kierkegaard, this aporetic problem of religious diversity takes the form of a sustained and multifaceted struggle to hold on to both universal and particular dimensions of human existence and divine revelation. This concern is pervasive in his entire authorship, but nowhere is it more vivid than in the first section of *Practice in Christianity*: "Come Here All You Who Labor and Are Burdened, and I Will Give You Rest."

In the first section of this discourse, "The Invitation," Anti-Climacus's whole focus falls on the word "all." Evoking the image of the crucified Christ, he vividly describes Jesus standing with open arms ready to embrace all without preference or condition: "[H]e who opens his arms and invites all — ah, if all, all you who labor and are burdened, were to come to him, he would embrace them all" (*PC*, 15).[10] Using repetition to underline key ideas, Anti-Climacus writes, "Come here, all, all, all of you; with him is rest" (*PC*, 19), and "Come here, come here all of you — and you and you and you, too, you loneliest of all fugitives" (*PC*, 16). The universality of Christ's saving intention sets him and his invitation in sharp opposition to prevailing society that is all about sorting people into categories and classes: "The invitation blasts away all distinctions in order to gather everybody together; it wants to make up for what happens as a result of distinction: the assigning to one person a place as a ruler over millions, in possession of all the goods of fortune, and to someone else a place out in the desert" (*PC*, 17).[11]

After vividly portraying the encompassing and unconditional character of the divine invitation, Anti-Climacus moves on in the next section, "The Halt," to portray vividly the dialectical counterpart to universality: radical

---

they often have difficulty putting biblical or theological confession ('Christianity is true and other religions are not, which spells dire eternal consequences for their adherents') together with existential or experiential confession ('Many non-Christian persons whom I know are highly moral and in their own ways devout — can their ultimate fate really be so bleak?')." Richard J. Plantinga, ed., *Christianity and Plurality: Classic and Contemporary Readings* (Oxford: Blackwell, 1999), pp. 3-4.

10. We find a similar declaration in "Two Discourses at the Communion on Fridays" (1851): "Allow me, however, to express only this, which in a way is my life, the content of my life, its fullness, its bliss, its peace, its satisfaction — this, or this view of life, which is the thought of humanity and of human equality; Christianly, every human being (the single individual), unconditionally every human being, once again, unconditionally every human being, is equally close to God." *WA*, 165. Jamie Ferreira discusses this passage in *Love's Grateful Striving: A Commentary on Kierkegaard's "Works of Love"* (Oxford: Oxford University Press, 2001), p. 47.

11. Sylvia Walsh highlights the universality of the invitation in her discussion of this passage in *Living Christianly: Kierkegaard's Dialectic of Christian Existence* (University Park: Penn State University Press, 2005), p. 64.

particularity: "That the inviter is and wants to be the specific historical person he was eighteen hundred years ago, and as that specific person, living under the conditions under which he lived at that time, he has spoken words of invitation" (*PC*, 23). Anti-Climacus insists that we come to terms with the particularity of the person of Christ:

> Let us talk about him quite frankly, just as his contemporaries talked about him and as we talk about a contemporary, a person just like ourselves, whom we see in passing on the street; we know where he lives, on what floor, what he is, what he does for a living, who his parents are, his kinfolk, what he looks like, what he wears, with whom he associates. . . . (*PC*, 40)

As we consider the particularity of Christ, we stand before the extraordinary, but not the extraordinary as we ordinarily understand it. With humans, that one exists is ordinary; one becomes extraordinary only by distinctive accomplishments. In contrast, when God comes to be as a particular person, it is this very particularity, the very fact of existing, that is the genuinely extraordinary: "But that God has lived here on earth as an individual human being is infinitely extraordinary. Even if it had had no results whatever, it makes no difference; it remains just as extraordinary, infinitely extraordinary, infinitely more extraordinary than all results." (*PC*, 31)

Though Anti-Climacus does not say a word in these passages about Christianity in contrast to Judaism or Islam or Hinduism or Buddhism, the issue of religious pluralism lurks massively just below the surface. For the very figure he invokes as an image of God's open-armed, all-embracing love, the figure of the crucified Christ, also stands as the devotional focus of a particular religious tradition, the Christian, and by its profound symbolic and historical associations unavoidably evokes deeply disparate responses from the wide range of individuals to whom his invitation extends. Inherent in the particularity, the specific individuality, of the person of Jesus is the scandal of disparate availability that seemingly runs counter to everything Anti-Climacus has to say about God's universal and undifferentiating love.[12]

12. For a very sharp and clear statement of this tension in Kierkegaard, see Gene Outka, "Equality and the Fate of Theism in Modern Culture," *Journal of Religion* 67, no. 3 (July 1987): 275-88. An earlier version of this paper was delivered at the 1983 Eastern Division meeting of the American Philosophical Association. I was present for that reading, and Outka's statement of this tension has stayed with me over the years and has significantly shaped my treatment

For, as he insists, here the helper is himself the help, even though that help appears very differently to those to whom he offers help. Accidents of time and space, the results of the birth lottery, allocate to individuals very different perspectives on this figure. Anti-Climacus gestures only occasionally and obliquely toward this issue, but what he says is striking. After stating emphatically that Christ's invitation goes out to all, Anti-Climacus locates responsibility for different responses squarely on the shoulders of the invitees: "How the single individual will understand the invitation he leaves up to the individual. His conscience is free, he has invited all who labor and are burdened" (*PC*, 14). As if to affirm this assignment of full responsibility to the invitees, Anti-Climacus reassures himself by asserting that "it is indeed certain enough that his name is proclaimed all over the world" (*PC*, 27). But, of course, the Christian imperative to preach the gospel everywhere remains an incomplete and deeply imperfect project. What is more, Anti-Climacus characterizes this very gospel in terms of its contrast with the religious traditions of most of humankind over most of history: he writes that when one leaves out the particularity of Christ, when one omits the distinctive feature of the Christian gospel, what one is left with is "paganism" (*PC*, 35).[13] So, the figure of Christ plays two dialectically opposed roles in Anti-Climacus's discussion: at one and the same time Christ embraces all as the incarnation of universal divine love and also fractures human solidarity by embodying the particularity of one religious identity in contrast to others.

This tectonic clash of universalist and particularist impulses that is so evident in *Practice in Christianity* runs like a fault line through all of Kierke-

---

of the issue of Kierkegaard and religious diversity offered in this book. See also Gene Outka, "Equality and Individuality: Thoughts on Two Themes in Kierkegaard," *Journal of Religious Ethics* 10, no. 2 (1982): 171-203. In addition, see M. Jamie Ferreira's discussion of equality in ch. 3 of *Love's Grateful Striving*. Ferreira (p. 47) quotes and discusses a passage from the preface to "Two Discourses at the Communion on Fridays" that captures this dialectical tension perfectly: "Christianly, every human being (the single individual), unconditionally every human being, once again, unconditionally every human being is equally close to God" (quoting *WA*, 165). Richard J. Plantinga offers a succinct but compelling reading of Christian Scripture (both Old and New Testaments) in terms of just this unresolved tension between universalist and particularist themes in ch. 1 of his *Christianity and Plurality*, pp. 11-25.

13. Stephen Evans usefully discusses Kierkegaard's use of the term "pagan" in *Kierkegaard's Ethic of Love: Divine Commands and Moral Obligations* (Oxford: Oxford University Press, 2004), p. 157. Evans notes that Kierkegaard characteristically uses the term to refer to the ancient Greeks, but Evans also notes wider use of the concept when distinctions are drawn between unspoiled pagans, spoiled pagans, and deluded pagans (pp. 114-17). I will discuss Kierkegaard's use of the term "pagan" in more detail in chapter 1.

gaard's writings on God and humans. God, for Kierkegaard, is the utterly other, the absolutely different, and thus is beyond all the particularities that characterize the created order. Unable to endure an awareness of such otherness, the religious imagination of humankind typically clothes the divine in gaudy, aesthetically appealing particularities through its characteristic idolatrous impulse (*PF*, 45). Thus, the universality of God is falsified by the human desire for particularity. But the unknowability of God implied by God's utter otherness also requires that God take the initiative in revealing Godself to us if we are to know and respond to God. And for Kierkegaard, that revelation characteristically comes in the form of particularities: a particular book, the Bible, and a particular person, Jesus.

Similarly, for Kierkegaard, the human self is caught in an essential dialectical opposition of particularity and universality. On the one hand, Kierkegaard insists that each of us is called to become the particular individual that we were created to be. To exist as spirit is to be aware that God knows us by name, as individuals, not merely as tokens of the type "human being." But the ethical and religious task of being a self is identical for all: while the external realm of social and physical interactions is subject to chance and full of inequalities of opportunities and results, Kierkegaard insists that when it comes to the essential task for each person, the ethical and religious task of becoming oneself, the differences between us disappear and we all face a single, universal challenge.

Critics of Kierkegaard no doubt perceive these contrasting claims as evidence of a failure on Kierkegaard's part to articulate clear and consistent positions on key issues. As King Lear puts it, " 'Ay' and 'no' too was no good divinity."[14] But for Kierkegaard, the unresolved tension between universality and particularity is enormously fecund; many of his key texts are explorations of just this dialectical opposition. *Either/Or* sets the self-indulgently idiosyncratic aesthete, A, over against the ethical Judge William, who calls on the wayward A to "realize the universal." *Fear and Trembling* stages an alternative confrontation of particular and universal by setting Abraham's exceptional duty to sacrifice Isaac over against the uniform duties that govern life on the plains below Moriah. The texts by Johannes Climacus, *Fragments* and *Postscript,* are structured around the juxtaposition of immanent religion, which assumes a universal eternal consciousness, with transcendent religion, which asserts that we only encounter the eternal as manifest in the particular moment, that we only relate to the divine as incarnated in a particular

14. *King Lear,* IV.vi.2708.

person. A similar juxtaposition runs through the discussion of revelation in *The Book on Adler,* in which Petrus Minor tells us that "Magister Adler's collision is easy to see: the collision of *the special individual with the universal*" (*BA,* 29). In *The Sickness unto Death,* Anti-Climacus makes the dialectical pairing of universality and particularity the basis of his theory of the self: on the one hand, he offers a universal structural framework — every human self is a relation that relates itself to itself — but key elements of this universal self-synthesis (e.g., finitude) consist in the specifics of the self's concrete particularity. And Kierkegaard argues in *Works of Love* that we fulfill our universal duty to love only by loving the particular neighbor before us.

Because Kierkegaard's thought is so pervasively structured around this juxtaposition of the particular and the universal, we can and indeed we must ask about its implications for our pressing issues of religious diversity. For the challenge presented by religious diversity is, at its core, a matter of balancing the demands of our particular identities, especially our particular religious identities, with the demands of our shared humanity, especially our common need to find ways to coexist harmoniously and appreciatively with people different from us. Whether through the large-scale relocations of contemporary life or through centuries-old patterns of settlement, members of different religious communities find themselves living side by side, interacting socially, economically, politically, and religiously. In this new age of instant communications, we are virtually living side by side with members of other religious communities beyond our physical locality, and this mode of presence carries with it its own forms of interaction. Will those interactions, both direct and electronically mediated, be harmonious and respectful or will they take the form of confrontation, contest, and exclusion?[15]

Many people of good will argue that societies can achieve harmonious coexistence only if their constituent religious communities minimize and/or fundamentally reappraise what is distinctive about themselves. Behind the pluralist philosophies of John Hick and Wilfred Cantwell Smith is a deep conviction that we must emphasize what is universal about our religious lives if religion is to be a force for peace and harmony rather than acrimony and

---

15. The relevance of this question was painfully reinforced when the Danish newspaper *Jyllands Posten* published a number of political cartoons depicting the prophet Muhammad. What seemed acceptable satire to many secularized Danes represented highly offensive blasphemy to their Muslim neighbors, both in Denmark and internationally. See Jytte Klausen, *The Cartoons That Shook the World* (New Haven: Yale University Press, 2009). In January 2015, two brothers identified with Al-Qaeda attacked the offices of *Charlie Hebdo,* a French satirical weekly, in response to similar cartoons.

war. Specifically, when Hick argues for moving from a Christocentric to a theocentric perspective, he accentuates what Christianity shares with other theistic faiths and demotes what is distinctive.[16] By the same logic, Hick is pushed away from "God-talk" toward the language of "ultimate reality" to avoid favoring theistic over nontheistic understandings of the object of religious devotion. In order to avoid contention-producing particularity, Hick moves toward a construal of the divine as a Kantian thing-in-itself, an object so general in character that every trace of particularity is bleached out.[17]

Corresponding to Hick's philosophical and religious movement from particularity to universality are a host of social and political developments that trace the same arc. We see this, for example, when John Rawls asks us to step behind the veil of ignorance, to abstract from all the particularities of our situations, our histories, our convictions (including religious convictions), in order to grasp the nature of justice.[18] It is this same trajectory that Thomas Friedman describes in *The Lexus and the Olive Tree*, where the Lexus symbolizes the enticing rewards of globalized standardization over against the rootedness in place and tradition symbolized by the olive tree.[19] Not least of the attractions of the Lexus is the implicit promise of a world harmoniously unified in a common consumer culture and so freed from conflict and war. This is the world Francis Fukuyama imagined in his already quaint prognostications in *The End of History and the Last Man*.[20]

In reaction to these universalizing tendencies, the twentieth century saw a wide array of movements whose impulse is particularist, which seek to

16. See, for example, his imaginative portrait of religious life in 2056: "In those sections of the universal church in which the pluralistic vision has become established, worship is explicitly directed to God, rather than to Jesus." John Hick, *A Christian Theology of Religions: The Rainbow of Faiths* (Louisville: Westminster John Knox, 1995), p. 136.

17. There are many critical discussions of this aspect of Hick's project, but Paul R. Eddy's "Religious Pluralism and the Divine: Another Look at John Hick's Neo-Kantian Proposal," in *The Philosophical Challenge of Religious Diversity*, ed. Philip L. Quinn and Kevin Meeker (Oxford: Oxford University Press, 1999), pp. 126-38, is especially useful in showing that the utter indeterminacy of Hick's "ultimate reality" undercuts his intended religious realism. Another critique, offered by Miroslav Volf, uncovers a sort of return of the repressed: Hick's deity is so abstract that worship of it leads back to religious tribalism. "The trouble is that an unknowable god is an idle god, exalted so high on her throne (or hidden so deep in the foundations of being) that she must have the tribal deities do all the work that every self-respecting god must do." Miroslav Volf, *Exclusion and Embrace* (Nashville: Abingdon, 1996), p. 44.

18. John Rawls, *A Theory of Justice* (Cambridge, MA: Harvard University Press, 1972).

19. Thomas L. Friedman, *The Lexus and the Olive Tree: Understanding Globalization* (New York: Farrar, Straus, Giroux, 1999).

20. Francis Fukuyama, *The End of History and the Last Man* (New York: Free Press, 1992).

return to the authentic specific identities of their faiths or nations or ethnic groups, which equate integrity with proudly affirming what is distinctive in those identities. To use Friedman's images, despite the glitz of the Lexus, the olive tree speaks to something deep in our souls. During the past century and now in the new millennium, almost every religious tradition has seen vigorous fundamentalist movements that seek to repristinate their faiths by zealously embracing what is distinctive about them.

What is true of the social dimension of religion has its counterpart in philosophy of religion. For example, in his critique of Hick's pluralism, Peter van Inwagen mockingly describes "a currently popular picture of what are called 'the World Religions'" that regards the various great religious traditions as "species of a genus."[21] The ideological point of this apparently inoffensive bit of classification is to valorize all that is purportedly universal in these religions and to deemphasize all that is particular. Speaking (derisively) in the voice of Hick and company, van Inwagen writes:

> What we can hope to see over the next couple of hundred years — as each of the great world religions becomes more and more separated from the geographical area in which it arose, and as the earth becomes more and more a single "global village" — is the sloughing off of the inessential elements of the world religions. And we may hope that among these discarded inessentials will be those particular elements that at present divide the world religions.[22]

Van Inwagen ends his restatement of Hick's pluralist vision by saying, "This is as much of the picture as I can bear to paint."[23] He goes on to offer his own theory of non-Christian faiths in terms of the specific commitments of Christian theology, especially the doctrine of original sin. Van Inwagen unapologetically acknowledges the specificity of his account: "I provide a perspective from which the traditional, orthodox Christian can view such topics as 'the world religions,' 'the scandal of particularity,' and 'religious pluralism.' I do not expect this theory to recommend itself to anyone who is not a traditional, orthodox Christian."[24]

21. Peter van Inwagen, "Non est Hick," in Rationality of Belief and the Plurality of Faith: Essays in Honor of William P. Alston, ed. Thomas D. Senor (Ithaca: Cornell University Press, 1996), pp. 216-17.

22. Van Inwagen, "Non est Hick," p. 218.

23. Van Inwagen, "Non est Hick," p. 218.

24. Van Inwagen, "Non est Hick," p. 219.

Hick's cosmopolitan religious dream is undeniably appealing with its prospect of a world freed from religious disrespect and conflict. In a very different but equally compelling way, van Inwagen's "muscular Christianity" has its own appeal, the appeal of a strong, uncompromising statement of a view that is theoretically powerful even if politically incorrect. But the very purity of both Hick's and van Inwagen's perspectives makes them ultimately suspect. There is something deeply inadequate about a one-sided focus on either the universal or the particular. As long as our options are framed in terms of a bland universalism and an assertive particularism, we are stuck in the Yeatsian either/or, making a Hobson's Choice between lack of robust conviction on the one hand and passionate religious tribalism on the other.

This is where Kierkegaard is able to speak a useful word to us. What I have sketched above and will develop in much more detail in subsequent chapters is that Kierkegaard, as a profoundly dialectical thinker, rejects any simple choice in favor of either the universal or the particular dimension of the human condition.[25] Throughout his works, he profoundly and sensitively investigates different ways selves negotiate living as both particular and universal at one and the same time. Because he lived in very different circumstances from our own, he did not apply his dialectical understanding to our question of how to live in community with people of other faiths. But the clear direction of his thought points us toward a vision of counterpoised particularity and universality. What are the implications of this vision? Does Kierkegaard's dialectical sense of counterpoised particularity and universality mean that, for Kierkegaard, fidelity to a specific faith should lead toward, not away from, mutual recognition of shared humanity, that delving more profoundly into the deepest sources of that faith should foster peaceful and appreciative coexistence rather than fomenting discord, that faithfulness invites us to attend with equal seriousness to the common convictions that unite as well as to the contrasting beliefs that distinguish one faith from another?

I believe the answer to these questions is yes. The reading of Kierkegaard on the issue of religious diversity that I will advance aligns in broad spirit

---

25. Merold Westphal effectively captures the sense in which Kierkegaard is a dialectical thinker: "[A]s the realm of opposition and contradiction, the dialectical is the realm of difference, otherness, alterity; and as the region in which the fixed determinations of thought dissolve in a flux that permits neither immediacy *(alpha, archè)* nor ultimacy *(omega, telos)*, it is a region of undecidability. It is the deconstruction of the desire to bring thought to a close and thus to the repose of eternity rather than the restlessness of time." Merold Westphal, *Becoming a Self: A Reading of Kierkegaard's "Concluding Unscientific Postscript"* (West Lafayette: Purdue University Press, 1996), p. 37.

with Jonathan Sacks's *The Dignity of Difference: How to Avoid the Clash of Civilizations*. Like Kierkegaard, Sacks argues for a vision of counterpoised particularity and universality. Also like Kierkegaard, he complains of a deeply rooted and long enduring philosophical bias against particularity that Sacks traces back to Plato:

> [A] certain paradigm that has dominated Western thought, religious *and* secular, since the days of Plato is mistaken and deeply dangerous. It is the idea that, as we search for truth or ultimate reality, we progress from the particular to the universal. Particularities are imperfections, the source of error, parochialism, and prejudice. Truth, by contrast, is abstract, timeless, universal, the same everywhere for everyone. Particularities breed war; truth begets peace, for when everyone understands the truth, conflict dissolves. How could it be otherwise? Is not tribalism but another name for particularity? And has not tribalism been the source of conflict through the ages?[26]

Against this bias for the universal, Sacks calls for a return to balance that will require recognizing "the dignity of difference," that is, the inherent value and essential role of distinctiveness, specificity, and particularity not only in the religious but in other spheres of life as well:

> It is time we exorcized Plato's ghost, clearly and unequivocally. Universalism must be balanced by a new respect for the local, the particular, the unique. There are indeed moral universals — the Hebrew Bible calls them "the covenant with Noah" and they form the basis of modern codes of human rights. But they exist to create space for cultural and religious difference. . . . The proposition at the heart of monotheism is not what it has traditionally been taken to be: one God, therefore one faith, one truth, one way. To the contrary, it is that *unity creates diversity.* The glory of the created world is its astonishing multiplicity: the thousands of different languages spoken by mankind, the hundreds of faiths, the proliferation of cultures, the sheer variety of the imaginative expressions of the human spirit, in most of which, if we listen carefully, we will hear the voice of God telling us something we need to know. That is what I mean by *the dignity of difference.*[27]

26. Jonathan Sacks, *The Dignity of Difference: How to Avoid the Clash of Civilizations* (New York: Continuum, 2003), pp. 19-20.

27. Sacks, *The Dignity of Difference*, pp. 20-21.

Here, Sacks emphasizes the particular not in contrast to the universal but as its necessary dialectical counterpart. For Sacks, understanding and accepting this juxtaposition are challenging (he calls this a "large and difficult idea"),[28] but he argues that only by holding the universal and the particular in tension do we have a chance of defusing Samuel Huntington's predicted "clash of civilizations."[29] Since Kierkegaard is a thinker of Sacks's "large and difficult idea" par excellence, looking at the issue of religious diversity through the lens of his thought is one way to move toward the paradigm shift Sacks advocates.

The parallelism of Sacks and Kierkegaard is both encouraging and instructive. For Sacks, an Orthodox rabbi, and Kierkegaard, a Lutheran Christian, move toward their visions of counterpoised particularity and universality by calling on the specific resources of their particular religious traditions. Sacks's argument, explicitly presented for an audience not just of fellow Jews but of people of other or no faiths, robustly calls on the specific resources of the Hebrew Bible and of Jewish religious tradition in presenting a case for a world of mutual appreciation among people of strongly differing viewpoints. Similarly, Kierkegaard calls upon specific biblical and theological resources in ways that sharply distinguish him from prevailing philosophical practice. Contrary to Richard Rorty's claims that reference to specific religious convictions and texts is a "conversation stopper," Kierkegaard, like Sacks, opens up those specific resources in ways that invite broader conversations.[30] This practice augers well for the prospect of articulating a constructive Kierkegaardian understanding of religious diversity.

Before I sketch out my plan for developing such a Kierkegaardian understanding of religious diversity, I need to address at least six foreseeable objections to my project. These objections can be succinctly labeled arguments from pseudonymity, anachronism, silence, misreading, suspicion, and unacceptable risk.

1. *Pseudonymity:* There are long-running disputes in Kierkegaard scholarship over the ultimate significance of Kierkegaard's pseudonymous approach to writing many of his books, some scholars even insisting that we treat the purportedly non-pseudonymous works as written by the pseudonym "Søren Kierkegaard," a figure as independent of the actual Kierkegaard

---

28. Sacks, *The Dignity of Difference*, p. 21.

29. Samuel Huntington, *The Clash of Civilizations and the Remaking of World Order* (New York: Simon and Schuster, 1996).

30. Richard Rorty, "Religion as a Conversation-stopper," *Common Knowledge* 3, no. 1 (Spring 1994): 1-6.

as any of the other pseudonyms. Clearly, one cannot blithely attribute to Kierkegaard any and all statements made by his various pseudonyms. That said, Kierkegaard leaves us a body of writing that offers a coherent if complex vision of the human condition. It is unconvincing to cite pseudonymity as an a priori reason to refuse to ask about the implications of Kierkegaard's thought for religious diversity. Clearly, one cannot take all texts in the same way. When citing, for example, something that Johannes de Silentio says in *Fear and Trembling,* it will be important to take the particularities of that pseudonym into account in contrast to the way we can read Kierkegaard's comments in *Works of Love* or Anti-Climacus's comments in *Practice in Christianity.* No blanket policy can productively inform the development of a Kierkegaardian perspective on religious diversity, but I have sought to remain attentive to the particular difficulties posed by Kierkegaard's pseudonymous style of writing as I discuss particular texts.

2. *Anachronism:* To have Kierkegaard speak relevantly to the issue of religious diversity requires transposing his thought from its actual situation, the Christendom of nineteenth-century Europe, into the fundamentally different context of religious diversity we face today. Christendom is the horizon against which all specific themes in Kierkegaard's writings are foregrounded. To place his specific statements against a fundamentally different horizon, religious diversity, is arguably to change the meaning of those specific statements. Since Kierkegaard is a situational and polemical thinker, shaping his writing to context, rather than an abstract, systematic philosopher, such a transposition is problematic, at best, and perhaps hopelessly anachronistic. Over the past several decades, a number of Kierkegaard scholars have shown how engaged with his local Danish context Kierkegaard was.[31] To call on the particularity-universality pairing discussed above, Kierkegaard incorporates his own particular context so deeply into his thought that it arguably resists transposition into our own particular context.

I agree with this challenge without seeing it as a reason not to proceed. The specific character of Kierkegaard's writings does resist such a transposition. But that is not to say that such a transposition is impossible or unfruitful. There is plenty of precedent for creative application of Kierkegaard's thought to situations unfamiliar to Kierkegaard himself. Kierkegaard remains a living and relevant thinker just to the extent he remains able to help us think through novel situations and challenges.

---

31. For a good example of this trend, see Bruce Kirmmse, *Kierkegaard in Golden Age Denmark* (Bloomington: Indiana University Press, 1990).

Further, serious consideration of religious diversity was part of the intellectual landscape well before Kierkegaard's time. Kierkegaard's enthusiasm for Lessing is familiar to every reader of the *Concluding Unscientific Postscript,* and it was, of course, Lessing's *Nathan the Wise* that framed the question of relations between the three Abrahamic religions in a way that has captured imaginations since its publication in 1779. Further, Kierkegaard studied Schleiermacher closely in his preparation for his theological examinations. Schleiermacher explicitly considers the issue of religious diversity in both his *On Religion* and *The Christian Faith,* arguing for a hierarchical view of faiths that places Christianity decisively above both paganism and Judaism, a tripartite pattern of classifying religions that we will see echoed in Kierkegaard's writings. Clearly, the issue of religious diversity is not an anachronism in the sense that the issue would have been unfamiliar or inconceivable to Kierkegaard.

3. *Silence:* That Kierkegaard was familiar with the issue of religious diversity as framed by Lessing and Schleiermacher, among others, but chose not to address the issue in an extended, explicit way might be given as a reason not to venture in where Kierkegaard himself chose not to tread. As I noted above, the issue of other religions does not seem to have been a major worry for Kierkegaard. Given his sense of the paradoxical character of the Christian faith, he would not have been impressed by Hume's argument that the miracle claims of *other* faiths decreased the calculated probable truth of Christianity. But as in the case of other topics, Kierkegaard does have substantial things to say on this issue even though he does not lay out a treatment of the issue in the way a systematic philosopher or theologian might. My task here is to draw on a variety of texts to show that Kierkegaard does have a coherent if implicit view on the question of religious diversity. Beyond pulling together what he does say, I have tried to trace out what he might have said, or, more plausibly, how we might think about this issue on the basis of our ongoing readings of Kierkegaard. To that extent, I hope to bring a silent dimension of Kierkegaard to voice, even if it would be a voice that might surprise him.

4. *Misreading:* To admit, as I have, that I intend to offer an imaginative, constructive reading of Kierkegaard on this issue, to go beyond what he does actually say to construct a "Kierkegaardian" understanding of religious diversity, raises questions about the appropriate latitude of the interpreter. To a significant degree, Kierkegaard himself disarms this objection. In *Point of View for My Work as an Author,* he disowns any privileged access to the meaning of his texts. He asks that we evaluate his overall interpretation of

his authorship by gauging its hermeneutic fit and fecundity.[32] As such, it is appropriate to discern a Kierkegaardian understanding of religious diversity if that proposed understanding similarly fits the texts and leads to helpful insights. That said, a possible objection remains: there is significant evidence both in his writings and in the testimony of contemporaries that Kierkegaard held what would be classified today as exclusivist views on the status of the various religions. To the extent that I develop a view other than straightforward exclusivism on the basis of my reading of his texts, am I not willfully misreading him? Given Kierkegaard's own views of the independence of the text from the author and also given his understanding that thinkers often have a deeply obscure grasp of the full implications of their own thought, I unapologetically offer a Kierkegaardian interpretation of religious diversity that declares a certain degree of independence from the conscious thoughts of the man Kierkegaard. I will devote the first chapter to reconstructing as far as possible Kierkegaard's own thoughts on the topic, but thereafter I propose to follow the implications of his thought where they take me.

5. *Suspicion:* In discussing the previous objection, I mentioned Kierkegaard's sense of the obscurity of human subjectivity, that is, the degree to which we are often mysteries to ourselves. In the murky twilight of self-deception, a hermeneutics of suspicion is called for, and such a hermeneutics might turn its gaze not only on my project but on the broader enterprise of philosophical pleas for harmonious coexistence of diverse religious communities. But what person of good will could raise a question about such a noble and necessary goal? Beyond question, Kierkegaard was willing to cast a suspicious gaze at all manner of noble goals that quicken the pulse of democratic liberals such as myself. Let us not forget his disparaging comments about democracy, freedom of the press, and women's equality. It seems plausible that were he to view the philosophical and theological industry that today brings forth so many publications in support of religious coexistence, he would suspect that economic and political interests operate behind the curtain. A bland pluralism that allows different peoples to keep their various faiths in an unobtrusive, privatized manner serves the interests of the globalized economic system, just as Kierkegaard noted that Christendom served the existing social

32. "*[Q]ua* author it does not help very much that I *qua* human being declare that I have intended this and that. But presumably everyone will admit that if it can be shown that such and such a phenomenon cannot be explained in any other way, and that on the other hand it can be explained at every point, or that this explanation fits every point, then the correctness of this explanation is substantiated as clearly as the correctness of an explanation can ever be substantiated." *PV,* 33.

and economic order of his day. To what extent do those of us who teach in contemporary colleges and universities use classroom discussions of religious diversity to divest our students of angular, inconvenient, particular religious convictions that might interfere with their smooth and efficient functioning as producers and consumers in the global economic structure? Even if we remain convinced of the need for interreligious dialog and understanding, it is good to have some Kierkegaardian suspicion of the way such noble ideals can serve less noble agendas. Keeping in view what Sacks calls "the dignity of difference," that is, keeping a dialectical tension in place between religious particularity and universality, can serve to keep us skeptical about the homogenizing agendas that serve corporate and national interests.[33]

6. *Unacceptable risk:* For many readers, to look to Kierkegaard to valorize particularity, especially religious particularity, is to open a Pandora's Box of divisiveness and discord. Where assertiveness about particular national identity fueled many of the conflicts of the nineteenth and twentieth centuries, present conflicts, like their sixteenth- and seventeenth-century predecessors, seem to be driven especially by assertive religious particularisms. Tensions between Islam and the West have grown significantly in the decades since the 1967 Arab-Israeli War that discredited the secular Arab nationalism of Nassr and helped inspire a widespread return to more assertive forms of Islam. Similarly, ultra-orthodox Judaism has driven national policies in Israel in directions that have persistently frustrated efforts to broker a just and lasting peace with the Palestinians. Resurgent Hinduism in India has transformed the political scene there, leading to interreligious violence between Hindus and Muslims and raising questions about India's identity as a secular democracy. Pakistan's formation through its separation from India as a specifically Islamic state continues to have fateful, often conflictual implications. Looking at the associations between assertive religious particularity and rising conflict, is it really advisable to enlist Kierkegaard in the issue on the side of particularism?

In fact, he has already been so enlisted. On November 13, 2009, Søren Krarup, the leader of the Tidehverv theological movement and a member of the Danish parliament from the ultra-right Dansk Folkeparti (Danish People's Party), specifically invoked Kierkegaard as providing the ideological basis for a nativist immigration policy. In an Op-Ed piece in a leading

33. Kierkegaard discusses a gap between the rhetoric of equality and the reality of distinctness in *WL*, 77. For an especially vigorous example of a hermeneutics of suspicion directed at religious pluralism, see Kenneth Surin, "Towards a 'Materialist' Critique of 'Religious Pluralism': A Polemical Examination of the Discourse of John Hick and William Cantwell Smith," *The Thomist* 53 (1989): 655-74.

Danish newspaper, *Politiken,* Krarup starkly summarizes an argument he made in an earlier book for the idea that Marx and Kierkegaard represent two fundamentally opposed ways of thinking between which Danes must choose in confronting the immigration issue:

> [I]t is all about the concept of existence. It all actually takes its departure point in Søren Kierkegaard's understanding of what it means to be human. It is all about how human life is about guilt and responsibility, not about ideology and utopia and the worship of progress.
>
> What is it to be human? In . . . *The Modern Breakdown,* I drew a line in Danish and European intellectual history with Søren Kierkegaard and Karl Marx as the two decisive opponents. I could just as well say Christianity and humanism. . . .
>
> Kierkegaard and Christianity preach respect for "the singular individual," the existing human being. Humanism and Marxism on the other hand denote contempt for the individual in the name of the idea and progress.
>
> Immigration in Denmark grossly disregarded consideration for the Danes. Svend Auken & Co. [i.e., the Social Democrats] were busily occupied taunting and chastising those Danes who could not rise above their increasingly intolerable conditions on the streets and staircases. It was "racism" when the tormented and concerned Danes cried for help. It was the "racist" Danes, which . . . the ideological Pharisees made into the problem.
>
> But reality is real. . . . The Danish population's needs and fears would not be abolished by Svend Auken's indignation over the Danes.
>
> Existence was real, and the real meaning of the change of system is the expulsion of abstract ideological lies by existential reality.
>
> The Danes had had enough of empty phrases! The Danes reacted spontaneously, immediately, yes, existentially to the threatened life they had come to live under immigration policy [when they voted in a Center-Right coalition, including the Danish People's Party in 2001].

Krarup sums up his message with a starkly simple plea: "Say yes to Kierkegaard and no to Marx."[34]

---

34. I first found this text at http://culturalmeanings.wordpress.com/2009/12/08/107/ and the quoted translation is from that site. The original Danish text of Krarup's editorial can be found at http://politiken.dk/debat/kroniker/article831285.ece.

Krarup's Kierkegaard/Marx opposition on the issue of individuality versus social identity is certainly familiar, but the leap from respect for the individual to xenophobic immigration policy seems a stunning non sequitur. When we make explicit Krarup's oblique reference to "intolerable conditions on the streets and staircases" as a comment on Denmark's Muslim immigrants, we face the disturbing reality that Kierkegaard is being invoked in support of ugly ethnic and religious rhetoric and policies. To non-Danish readers, this linkage is so implausible as to solicit immediate dismissal. For progressive Danes, any comments by "the black priest," as Krarup is labeled, are likely to be dismissed with equal speed. But Krarup's invocation of Kierkegaard's name is not something we should dismiss lightly, for Krarup speaks as the undisputed leader of the Tidehverv movement. Since its founding in 1926 by a group of young neo-orthodox theologians, Tidehverv has been identified as the Kierkegaardian wing of the Danish church. Stylistically, it has always been marked by harsh polemics that recall Kierkegaard at his most vituperative; and, substantively, figures associated with Tidehverv, especially K. Olesen Larsen, one of the movement's founders, have explicitly grounded their thought in Kierkegaard's writings.[35] The most significant Danish ethicist of the twentieth century, K. E. Løgstrup, was long involved in the movement, but broke with it at the same time he articulated a critique of Kierkegaard's account of the Christian obligation to love the neighbor. Given over eighty years of close, deep, and very public association between Kierkegaard and the Tidehverv movement, Krarup's appeal to Kierkegaard to validate Danish People's Party policies and rhetoric cannot be left unanswered.

Fortunately, Krarup makes it easy to debunk his appeal to Kierkegaard. It is hard to imagine anything less Kierkegaardian than Krarup's defense of the state church and his opposition to immigration as threatening Denmark's identity as a Christian culture. One wonders whether Krarup has read *The Moment* and the other texts from Kierkegaard's final attack on Christendom. Or, for that matter, whether he has noticed the derision Kierkegaard heaps on N. F. S. Grundtvig for his enthusiasm about the church as a locus of specifically Danish cultural identity.

But that leaves one to wonder why Krarup insists on the Kierkegaardian basis of his views. Is it completely imaginary, or is there some real aspect of Kierkegaard's thought that Krarup is twisting to make it support exclusionary policies? I think there is a real basis: the valorization of particularity. The Ti-

---

35. K. Olesen Larsen, *Søren Kierkegaard læst af K. Olesen Larsen* (Copenhagen: Tidehverv, 1966).

dehverv movement began as a rejection of the bland, sentimental pietism of the Student Christian movement of the 1920s. In place of a general linkage of Christianity, morality, and civilization, the founders of Tidehverv promoted a sharp, specific gospel message based on readings of Luther and Kierkegaard, thus emphasizing particularity of the Christian gospel over generic religiosity. Their formulation of Lutheranism, with its message of sin, forgiveness, and responsibility, led the Tidehverv theologians to an ethical particularism: ethics does not involve obedience to general rules but responsibility for the particular Other before one. This ethical particularism obviously follows the direction of Kierkegaard's *Works of Love.* The fullest flowering of this particularist tendency comes in K. E. Løgstrup's *The Ethical Demand,* a book that deserves more attention in English-language philosophy and theology than it has so far received. But where Kierkegaard and Løgstrup keep the focus squarely on the human Other before one, a number of the Tidehverv thinkers expand this idea of particular responsibility to one's particular place in the world. N. Otto Jensen, one of the movement's founders, wrote thus in 1930:

> All of God's creation is good, and the stance humans are obligated to take toward it is therefore thankful joy. But that one is obligated shows that there is no talk at all about natural inclination, about whether one enjoys one's situation or not. It is not the self's satisfaction but the created person's guilt before his Creator that matters. The stance toward creation is the same as to the neighbor. I have not chosen him, being around him may annoy me, he may compete with me, but he is given to me, and I shall love him. I have not chosen the existential situation I have been placed in [*Jeg har ikke valgt den Tilværelese, jeg er stillet i*], but whether it suits me or not, I shall love it, such as it is, and know that here is my place [*Plads*].[36]

For the early Tidehverv thinkers, this vivid notion of *place* works to root humans in the here and now of reality as opposed to an abstract elsewhere of ideals. Citing Eduard Thurneysen, Karl Barth's early collaborator, Jensen speaks approvingly of *Dennesidigheden,* literally of "this-sideness," which seems an anticipation of Bonhoeffer's notion of a purely this-worldly faith.[37]

This powerful existentialist and neo-orthodox anti-idealism, this robust attempt to couch the concept of facticity in terms of a Lutheran understand-

36. In *Tidehverv: En Antologi,* ed. Leif Grane (Copenhagen: Gyldendal, 1967), p. 22. (My translation.)

37. *Tidehverv: En Antologi,* p. 26.

ing of creation, is an authentic extension of Kierkegaard's legacy into the twentieth century. But, under the impact of increasing immigration that began in Denmark in the 1960s and intensified in the 1980s and 1990s, this concept of place has shown itself to be terribly vulnerable to misuse. Krarup, especially after 1986, has used the idea of God's assigning each human a particular existential situation as the basis for a nativist politics and rhetoric. This usage is undoubtedly tendentious and selective, using a Kierkegaardian trope to support the very Christendom Kierkegaard railed against. It has, however, succeeded beyond all reasonable expectation. When I first attended a Tidehverv summer meeting in 1980, the movement was, as it had always been, a small but vocal part of the Danish religious scene. When I visited again in 1991, the movement had become much more politicized and contentious, taking a strong stance not only against immigration but also against Danish involvement in the European Union. By 2001, Krarup and another Tidehverv figure, his cousin Jesper Langballe, as parliamentary representatives of the Danish People's Party entered into a Center-Right coalition that displaced a more progressive government from power.

And so, an ideology with undeniable Kierkegaardian lineage has played a crucial role in sharpening tensions between Christians and Muslims in Denmark, unfortunately contributing to a general pattern of suspicion, misunderstanding, and limited integration into society that prevails among Muslim immigrant populations throughout Western Europe.

It was with this backdrop in mind that I said earlier that we not only may but must ask the question of the implications of Kierkegaard's thought for the question of religious diversity. Does Kierkegaard's multidimensional emphasis on particularity leave his thought irremediably prone to the sort of exclusivist use to which Krarup puts it? Or does the dialectical tension Kierkegaard himself maintains between the universal and the particular poles of the human condition, specifically the human religious condition, guard against such use? Should specific religious traditions deemphasize what is distinctive about themselves, moving, as Philip Quinn puts it, toward "thinner theologies"?[38] Or does the concrete richness of the specific faiths offer ethical and religious resources to promote respectful and harmonious relations with religious Others that thinner theologies simply lack? In these either/ors lies the twofold task of this book: on the one hand, to use the issue of religious diversity to read Kierkegaard in fresh ways; and on the other hand, to use

---

38. Philip L. Quinn, "Toward Thinner Theologies: Hick and Alston on Religious Diversity," in Quinn and Meeker, eds., *The Philosophical Challenge of Religious Diversity*, pp. 226-43.

Kierkegaard to prompt us to think anew about the pressing issues of living both peacefully and authentically in a world of religious difference.

In chapter 1, I approach these tasks directly by looking at what Kierkegaard, both in his own voice and through his pseudonyms, says explicitly about other religions and their relation to Christianity. Since Kierkegaard never takes on this issue in a systematic way (as, for example, Schleiermacher does), this will involve pulling together a variety of passages from a wide range of texts from the early journals to the late non-pseudonymous works.

While developing a Kierkegaardian understanding of religious diversity requires beginning with Kierkegaard's direct statements about other faiths and their relation to Christianity, it cannot stop there. What Kierkegaard writes specifically on the matter of other religions is too fragmentary and scanty for a purely direct approach to succeed. Accordingly, in the remaining chapters I will proceed indirectly, constructing a Kierkegaardian understanding of religious diversity by focusing on the issues such diversity raises and asking what Kierkegaard has to say about them. In his survey article for *The Oxford Handbook of Philosophy of Religion,* Philip Quinn identifies four prominent philosophical challenges posed by religious diversity.[39] He divides these challenges into two broad categories:

Familiar Problems	Novel Opportunities
Epistemological Conflict: How should we understand the conflicting truth-claims of the various religions? Do these conflicting truth-claims mutually destroy the rational warrant of those claims? Is there a way to understand these apparently conflicting claims as somehow mutually compatible?	**Definitions of Religion**: Can we state the necessary and sufficient conditions for being a religion such that our definition captures the full range of human religions without also including other nonreligious phenomena?
Religious Intolerance: What is religion's role in fomenting intolerance and violence? What understanding(s) of religion can ameliorate such tendencies?	**Constructive Comparisons**: How can balanced comparisons of different religions contribute to a deeper understanding both of particular religions and of religion as a broader phenomenon?

39. Philip L. Quinn, "Religious Diversity: Familiar Problems, Novel Opportunities," in *The Oxford Handbook of Philosophy of Religion,* ed. William J. Wainwright (Oxford: Oxford University Press, 2005), pp. 392-417.

Quinn's classification is admirably lucid in its own right, but it is also ideal as a way of framing the issue of Kierkegaard and religious diversity, for each of Quinn's four questions suggests natural links to Kierkegaard's philosophical and theological reflections. Accordingly, I will devote chapters 2 through 5 to posing Quinn's four questions in a Kierkegaardian manner and asking what resources Kierkegaard offers to respond to those questions.

In chapter 2, I ask what perspective Kierkegaard brings to the vexed question of the conflicting truth-claims of the various religions. To ask this question, is, of course, to bring Kierkegaard's (in)famous declaration that "truth is subjectivity" immediately to the fore. If this phrase represented the straightforward statement of relativism it is often taken to be, then Kierkegaard's relevance to the conflicting truth-claims of various religions would not be far to seek: each believer who authentically believes the articles of faith of his or her religion would believe truly. As truth is, on such a view, purely a matter of conviction, the issue of conflicting truth-claims advanced by different religions would disappear (unless a particular believer tried to believe the conflicting claims of multiple religions simultaneously).

Such a simplistic reading of the phrase "truth is subjectivity" does not, however, bear scrutiny. Once it is cleared away, the deeper significance of Kierkegaard's slogan becomes available. In saying that "truth is subjectivity," Kierkegaard problematizes the relation of the believer to the belief. Drawing on Kierkegaard's theory of moods, I will reframe the question of conflicting claims from an objective form (which of these views is true?) to one that is subjective in Kierkegaard's sense of the term (given the existence of incompatible truth-claims by the various religions, what stance toward them should I take?). Specifically, I will argue that Kierkegaardian humor represents an existential stance toward religious diversity that has significant advantages over the moods of seriousness and irony that lie behind exclusivism and pluralism, respectively.

While Kierkegaard's theory of truth puts in question Quinn's separation of epistemological from ethical-political dimensions of religious diversity, chapter 3 focuses in particular on the implications of Kierkegaard's thought for the issue of peaceful coexistence of differing religious groups. On the one hand, there is much in Kierkegaard that reassures on this front. Kierkegaard is so concerned about each individual's personal responsibility for his or her own convictions that he rejects direct communication of religious beliefs. How then could he countenance using power of whatever sort to impose beliefs on others? Further, Kierkegaard's account of neighbor love in *Works of Love* specifically enjoins love of the Other who is not like one.

Where preferential love seeks out some favored form of likeness in the beloved, neighbor love loves the Other as genuine other. That would clearly include the Other who differs from one in religious faith as well as class or educational level or nationality.

All that said, there is nonetheless a pressing concern as regards Kierkegaard and religious violence. In the aftermath of 9/11, Kierkegaard's treatment of the Akedah, of God's command that Abraham sacrifice Isaac, must give us pause. Johannes de Silentio's discourse of absolute obligation, of suspension of ethical norms, and of the impossibility of rational explanation raise troubling questions about the use to which *Fear and Trembling* might be put. Accordingly, I devote chapter 3 entirely to asking what stands in the way of reading *Fear and Trembling* in such a way as to legitimate religious violence. With the help of several Danish films inspired by *Fear and Trembling*, I argue that this text, which Kierkegaard regarded as his masterpiece, cannot be plausibly invoked as an apologetic for terrorist religious violence.

While the first two of his questions have long philosophical pedigrees, Quinn believes that our new conditions of interreligious awareness and interaction create new philosophical opportunities. Specifically, he highlights the issues of defining religion and of constructively comparing different religions to each other. In chapter 4, I take up the definitional issue by looking at Kierkegaard's use of the concept "religion." Using the term "religion" as the genus of which the various faiths are the species was a relatively recent linguistic and philosophical practice in Kierkegaard's day. And it was a practice about which he seems to have been ambivalent. On the one hand, Kierkegaard and his pseudonyms treat religion as a universal human phenomenon, describing religious life as a spiritual possibility entirely independent of any specifically Christian message. Such strong statements about the ultimate equality of all humans indicate sympathies to religious pluralism. On the other hand, Kierkegaard and his pseudonyms speak of Christianity as a reality that is not only *sui generis* but is specifically opposed to all other forms of religious life. This appears to underwrite exclusivist views of both truth and salvation. In the dialectical tension between the universalism of his account of immanent religion and the particularism of his treatment of transcendent religion (Christianity) lies the genius of Kierkegaard's treatment of this matter: as we examine the broad and variegated phenomena of human religious life, we must hold in unresolved tension the family resemblances of those faiths and their particular, individual, distinctive features.

Cultivating a simultaneous awareness of similarity and difference invites comparison, and Quinn makes a strong case for comparative philosophy of religion as an area of particular promise today. I explore that promise as it relates to Kierkegaard in chapter 5 by placing him in comparison to the ancient Chinese thinker Confucius. Through this single juxtaposition, I hope to raise more general questions about the prospects and perils of such comparisons.

CHAPTER 1

Pagans and Jews: Kierkegaard's Religious Others

A Hermeneutic Preamble

If we were, *per impossible,* to transport Kierkegaard from his own religious situation into the kaleidoscopic religious world we inhabit today, it is hard to know what his reaction would be. Perhaps he would welcome the demise of Christendom (assuming that reports of its death, like Mark Twain's, are not greatly exaggerated). Perhaps he would be surprised at how much he missed even nominal commitment to, knowledge of, and interest in the Christian faith as a social given. Surely he would feel disoriented by the variety and even exoticism of faiths on offer today. When confronted by the case of a lone eccentric religious visionary, Adolph Adler, a Lutheran pastor from the Baltic island of Bornholm, Kierkegaard wrote but never published a whole book on the questions Adler's case posed *(The Book on Adler).* What questions would the more florid manifestations of the contemporary religious scene spark in his mind?

I raise these counterfactual speculations about a time-traveling Kierkegaard only to highlight their fecklessness. In writing this study on Kierkegaard and religious diversity, I am not only or even principally interested in recovering Kierkegaard's own mindset on other faiths. Rather, I want to ask what we see when we look at our own pluralistic religious context through the lenses of Kierkegaard's texts, concepts, theories, and themes. Kierkegaard the man belongs to his native nineteenth century. He is the appropriate object of concern for biographers and historians. Kierkegaard's texts, in contrast, are living documents whose meanings emerge in ongoing encounters between author, text, and readers, where changing reading contexts bring to the fore different configurations of significance.[1]

A review of the history of Kierkegaard reception reflects how differently Kierkegaard's texts have been read in different times and contexts. Kierkegaard's discussions of anxiety had a distinctive resonance for those of us who grew up under the threat of nuclear Armageddon. While Kierkegaard was an archetypal existentialist for readers in the 1950s, he emerged as a postmodernist *avant la lettre* by the 1980s. At a recent Kierkegaard Conference at St. Olaf College, a young Romanian scholar spoke movingly of the earthshaking significance Kierkegaard's category, the individual, had for him as he suffered through the dark final years of the Ceausescu regime, that at a time when emphasis on the individual was becoming passé in Western philosophical circles. Kierkegaard's discussion of the Akedah has a changed resonance after 9/11, just as his often harsh comments on Judaism read differently after Auschwitz.

In light of these and many more examples of emerging and shifting significance, I propose to ask how we should read Kierkegaard in our own pluralistic religious context. I will, that is, practice a Gadamerian hermeneutic, reading Kierkegaard's texts as much constructively as descriptively, asking what these texts mean for us today rather than what Kierkegaard had in mind at the time he wrote them.[2] I undertake this study with a strong conviction that Kierkegaard's texts are not captive to the more religiously homogeneous context within which they were written, that they prompt us to ask about and look at our very different religious situation in fruitful ways, and that we can find in his writings important suggestions about how to combine authentic religious conviction with respectful coexistence with people of other faiths or no faith at all.

While subsequent chapters of this study will undertake this simultaneously constructive and interpretive project, I devote this first chapter to

1. David Possen makes the point that Kierkegaard's own approach to biblical interpretation reflects such a hermeneutic: "[Kierkegaard's] goal is not to *interpret* the above lines [Matt. 6:24-34] in their first-century Judean context, but to *apply* them to his own nineteenth-century Danish 'Christendom.'" Possen, "On Kierkegaard's Copenhagen Pagans," in *International Kierkegaard Commentary*, vol. 17: *"Christian Discourses" and "The Crisis and a Crisis in the Life of an Actress,"* ed. Robert L. Perkins (Macon, GA: Mercer University Press, 2007), p. 35.

2. For a helpful introduction to hermeneutics in general and Gadamer in particular, see Merold Westphal, *Whose Community? Which Interpretation? Philosophical Hermeneutics for the Church* (Grand Rapids: Baker, 2009).

a more purely descriptive project, one shaped by an interpretive approach more in the spirit of E. D. Hirsch than H. G. Gadamer.[3] To borrow terms from constitutional law, I plan to proceed as a "strict constructionist" in this first chapter before offering "living text" readings in subsequent chapters. Why the shifting hermeneutics?

Before moving on to constructive readings of Kierkegaard's texts, it is important to establish a sense of Kierkegaard's own understandings of and attitudes toward other faiths and their adherents. In order to appreciate the vitality of Kierkegaard's texts, we need to have a sense of the distance between our constructive readings of them and the ways they would have resonated in his own time. Reconstructing at least in broad outline Kierkegaard's understandings of his "religious Others" will help us to acknowledge appropriately the ways our own readings of his texts have developed in response to our massively changed circumstances.

Pagan-Jew-Christian: Kierkegaard's Schema of Religions

Scandinavia's greatest contribution to biology is surely Carl Linneaus, the developer of modern taxonomy. Scandinavia's greatest contribution to philosophy and theology, Søren Kierkegaard, displays a taxonomic impulse parallel to that of his Swedish predecessor. Kierkegaard's theory of the stages, the basic organizing principle of his thought and writings, boldly presumes to classify *all* manifestations of human life into three encompassing categories: the aesthetic, the ethical, and the religious. When faced with forms of life, such as irony and humor, that do not fit neatly into any of the three "existence spheres," Kierkegaard designates them as "confinia" that he places at the boundaries between the spheres, thus giving them a definite location in his categorial scheme.[4] Kierkegaard's taxonomic impulse also directs his presentations of the particular spheres: *Either/Or's* depictions of aesthetic existence are structured by a distinction between immediate and reflective forms, just as the Climacus texts explore religious existence by differentiating between "Religiousness A" (immanent religion) and "Religiousness B" (transcendent religion). Anti-Climacus's *The Sickness unto Death* offers a sort of periodic chart of despair with the classifications emerging directly out of the theory

---

3. E. D. Hirsch, *Validity in Interpretation* (New Haven: Yale University Press, 1967).

4. See John Lippitt, *Humor and Irony in Kierkegaard's Thought* (London: Macmillan, 2000).

of selfhood laid out at the start of the book. Kierkegaard repeatedly affirms that the mark of a good dialectician is careful delineation of categories, and categories are ways of ordering the world.

To make sense of Kierkegaard's statements about non-Christian religions and their adherents, we need to appreciate that Kierkegaard situated these "religious Others" either explicitly or implicitly within a strikingly simple tripartite scheme: pagan-Jew-Christian. One could multiply passages at great length, but I will cite two on the theme of suffering, one quoted by Sylvia Walsh and another by Bruce Kirmmse in their discussions of Kierkegaard's tripartite scheme:

> Reconciling oneself to unavoidable loss is also seen in paganism. Reconciling oneself to unavoidable loss in such a way that one not only does not lose faith in God but in faith worships and praises his love — that is Jewish piety. But to give up everything *voluntarily* — that is Christianity. (*CD*, 178)[5]

> The pagan will not suffer at all. The Jew will endure [suffering] for a number of years, but nonetheless desires to be a victor in this world and to enjoy life. The Christian will suffer his entire life. (*JP* 3, 4700)[6]

The two passages are somewhat divergent in their content, but both display the way Kierkegaard characteristically identifies the distinctively Christian by setting it over against Christianity's "near Other" (Judaism) and "far Other" (paganism).[7] The specific character of the scheme changes at various points in Kierkegaard's writings; at times the scheme represents three

---

5. Sylvia Walsh quotes and discusses this passage in *Living Christianly: Kierkegaard's Dialectic of Christian Existence* (University Park: Penn State University Press, 2005), p. 127.

6. Bruce Kirmmse quotes and discusses this passage in "Kierkegaard, Jews, and Judaism," in *Kierkegaardiana*, vol. 17, ed. Joakim Garff, Arne Grøn, Eberhard Harbsmeier, Bruce H. Kirmmse, and Julia Watkin (Copenhagen: C. A. Reitzel, 1994), p. 87.

7. My labels "near Other" and "far Other" echo the Soviet terminology of the "near abroad" and the "far abroad" that entered English as familiar terms in the 1990s. See William Safire's discussion of the terms in his "On Language" column in the *New York Times* from May 22, 1994 (http://www.nytimes.com/1994/05/22/magazine/on-language-the-near-abroad .html). "Near" and "far" in my use of the terms here have multiple dimensions: Judaism is the "near other" both in the sense that Christianity is deeply connected with Judaism, sharing history and sacred texts, and that Jews were geographically near, living as a religious minority in Kierkegaard's Copenhagen. Pagans, in contrast, are "far" temporally (the ancient Greeks) and geographically (non-European religious Others).

robustly distinct options, while at other times paganism and Judaism tend to merge as an undifferentiated Other to Christianity.[8] While there are such changes of emphasis, the habit of juxtaposing paganism, Judaism, and Christianity is deeply engrained in Kierkegaard and informs his thinking even when he is speaking exclusively about one or the other of Christianity's two "religious Others" (as he counts them).

Kierkegaard's reliance on this tripartite scheme represents a significant "stumbling block" for contemporary readers. First, the catch-all character of the term "pagan" is highly problematic. The idea that all religions other than the historically interconnected Jewish and Christian faiths belong in a single undifferentiated category is implausible on its face. This category effectively lumps together the polytheisms of ancient Greece and Viking Scandinavia with nontheistic religions such as Buddhism and Daoism and even with non–Judeo-Christian monotheisms such as Ramanuja's Vishishtadvaita Vedanta. The overt omission of Islam from the scheme is striking even in Kierkegaard's day. That Kierkegaard could categorize so many different forms of religious faith in an undifferentiated mass indicates that he was not really very interested in them for their own sakes but spoke of them only so as to illuminate Christianity. As he puts it starkly, "Paganism forms the opposition to Christianity" (CD, 9).

Second, the term "pagan" is decidedly pejorative; it occupies the same semantic space as "infidel" and is a counterpart to "heretic": the incorrectly believing religious outsider is a pagan even as the incorrectly believing religious insider is a heretic.[9] Kierkegaard's lumping all non–Judeo-Christian faiths under a single negative label leads Karen Carr to question his value as a guide to thinking about other faiths: "his strict, even unrelenting, focus on Christianity and characterization of all other religious paths as 'paganism' suggest that Kierkegaard scholarship has little to contribute to discussions of religious pluralism. Certainly, Kierkegaard himself seems little concerned with this issue."[10]

8. After discussing Kierkegaard's tripartite scheme, Kirmmse writes, "But there is also a development toward a *dualistic* structure, a two-stage either/or: *either* paganism, Judaism, or whatever. As time goes by this shift becomes quite clear." Kirmmse, "Kierkegaard, Jews, and Judaism," p. 87.

9. Summarizing Jan Assman's work, Eric Santner writes, "Monotheism . . . because grounded in (revealed) scripture, tends to erect a rigid boundary between true religion and everything else, now rejected as 'paganism.'" Santner, *On the Psychotheology of Everyday Life: Reflections on Freud and Rosenzweig* (Chicago: University of Chicago Press, 2001), p. 3.

10. Karen Carr, "Sin, Spontaneity, Nature and God: Comparative Reflections on Kierke-

Third, while Kierkegaard recognizes Judaism as a specific faith, he places it as an intermediate, transitional stage in a teleological process that culminates in Christianity. Thus, Kierkegaard's tripartite scheme succinctly expresses a supersessionist Christian theology that poses a challenge to interfaith dialog.[11] Further, Kierkegaard's placement of Judaism in his scheme involves a homogenization of complex phenomena parallel to his inclusion of all non–Judeo-Christian faiths in the single category "pagan"; as Peter Tudvad stresses, Kierkegaard makes no differentiation between biblical Judaism (in all its varied forms) and the Judaism of mid-nineteenth-century Copenhagen.[12]

Having acknowledged that Kierkegaard's framework for thinking about other faiths raises problems for contemporary readers, I turn to asking why he adopted it. What motives and what influences lie behind his paradigm for thinking about varied religious phenomena?

First, as a deeply biblical thinker, Kierkegaard reflects Pauline categories in his tripartite schema. A passage central to Kierkegaard's thought is 1 Corinthians 1:23: "but we proclaim Christ crucified, a stumbling block to Jews and foolishness to Gentiles [ἔθνεσιν]." In neighboring verses, the Gentiles are specifically identified as Greeks, but in this verse Paul uses the generic biblical term for non-Jews, *ethnos* (ἔθνος). Danish translations of the New Testament render *ethnos* as *Hedning*, which the Hongs translate as "pagan" but which Swenson and Lowrie sometimes render with the cognate English term "heathen." Finding this tripartite scheme "ready to hand" in Paul's epistles, Kierkegaard easily adopts it.

Second, Kierkegaard's taxonomy of religions parallels his theory of the stages so closely that the two schemas clearly influence each other. In a journal entry from 1847, Kierkegaard writes, "The pagans believed that the gods claimed revenge as their exclusive property because it was sweet; the Jews think revenge belongs to God because he is just; the Christians, because he is merciful" (*JP* 4, 6044). Bruce Kirmmse writes of this passage, "Kierkegaard's remarks fit in nicely with his well-known theory of stages: the Aes-

---

gaard and Zhuangzi," in *Acta Kierkegaardiana*, vol. 5: *Kierkegaard: East and West* (Toronto: Kierkegaard Circle, Trinity College, and Šalià, Slovakia: Kierkegaard Society in Slovakia, 2011), p. 109. Carr argues for overcoming this initial resistance in order to study Kierkegaard in comparison with kindred spirits from other religious traditions, specifically the Daoist Zhuangzi.

11. For a critical discussion of Christian supersessionism, see R. Kendall Soulen, *The God of Israel and Christian Theology* (Minneapolis: Fortress, 1996).

12. Peter Tudvad, *Stadier på Antisemitismens Vej: Søren Kierkegaard og Jøderne* (Copenhagen: Rosinante, 2010), p. 166.

thetic *(sweetness)*, the Ethical *(justice)*, and the Religious *(mercy)*."[13] Kirmmse then references another journal entry in which Kierkegaard specifically uses the term "stages" *(Stadier)* to describe the "Gradations in the Relationship to God" represented by paganism, Judaism, and Christianity *(JP* 2, 1433).

From his earliest to his latest writings, Kierkegaard presents paganism as a religious manifestation of aestheticism. In 1838, he writes, "Paganism is the sensuous [*sandselig*], the full development of the sensuous life" *(JP* 3, 3059). This association is just as clear in his 1855 attack on the Danish church when he writes that clerics enjoy "the most select refinements, for which the pagan has in vain had itchy fingers" *(M,* 21).[14]

The association of Judaism with ethical existence is less consistent; at times, especially in his later years, Kierkegaard collapses paganism and Judaism as two corollary forms of worldly self-indulgence.[15] Still, from his Lutheran theological perspective, Kierkegaard naturally associates Judaism with the law over against Christianity's message of grace, making the Judaism–ethical stage association almost inevitable.[16] Kierkegaard associates Judaism with a focus on family and children, an emphasis (somewhat) shared by Kierkegaard's iconic ethical self, Judge William.[17] It is evident that Kierkegaard's theory of stages and his taxonomy of religions are parallel and mutually reinforcing. What is most striking is that Kierkegaard assimilates major religions to his theory of stages not principally by placing them within the religious stage but by aligning them with the apparently pre-religious existential stages.

Beyond biblical sources and his theory of stages, the whole intellectual context within which Kierkegaard moved reinforced a broadly triadic classification of religions, more or less along the lines he proposes. Peter Tudvad identifies quite a list of now largely unfamiliar figures who proposed a pagan-Jewish-Christian developmental scheme: Johann Rosenkranz, Immanuel Fichte, Leopold Rückert, Johann Billroth, August Twesten,

---

13. Kirmmse, "Kierkegaard, Jews, and Judaism," p. 87.

14. Kierkegaard associates dissoluteness (Lowrie translates as "lewdness") and brothels (Lowrie translates as "whorehouses") with paganism. Lowrie's alliterative phrase, "pleasure-loving pagans" *(AC,* 158), is replaced in the Hongs' more recent translation with "the indulgent pagan" *(M,* 178).

15. Kirmmse, "Kierkegaard, Jews, and Judaism," p. 89.

16. See, for example, *EO* 1:150, where A contrasts the "ethical maturity" of Judaism with the "esthetic ambiguity" of the Greeks. In *Concept of Anxiety,* Vigilius Haufniensis writes, "It is usually said that Judaism is the standpoint of the law." *CA,* 103.

17. Tudvad, *Stadier på Antisemitismens Vej,* p. 249. While Judge William speaks in glowing terms about family life, he rejects the idea that raising children is the goal of marriage.

and Philipp Marheineke (whose lectures Kierkegaard attended during his 1841-42 residence in Berlin).[18] While this list shows how pervasive the basic idea of a developmental religious taxonomy was, we should pay particular attention to two thinkers whose articulation of such a scheme had significant direct influence on Kierkegaard: Friedrich Schleiermacher and Hans Lasson Martensen (Kierkegaard's tutor, professor, and ultimately adversary).[19]

In *The Christian Faith,* Schleiermacher organizes religious phenomena into triads within triads. His most basic triad is fetishism-polytheism-monotheism. Fetishism is marked by idol worship, the worship of a sensible object regarded as having a limited field of power, interest, and sympathy. Where fetishism's objects are particular and local, polytheism rises toward a sense of the totality of the divine through its worship of an ordered system of deities. Only with monotheism does the essential unity of the divine emerge, and therefore Schleiermacher without hesitation ranks monotheism above the other modes of religious consciousness. Since, for Schleiermacher, religious faith is the feeling of ultimate dependency, that feeling can never gain full development when focused on a particular object within the world (fetishism) or a pantheon above but still part of the world (polytheism). Only in monotheism can piety "express the dependence of everything finite upon one Supreme and Infinite Being" and therefore "the monotheistic forms occupy the highest level; and all others are related to them as subordinate forms, from which men are destined to pass to those higher ones."[20]

Schleiermacher's eagerness to rank faiths extends into the domain of monotheisms, where he places Judaism lowest, "Mohammedanism" intermediate, and Christianity highest. He argues for this triadic ranking by invoking the previous one: Judaism, with its notion of God's particular selection of Israel as the chosen people, smacks of fetishism; Islam, because of its "passionate character" and "influence of the sensible," manifests residual polytheism, leaving Christianity as the monotheistic monotheism.[21] Obviously, Schleiermacher's charge of residual polytheism could have been leveled against trinitarian Christianity. Further, Schleiermacher's demotion of Islam

---

18. Tudvad, *Stadier på Antisemitismens Vej,* pp. 284-85.

19. While Hegel belongs at the top of any list of nineteenth-century thinkers who presented religions in terms of a developmental hierarchy, Kierkegaard knew his *Lectures on Religion* only indirectly, especially as mediated by Martensen, and so I will not specifically discuss those lectures here.

20. Friedrich Schleiermacher, *The Christian Faith,* trans. H. R. Mackinosh and J. S. Stewart (Edinburgh: T&T Clark, 1928), pp. 34-35.

21. Schleiermacher, *The Christian Faith,* p. 37.

to secondary status is a rare departure from seeing unidirectional progress in religious history so that later phenomena are typically more developed than earlier ones.[22] The task here is not to assess the merits and demerits of his assertions, but to note that Kierkegaard, having studied Schleiermacher intensely as a dominant theologian of his day, would have come to feel quite at home with schematic, developmental arrangements of the world's religions.

While Schleiermacher's fondness for triads and willingness to rank are formally parallel to Kierkegaard's scheme, Martensen's *Lectures on Speculative Dogmatics* is much closer both in terminology and in substance to Kierkegaard's ideas. Kierkegaard attended Martensen's course during the summer semester of 1838 and winter semester of 1838-39. He transcribed a lengthy "referat" of the course in Notebook XX, as well as acquiring a second set of notes on the course from another theology student.[23] While Martensen's speculative development of faith later becomes a target of Kierkegaard's anti-Hegelian polemic, just as Martensen himself becomes the immediate target of Kierkegaard's attack on the Danish Lutheran Church, Curtis Thompson is clearly correct in calling for a reappraisal of Martensen's positive influence on Kierkegaard's development.[24] Nowhere is that influence more evident than in Martensen's taxonomy of religions, which anticipates Kierkegaard's in a number of ways.

In §7 of the *Lectures* as transcribed by Kierkegaard, Martensen identifies paganism, Judaism, and Christianity as the three "fundamental forms [*Grundformer*] in which the ideas of religion and revelation have historically realized themselves." The reference to history here is key. Martensen follows Hegel in asserting that divine revelation is never direct but is mediated historically, so that we can see religions as stages of a developing religious consciousness *(Bevidsthedstrin)*. Paganism corresponds to an awareness of the divine as substance (i.e., as object), while Judaism experiences God as subject.

22. In a sort of religious version of the "Brezhnev Doctrine," Schleiermacher insists that history shows no examples of regression from polytheism to fetishism or monotheism to polytheism: "there is strictly speaking no such thing as wholesale relapse from Christianity to either Judaism or Mohammedanism, any more than from any monotheistic religion to Polytheism or idol-worship." Schleiermacher, *The Christian Faith*, p. 38. Religious history for him is one of inexorable and irreversible progress from less to more fully developed forms of religious awareness.

23. *SKP* XIII, II C 26-27 (p. 3).

24. Hans L. Martensen, *Between Hegel and Kierkegaard: Hans L. Martensen's Philosophy of Religion,* trans. Curtis L. Thompson and David J. Kangas, intro. by Curtis L. Thompson (New York: Oxford University Press, 1997).

Only in Christianity is there a reconciliation of these two "abstract moments" of religious consciousness leading to a fully developed notion of a personal God. Martensen's notion of revelation playing out in the course of history leads him to identify paganism and Judaism as "elementary presuppositions [*elementariske Forudsætninger*] and points of passage [*Gjennemgangspunkter*] for Christianity." They each contain true insights into the God-idea, but these insights are fragmentary and incomplete *(membrum disjectum)*.[25]

Even in this little sketch of Martensen's *Lectures,* we see the "world historical perspective" and inexorable dialectical development of ideas that Kierkegaard goes on to ridicule, especially in the Climacus texts. But reading over his notes from Martensen's *Lectures,* it is clear that Kierkegaard came away from the course with lasting influences. First, as we have noted, Kierkegaard consistently thinks and writes about religion in terms of a pagan-Jew-Christian triad. While others also used this scheme, Kierkegaard heard and transcribed Martensen's presentation of it. Second, many of Martensen's specific statements about the particular forms of religious consciousness, especially paganism, echo in Kierkegaard's later writings. (I will describe these parallels more specifically in the next section of this chapter.) Clearly, Martensen's views of other religions made an impact on Kierkegaard as he sat in his antagonist-to-be's lectures over weeks and months in 1838-39.

Placing Kierkegaard's taxonomy of faiths alongside those proposed by his contemporaries shows that, in this regard at least, Kierkegaard is very much a man of his own time. He not only reflects the dominant nineteenth-century paradigm for thinking about religious diversity but apparently took it as entirely unproblematic. Later, I will argue that, while accepting a thoroughly conventional taxonomic scheme, Kierkegaard puts it to radically different use than did his contemporaries. But before making that case, we should look more closely at the specific ways paganism and Judaism figure in Kierkegaard's thought and writings.

Kierkegaard's Pagans

In classifying all religious faith into three categories — pagan, Jew, Christian — Kierkegaard represses the diverse reality of religious life. This repressed diversity reasserts itself in the ambiguous, multiple, and shifting senses of the terms of his triad. In this section, I will focus specifically on the figure

25. *SKP* XIII, II C 26-27 (pp. 14-15).

of the pagan in Kierkegaard's writings. Who is Kierkegaard's pagan? In what guises does the pagan appear in Kierkegaard's texts? What rhetorical purposes does the pagan serve? How do the shifting appearances of the pagan reflect changes in Kierkegaard's thought about Christianity, his project as a writer, and his stance toward church and society?

Rather than trying to survey the comments on pagans scattered throughout Kierkegaard's published works and journals, I will focus on four scenes in Kierkegaard's writings where the pagan figures significantly: (1) "The Tragic in Ancient Drama as Reflected in the Tragic in Modern Drama," from the first volume of *Either/Or;* (2) the discussion of truth as subjectivity in *Concluding Unscientific Postscript;* (3) the extended discussion of the "Cares of the Pagans" that makes up Part One of *Christian Discourses;* and (4) texts from Kierkegaard's final attack on the Danish Lutheran establishment. These four scenes show real variation in the meanings and uses of the term "pagan," but they also show that key themes persist.

In the previous section, I observed that many specific themes from Martensen's discussion of pagans in his *Lectures on Speculative Dogmatics* reverberate through Kierkegaard's texts. According to Martensen, the pagan

1. represents "the spiritual standpoint of the natural human" (§8)
2. lacks a full sense of the divine as qualitatively different from nature (§9) and thus conflates creation and creator (§8)
3. is thus destined to idolatry *(Afguderie)* (§8) and polytheism (§9)
4. fails fully to differentiate self from nature and society (§8 and §10)
5. never having discovered the true independence of subjectivity, lives under the dominance of "a dark fate" (§10)
6. lacks a fully developed moral conscience and consciousness of sin (§10)
7. understands religion as an "elevated enjoyment of life" (§10), thus expressing an aesthetic rather than moral or religious outlook on life (§9)[26]
8. is haunted by unresolved care and sorrow despite having an enjoyment-oriented life-view (§10)
9. is ultimately "God-forsaken" *(gudforladt)* (§8)

26. Kierkegaard's own notes from Martensen's *Lectures* read, "for the ethical moment, which is the deepest core of personality, is suppressed by the aesthetic" (*SKP* XIII, II C 26-27 [p. 29]); the other set of notes from an unnamed student reads, "Individuality is still only aesthetic, not ethical, and the spiritual is only present in so far as it is expressed corporeally" (*SKP* XIII, II C 26-27 [p. 22]). The latter passage not only parallels Kierkegaard's treatment of paganism as aesthetic in character but suggests that Martensen used the categories "aesthetic," "ethical," and "religious" in ways that anticipate Kierkegaard's theory of the stages.

As we make our way through the four scenes, it will be useful to pay particular attention to the ways these motifs from Martensen show up in Kierkegaard's texts.

The Tragic Pagan

In Kierkegaard's early journals and published texts, "pagan" has a single predominant reference, the ancient Greeks, with a secondary, penumbral reference to the classical Romans. This focus reflects Kierkegaard's classical education. More significantly, it reflects the widely held conviction behind an education so focused on classical languages and literature: in ancient Greece and Rome, the natural human achieved its fullest flowering. If one wants to see what humans can achieve without the particular revelations God granted to Judaism and Christianity, one must look to classical antiquity. As such, Greek paganism serves as a key benchmark for Kierkegaard. In trying to identify what is distinctively and decisively Christian as well, he consistently refers to a sort of ideal Greek mentality *(Græciteten)* as a foil.

If the Greeks as a group manifest the humanly possible, Socrates figures for Kierkegaard as the individual fulfillment of what is possible as a Greek. Looking to his many discussions of Socrates is not, however, the best way to pin down Kierkegaard's understanding of Greek paganism, for Socrates represents for Kierkegaard a transitional figure, a figure who already presses beyond paganism.[27] We get a better picture of Kierkegaard's understanding of Greek paganism by looking instead at an essay that never uses the term "pagan": A's speech to the *Symparanekromenoi,* "The Tragic in Ancient Drama Reflected in the Tragic in Modern Drama."

As is often the case in *Either/Or* 1, A focuses here on suffering, specifically on the contrasting portrayals of suffering in classical and modern tragedy. Modern tragedy presents the tragic hero as culpable, as directly responsible for his or her suffering: "the hero stands and falls entirely on his own deed" (*EO* 1:144). In challenging the aesthetic credentials of such moralized drama, A invokes the genius of Greek tragedy, and his characterization of that tragedy gives us key features of Greek paganism as Kierkegaard understands it. Above all, Greek tragedy denies the total culpability of the

---

27. After writing "I calmly stick to Socrates" in matters of method, Kierkegaard makes a striking statement: "True, he was no Christian, that I know, although I also definitely remain convinced that he has become one" (*PV,* 54).

tragic hero. Rather, the hero's downfall is fated; it reflects the hero's unchosen involvement in given, opaque realities that shape his or her life apart from free action or even clear knowledge.

> [T]he ancient world did not have subjectivity reflected in itself. Even if the individual moved freely, he nevertheless rested in substantial determinants, in the state, the family, in fate. This substantial determinant is the essential fateful factor in Greek tragedy and its essential characteristic. (*EO* 1:143)

In this central idea of the essay, we can see key features of Kierkegaard's notion of paganism.

First, paganism is a pre-ethical, and therefore aesthetic, mode of consciousness. A emphasizes that tragic guilt *(harmatia)* is not moral guilt because libertarian freedom, the ability to do otherwise, is missing. Just as tragic heroes are pre-moral, so are the Greek gods. In contrast to the righteous punishment meted out by Jehovah, A says, "It was not this way in Greece; the wrath of the gods has no ethical character, only esthetic ambiguity" (*EO* 1:151). With neither a full sense of moral responsibility nor an awareness of God as righteous judge, the pagan is incapable of a consciousness of sin.

Second, paganism is collectivist or organicist. A explains that the tragic hero is only tragically, not morally, guilty, because he or she "rested in substantial determinants, in the state, the family, in fate" (*EO* 1:143). That is, the tragic hero is essentially involved in larger, opaque, unchosen realities. For Kierkegaard, paganism typically takes the form of ethnic or tribal religion where one's involvement in the social collective determines one's religious identity. In *The Concept of Irony,* Kierkegaard presents Socrates as using irony to separate himself from the social collective to emerge as the first true individual and therefore, in some sense, the first "post-pagan" self.[28]

Third, paganism is heteronomous. The common thread in the previous characterizations of paganism is the determination of the self by forces beyond itself. A emphasizes this by repeatedly asserting that, for the Greeks, "Tragic action always contains an element of suffering" (*EO* 1:150). Even in his or her actions, there is a key element of passivity.

---

28. "But if irony is a qualification of subjectivity, then it must manifest itself the first time subjectivity makes its appearance in world history. Irony is, namely, the first and most abstract qualification of subjectivity. This points to the historical turning point where subjectivity made its appearance for the first time, and with this we have come to Socrates" (*CI,* 264).

Finally, paganism is haunted by anxiety and melancholy. Though paganism is a form of aestheticism, its inchoate awareness of its determination by forces beyond its control gives it a pervasive undertone of melancholy: "Or is this not the striking feature of everything that originates in that happy people — a depression of spirit, a sadness in their art, in their poetry, in their life, in their joy?" (*EO* 1:146).

Parallels between this picture of paganism and Martensen's *Lectures* are multiple and evident. Both offer a broad picture of paganism as a pre-ethical, aesthetic mode of consciousness resulting from an incomplete development of the self's awareness of itself as a moral subject. Two specific parallels to Martensen deserve particular mention. First, Martensen says that paganism conceives of God in terms of "manifest substantiality" *(manifesterede Substantialitæt)* rather than as subjectivity. That is, the divine appears to pagans as immanent in the surrounding world rather than as a personal subject. Kierkegaard uses similar terminology, "substantial determinants" *(substantielle Bestemmelser),* in describing family, state, and fate as the realities in ultimate control of the tragic self's life. Second, Martensen anticipates Kierkegaard's analysis of Greek tragedy and his comments on Greek melancholy when he writes of a "premonition of dark fate" that casts a shadow of "unresolved sorrow over paganism's cheerful outlook."[29]

Martensen and Kierkegaard employ basically the same conceptual frameworks in discussing paganism, but they use them in strikingly different ways. Martensen presents paganism as a deeply limited but necessary transitional stage on the way to Christianity. Kierkegaard's aesthete, in contrast, appeals to classical tragedy, an artistic expression of a pagan mindset, to critique contemporary drama as moralistic. Against the "Pelagian" overestimation of personal autonomy implicit in contemporary tragedy, A cites *both* a pagan mindset (which sees the self in the hands of fate) *and* a Christian mindset (which recognizes sin and appeals to grace) as superior alternatives. A's polemic against modern tragedy is implicitly directed against the ethical life-view represented in *Either/Or* by Judge William. It is as if A is saying, "There are worse things than being a pagan; one can be a sanctimonious moralist like Judge William." Thus, Kierkegaard's aesthete wrests Martensen's conception of paganism away from a conception of necessary, unilinear advancement over the course of history to present paganism and Christianity as a currently valid either/or. This is potentially very significant for our estimation of Kierkegaard's view of religious pluralism: against the

---

29. *SKP* XIII, II C 26-27 (p. 22).

spirit of his times, which wants to treat other religions as bypassed relics of a developmental process, Kierkegaard and his pseudonyms present multiple religious perspectives as existential "live options."

The Fervent Pagan

Of all references to pagans in Kierkegaard's authorship, the most (in)famous is surely the parable of the fervent idolator:

> If someone who lives in the midst of Christianity enters, with knowledge of the true idea of God, the house of God, the house of the true God, and prays, but prays in untruth, and if someone lives in an idolatrous land but prays with all the passion of infinity, although his eyes are resting upon the image of an idol — where, then, is there more truth? The one prays in truth to God although he is worshiping an idol; the other prays in untruth to the true God and is therefore in truth worshiping an idol. (*CUP* 1:201)[30]

This short passage has long been the site of fierce interpretive battles over the meaning of Climacus's cryptic slogan, "truth is subjectivity." Some, such as Herbert Garelick, see it as endorsing radical relativism: "*Whatever* a man feels to be edifying is. As long as there is something which edifies *him* and to which he relates himself absolutely, he is in subjective truth, even if he relates himself to an admitted, objective falsehood."[31] If Climacus or his creator actually held any such view of truth, religious pluralism would pose no particular difficulty for them, but more careful interpreters of the *Postscript,* notably Stephen Evans and Merold Westphal, show that Climacus distinguishes between existential appropriation of a belief (subjective truth) and adequation of belief to a state of affairs (objective truth) without denying the (provisional) possibility of the latter.

My next chapter will focus specifically on issues of truth and religious pluralism, and I will return to this passage then. Here, I want to look at this parable specifically for what it shows us about how the pagan figures in Johannes Climacus's *Concluding Unscientific Postscript.* How does Climacus

30. In referring to this as a parable, I follow Merold Westphal, *Becoming a Self: A Reading of Kierkegaard's "Concluding Unscientific Postscript"* (West Lafayette: Purdue University Press, 1996), p. 118.

31. Herbert Garelick, *The Anti-Christianity of Kierkegaard: A Study of "Concluding Unscientific Postscript"* (The Hague: Nijhoff, 1965), p. 21.

conceive pagans, and for what rhetorical purposes does he invoke them? Where most interpreters approach this text in terms of Climacus's statements about truth and subjectivity, here I propose to read it in light of his references to pagans. Far from engulfing religious difference in a relativistic dark night in which all cows are black, as per Garelick and company, Climacus appeals to multiple differences as he sets paganism and Christianity off against each other. That is, what matters to Climacus is not the putative sameness of religions as equally valid subjective responses. Rather, the multiple differences between paganism and Christianity place readers in a dilemma.

On the one hand, here and elsewhere in the *Postscript,* Climacus presents a sharply negative picture of paganism. At the center of this parable is the figure of the pagan prostrate before an idol, a physical, sensible object that is the work of his own hands. There is no ambiguity in Climacus's negative judgment of idolatry. In both *Fragments* and *Postscript,* he ridicules the idea that divinity is discernible by sensory experience. He argues at great length that neither historical study nor firsthand observation could possibly settle the question of Christ's divinity because divinity is necessarily incognito; it is in principle unavailable to empirical confirmation or disconfirmation. In *Postscript,* he mocks an agnostic awaiting some sort of sensory experience of the divine:

> If God had taken the form, for example, of a rare, enormously large green bird, with a red beak, that perched in a tree on the embankment and perhaps even whistled in an unprecedented manner — then our partygoing man would surely have had his eyes opened. (*CUP* 1:245)

For Climacus, "paganism" is not first and foremost a term for historically specific forms of religious life, whether from classical Greece and Rome or contemporary non-European countries. Rather, it primarily designates false belief in the sensory availability of the divine, wherever and whenever that belief occurs. Right after mocking the idea of God appearing as a large green bird with a red beak, Climacus writes, "All paganism consists in this, that God is related directly to a human being, as the remarkably striking to the amazed" (*CUP* 1:245). Later in the *Postscript,* he states succinctly, "Direct recognizability is paganism" (*CUP* 1:600). When Climacus presents his parable of the fervent pagan, when he includes the detail that "his eyes are resting upon the image of an idol," we need to read it against the background of his sustained critique of sensory awareness of divine reality. As even deeper context, we need to feel the full weight of the Second Commandment prohibition on graven images bearing down on this scene of pagan worship. Far from equating paganism and Christianity, Climacus describes the Christian worshiper as entering "the house of the true God" and "worshiping with knowledge of the true idea of God," implying by contrast that the pagan lacks an adequate idea of God and that the pagan's temple is not a true house of God.

Only against the background of this sharply negative depiction does Climacus's positive judgment of the pagan achieve its impact. When he contrasts the authentic inwardness, the fervor and wholeheartedness, of the pagan worshiper with the desultory, disengaged worship of the nominal Christian, Climacus puts his readers in a condition of cognitive dissonance. The unresolved tension of the contrasting judgments of the two is essential to the effect Climacus seeks. His scene parallels quite closely Jesus' parable of the Good Samaritan: Jesus doesn't deny the superiority of Judaism over the heterodox Samaritan faith when he contrasts the responses of the priest, the Levite, and the Samaritan to the man fallen on the road to Jericho. Rather, he contrasts their existential responses to one in need. Just as Jesus asks who the true neighbor is, Climacus asks who the true worshiper is. To ask the question in this way is to answer it: the authenticity of the pagan's worship matters more to Climacus than the pagan's deeply flawed conception of the divine. But that is not, of course, to say that a flawed conception of the divine does not matter to him.

The Worried Pagan

For the most part, Kierkegaard's references to pagans are scattered and isolated. The striking exception is Part One of *Christian Discourses,* "The Cares of the Pagans" *(Hedingenes Bekymringer),* where Kierkegaard offers seven separate meditations on Matthew 6:24-34. In this passage from the Sermon on the Mount, Jesus calls on his listeners not to worry about what to eat, what to drink, what to wear, but instead to follow the example of the birds of the air and the lilies of the field who "neither sow nor reap nor gather into barns" but for whom God provides. In his meditations, Kierkegaard explores seven different cares or worries (poverty, abundance, lowliness, loftiness, presumptuousness, self-torment, and vacillation). In each case, he begins by poetically evoking the bird's lack of the particular care; as immediate, as entirely immanent within nature, the bird lives wholly in the moment, oblivious of the future and therefore immune to worry. For each care, Kierkegaard then shows that the Christian, like the bird, lacks the care, but where the bird

42

is naturally and inevitably free of the care, the Christian overcomes (better, by divine grace is freed from) the care through his or her awareness of existing *coram Deo* (before God). Kierkegaard concludes each meditation with a devastating account of how each care consumes the pagan. In each case, Kierkegaard depicts the frantic efforts of pagans to secure themselves and allay the care as entirely counterproductive; as pagans struggle to overcome the cares, they sink ever deeper into the quicksand of worry (which no doubt is located somewhere in the vicinity of the slough of despond).

Kierkegaard's worried pagan is a strikingly different figure from the tragic pagan and the fervent pagan of earlier texts. Where A and Climacus invoke the pagan as a comparatively positive figure by means of which to critique contemporary moralism and religious complacency, Kierkegaard delivers an unremittingly negative assessment of the pagan in *Christian Discourses*. In a passage from his discourse on the Care of Loftiness, Kierkegaard abandons all rhetorical restraint in describing the pagan's dire condition:

> Just as pithless rotten wood glows in the dark, just as the nebulous will-o'-the-wisp of miasma tricks the senses in the fog, so in this glittering of his earthly loftiness he exists before others. But his self does not exist; his innermost being has been consumed and depithed in the service of nothingness; slave of futility, with no control over himself, in the power of giddy worldliness, godforsaken, he ceases to be a human being; in his innermost being he is as dead, but his loftiness walks ghostlike among us — it lives. (*CD*, 58)

As he moves from the earlier mixed assessment of pagans to a stance of unrelenting negativity, Kierkegaard also moves toward a binary logic in which the Christian and the pagan stand in utter contrast: "According to the doctrine of Christianity . . . there is only one loftiness: to be a Christian — and one abyss: paganism" (*CD*, 59). Where Climacus asks whether the fervent pagan or the desultory Christian has "more truth," thereby implying that religious truth admits of degrees, Kierkegaard here speaks of absolute distinctions and uncrossable distances:

> The greatest distance, greater than any human skill can measure, is the distance from God's grace to God's wrath, from the Christian to the pagan, from being blessedly saved in grace to "eternal perdition [*Fortabelse*] away from the face of God," from seeing God to seeing from the abyss that one has lost [*tabt*] God. (*CD*, 69)

What are we to make of this striking shift in tone and substance? Why does the pagan become a figure of perdition and wrath in the post-1848 writings in contrast to earlier texts? Several answers seem possible. First, one could appeal to the contrast between pseudonymous and signed texts. The earlier texts discussed above are by pseudonyms, so perhaps in the later texts authored by Kierkegaard himself (and by his hyper-Christian pseudonym, Anti-Climacus) we hear Kierkegaard's own judgment, spoken from an unambiguously Christian perspective. That reading carries the disturbing suggestion that, on Kierkegaard's view, as one's commitment to one's own faith deepens, there is progressively less room for appreciation of other faiths. Second, one could take a biographical angle. In general, Kierkegaard's tone becomes harsher and his judgments more absolute in his final years, especially after his embittering experiences with *The Corsair.* Perhaps we hear some of that bitterness in his devastating analyses of the pagan in *Christian Discourses.* As I will discuss later in this chapter, there is a parallel shift in Kierkegaard's final years toward a harsher rhetoric about Jews and Judaism.

While I don't discount either of these interpretive angles, the fundamental reason for the shift in Kierkegaard's discourse is a profound change in the reference and the rhetorical function of the term "pagan" in his post-1848 texts. A and Climacus both invoke the pagan as a social and religious Other by means of which to critique the Danish status quo. As we have seen, A calls on the pagan mindset of ancient tragedy to critique moralistic contemporary drama, while Climacus invokes an idolator of indefinite provenance to challenge complacent Danish Lutheranism. In *Christian Discourses,* in contrast, the pagan *is* the contemporary Dane. "Pagan" entirely loses the ethnographic significance it had in Martensen's *Lectures* where it designates peoples from non-Christian and non-Jewish societies. When Martensen talks about pagans, he is speaking in terms a sociologist of religion would recognize. In contrast, Kierkegaard here speaks of a paganism that prevails in the heart of Christendom, rather than a paganism that would be picked up by a survey of religious affiliation or an ethnographic study of another culture.[32] Throughout *Christian Discourses,* Kierkegaard repeatedly identifies the pagan as one who exists "without God in the world" (Eph. 2:12). In his seven analyses of care, he argues that since Christians, like the bird, lack these cares, anyone

---

32. Climacus mocks the sociological use of religious categories when he has a wife dismiss her husband's concerns about whether he is genuinely Christian: "Hubby, darling, where did you ever pick up such a notion? How can you not be a Christian? You are Danish aren't you? Doesn't the geography book say that the predominant religion of Denmark is Lutheran-Christian? You aren't a Jew, are you, or a Mohammedan? What else would you be, then?" (*CUP* 1:50).

who continues to have these worries is *eo ipso* a pagan, whether he or she is on the rolls at the local Lutheran church or not. Where formerly "pagan" designated non-Jewish and non-Christian religious commitment, here it designates secularism, an absence of any genuine religious commitment.[33]

Labeling an absence of religious commitment with an overtly religious term is tendentious, but Kierkegaard is convinced that the religious impulse can never be eliminated, only misdirected. When people refuse to acknowledge the true God, they instead invest some worldly object with ultimate importance and fall down on their knees before it. Speaking of the rich pagan, Kierkegaard writes: "Not only is he without God in the world, but wealth is his god, which attracts to itself his every thought. He has only one need, wealth, the one thing needful — therefore he does not even need God" (*CD*, 33). Thus, idolatry is the middle term that links secularism and paganism. But where Climacus acknowledges the authentic worship of the pagan before the idol, Kierkegaard here drips contempt on the worshiper of mammon: "to oneself a curse, to nature an abomination, to the human race a defilement" (*CD*, 35).

As is evident in this quotation, the fundamental change in the reference of the term "pagan" corresponds to a profound shift in the rhetorical role of the term. In *Postscript*, Climacus challenges his readers by implying that their piety falls short of that of the pagan. In *Christian Discourses*, Kierkegaard goes more directly at his readers by telling them that, insofar as their lives are guided by the seven enumerated cares, they *are* pagans. In both instances, "pagan" serves the same project of critique of the contemporary religious situation, but it serves that role in very different ways. In the first case, "pagan" has to carry a positive charge in order to serve its critical role; in the latter case, Kierkegaard's polemic against contemporary secularism requires a purely negative deployment of the term. The semantic and rhetorical shift in Kierkegaard's use of "pagan" is thus tactical rather than strategic; that is, it is opportunistic rather than principial.

Kierkegaard is fully aware of the two distinct senses of "pagan" and calls attention to those senses in his introduction to *Christian Discourses*:

33. Merold Westphal writes, "In biblical times [pagan] would include Egyptians, Canaanites, Babylonians, Assyrians, Greeks, and Romans, among others. For Kierkegaard, who did not see himself facing a religiously multicultural world as we might see ourselves today, the pagans would be secularists, whether the proletarians who saw the church as nothing more than a prop for the privileged or those whom Schleiermacher called 'the cultured among the despisers of religion.'" Westphal, "Paganism in Christendom: On Kierkegaard's Critique of Religion," in Perkins, ed., *International Kierkegaard Commentary*, vol. 17: *"Christian Discourses" and "The Crisis and a Crisis in the Life of an Actress,"* pp. 18-19.

> [L]et us never forget . . . that the pagans who are found in Christendom have sunk the lowest. Those in pagan countries have not as yet been lifted up to Christianity; the pagans in Christendom have sunk below paganism. The former belong to the fallen race; the latter, after having been lifted up, have fallen once again and have fallen even lower. (*CD,* 12)

In Kierkegaard's equivocal use of "pagan," we can discern an important modification of prevailing ideas about the hierarchical ordering of religions. On the one hand, Kierkegaard here adopts the standard conception that Christianity is "higher" than paganism. That is, Christianity represents a later, fuller, more developed stage of religious consciousness than does paganism. Schleiermacher, Martensen, and most other nineteenth-century theologians take such a developmental scheme as a reason for Christian self-congratulation. In contrast, Kierkegaard uses the scheme to combat complacent triumphalism by locating apostate paganism, the paganism of purported Christians, as even lower than authentic paganism. Why that lower rank? Where the pre-Christian pagans are ignorant of the Christian truth and therefore nonculpable for their paganism, the apostate pagans of Christendom culpably close themselves off from all that is higher in order to focus their attention and efforts entirely on worldly goods, whether material (the cares of poverty and abundance) or reputational (the cares of lowliness and loftiness):

> So it is with the pagan, for paganism is without God in the world, but Christianity makes it quite evident that paganism is ungodliness. The ungodliness is not so much being worried, although it is certainly not Christian to be that; the ungodliness is being totally unwilling to know anything else. . . . He has sunk the deepest when he *wills* not to know anything higher. (*CD,* 19-20)

Paganism in Christendom, because it is chosen, is not just religious error; it is rebellion against God (*CD,* 66, 87).

The Apostate Pagan in The Moment *and Other Late Writings*

In *Christian Discourses,* Kierkegaard clearly uses the epithet "pagan" to critique Danish Christendom, but he does so with a comparatively light touch. In his Introduction to "The Cares of the Pagans," he says that one *might* offer a "subtle mockery" of a purportedly Christian country by noting that the cares of the pagans are all too prominent in it, leading to the paradoxical conclusion that "this Christian country is pagan." Kierkegaard mentions this mockery only to back away from it as one that would "backfire on the speaker himself, who certainly is not such a perfect Christian either." He notes, however, that it is a good discourse to have "up his sleeve" in case it is needed (*CD*, 11).

When he launches his final attack on the Danish Lutheran establishment six years later, Kierkegaard doesn't so much pull the discourse "out of his sleeve" as he wields the term "pagan" like a cudgel. The tone of his critique here is much sharper than in earlier texts, but the substance was already laid out in his earlier writings. As before, pagans are aesthetes and idolators. He repeatedly associates them with the crass pursuit of sensory pleasures and caricatures them as worshiping "a stone, an ox, an insect as God" (*M*, 122). However judgmental Kierkegaard sounds about paganism, he is not really interested in it as a religious phenomenon in its own right; it serves only as a foil for his critique of Christendom. Strikingly, Kierkegaard does not choose between the two different critical approaches deployed in the earlier texts. Rather, he alternates back and forth between the Climacus critique in *Postscript* (that however low the pagan is, the "Christians" of Christendom are still lower) and the *Christian Discourses* critique (that the "Christians" of Christendom are in reality pagans). We see an example of the first approach in "The Medical Opinion" from the fourth issue of *The Moment*:

> But the truth is this: not only are we not Christians, no, we are not even pagans, to whom the Christian doctrine could be proclaimed without hesitation, but by means of an illusion, an enormous illusion ("Christendom," a Christian state, a Christian country, a Christian world), we are even hindered in becoming that. (*M*, 157)

In the next issue of *The Moment*, Kierkegaard deploys the second approach, asserting that contemporary "Christians" are thinly disguised pagans:

> Christianity's idea was: to want to change everything.
>
> The result, "Christendom's" Christianity is: that everything, unconditionally everything, has remained what it was, only that everything has taken the name Christian — and so (strike up, musicians!) we are living paganism, so merrily, so merrily, around, around, around; or more accurately, we are living paganism refined by means of eternity and by means of having the whole thing be, after all, Christianity.

Test it, take whatever you want, and you will see that it does fit, is as I say.

Was it this that Christianity wanted: chastity — away with brothels. The change is this, that brothels have remained the same as in paganism, dissoluteness proportionately the same, but they have become "Christian" brothels. The brothel keeper is a "Christian" brothel keeper; he is a Christian just like the rest of us. (*M*, 185)

Kierkegaard's opportunistic alternation between these two ways of wielding the cudgel of paganism reinforces the point that he is only interested in paganism as a contrast to Christianity, not as a specific, rich human religious experience in its own right. Just as Kierkegaard invoked a generic bird in *Christian Discourses* as a dialectical third to the Christian and pagan without any specific interest in the details of ornithology, so Kierkegaard invokes an utterly generic pagan as Christianity's other.[34] This conclusion has two contrasting implications as we assess Kierkegaard's stance toward other religions: on the one hand, it gives us reason not to take his harsh language as evidence of religious intolerance since the harshness is all actually directed back on his purportedly Christian co-religionists; on the other hand, it indicates that Kierkegaard was not really very interested in the wide range of human religious experience that was becoming increasingly available to Europeans in his day.

Kierkegaard and Judaism

Implicitly or explicitly, Judaism is the ever-present background to Kierkegaard's thought and writings. The Jewish provenance of his ideas is most obvious when Kierkegaard takes texts from the Hebrew Bible as occasions of philosophical and theological questioning: the Akedah from Genesis 22 in *Fear and Trembling*, Job in *Repetition*, the Fall from Genesis 3 in *The Concept of Anxiety*, the injunction to love the neighbor from Leviticus in *Works of Love*.[35] Other ties are less specific but equally clear. Kierkegaard's

---

34. Merold Westphal makes a similar point when he notes that Kierkegaard's pagan is an ideal type rather than an object of empirical investigation. "Paganism in Christendom," p. 22.

35. For discussions of the Jewish origin of the command to love, see C. Stephen Evans, *Kierkegaard's Ethic of Love: Divine Commands and Moral Obligations* (Oxford: Oxford University Press, 2004), pp. 157, 314; and Merold Westphal, *Levinas and Kierkegaard in Dialogue* (Bloomington: Indiana University Press, 2007), pp. 68, 89.

denunciation of the unholy alliance between clerical, social, and political establishments resonates with cries of the Hebrew prophets. His close exegesis, especially of biblical texts, stands in the tradition of Midrash. His distinctive literary approach to philosophical writing, which often opts for character and story over abstraction and argument, recalls Hebrew literary preferences. The idea of Israel as God's chosen people is structurally analogous to Kierkegaard's emphasis on Jesus as the saving presence of God in a particular individual at a particular time and place. At the deepest level, Kierkegaard's overwhelming sense of the responsible individual existing naked before the all-seeing gaze of a moral God has its basis in the Jewish religious imagination.

But across this profoundly Jewish background, Kierkegaard all too frequently scrawls, like impudent graffiti, dismissive and derogatory comments about Jews and Judaism. Beyond question, Kierkegaard uncritically absorbed many negative stereotypes about Jews that circulated freely in mid-nineteenth-century Copenhagen, precisely at the time Denmark was normalizing the legal status of Jews. Even though he had personal contacts with several members of Copenhagen's small Jewish community, and even though his father seems to have actively opened doors for Jews into the Copenhagen business community, Kierkegaard lightly throws out comments stigmatizing Jews in a variety of ways, some of them all too familiar. According to Kierkegaard, Jews are:

1. fixated on money and talented at usury (*KJN* 2: FF, 187)
2. distinctive in appearance (*KJN* 1: BB, 19)
3. worldly (*KJN* 1: DD, 44; *KJN* 5: NB 49; *CUP* 1:402)
4. envious (*SKP* VIII, 1 A 131)
5. passionate (*BA,* 309)
6. obsessed with procreation and family (*KJN* 2: EE, 29; *JP* 2, 2225; *JP* 2, 2227)
7. absorbed in group identity/nationalism (*JP* 2, 2072)
8. devoid of a proper sense of eternity (*JP* 2, 843; *JP* 2, 2222)
9. turned toward the past, and thus incapable of developing (*KJN* 2: EE, 13; *KJN* 2: EE, 27; *JP* 2, 2220)
10. despairing (*SKP* VIII, 1 A 252)

While we find negative stereotypes of Jews throughout Kierkegaard's writings from his earliest journals, such comments become harsher and more frequent after Kierkegaard's painful clash with the satirical journal

The Corsair in 1846. As Kierkegaard never hesitated to note, *The Corsair* was edited by a Jew, Meïr Aaron Goldschmidt. After himself experiencing pervasive social opprobrium and exclusion, which he vividly fictionalized in his novel *A Jew,* Goldschmidt turned the tables, using crude but effective writings and drawings to render Kierkegaard an object of public mockery. (Kierkegaard provoked this attack after having been treated rather well by the journal.) After a relatively brief but devastating campaign, Goldschmidt himself became disgusted at the sorry spectacle and abandoned *The Corsair* in 1847. While Goldschmidt was able to separate himself from *The Corsair* and go on to a distinguished literary career, Kierkegaard's life was profoundly changed by the clash, leaving him isolated and embittered during his remaining years. We may have reason to be grateful for *The Corsair's* role in occasioning Kierkegaard's "second authorship," the largely non-pseudonymous and decisively Christian texts written after 1846, but we should not underestimate the suffering it caused Kierkegaard.

The Corsair Affair certainly does not excuse Kierkegaard's negative statements about Jews and Judaism. It is, though, a context within which his harsh later statements need to be placed in order to be understood. That said, the Corsair Affair represents a significant potential barrier to an honest reckoning with Kierkegaard's views of Jews and Judaism. The ugly business with Goldschmidt and his scandal rag makes it all too easy for readers of Kierkegaard to write off his comments about Jews as understandable if regrettable responses to personal injury. But that will not do. As noted, problematic passages on Jews appear from his earliest journals and throughout his writings, both published and unpublished. While the encounter with *The Corsair* influences both the tone and the substance of his comments, we have to look deeper to come to terms with Kierkegaard's conception of Jews and Judaism. As Peter Tudvad states, we should not let the Corsair Affair hide the connections between Kierkegaard's views of Judaism and his deepest conceptions of religion and human nature.

> Undoubtedly, an essential factor in the development of Kierkegaard's anti-Semitism is the injury he felt when *The Corsair* with the Jew Goldschmidt at its helm undertook in 1846 to make him ridiculous in an unfamiliar language and medium, coarse personal satire. But that injury was not the underlying cause, for his anti-Semitism fundamentally had its roots in his theological understanding of Christianity as polemical against various aspects of human nature, which he increasingly identified as Jewish. In other words, one cannot reduce his comments to a desperate reaction to an acute

crisis in his relation to his surroundings, as if his anti-Semitic expressions were just jargon that should compensate for his lack of adequate language to respond to Goldschmidt. The conflict with Goldschmidt, who in Kierkegaard's universe wasn't young, obstreperous, and republican but purely and simply a Jew, exacerbated the anti-Semitic tendencies he had in advance, tendencies which researchers have had trouble seeing as tendencies because they have made them products of the conflict with *The Corsair*.[36]

Tudvad offers here the important insight that behind Kierkegaard's anti-Jewish rhetoric lie key convictions about the character of Christian existence, convictions that Kierkegaard often expresses by setting up polar contrasts between Christianity and Judaism. Tudvad opens his compendious book with ten sharply drawn theses, the third of which reads:

> In his authorship, Kierkegaard develops an understanding of Judaism as Christianity's absolute opposite, so that it is by nature un- or anti-Christian (understood as Jewish optimism over against Christian pessimism, zest for life [*livslyst*] over against world weariness [*livslede*], enjoyment over against suffering, temporality over against eternity, fertility over against virginity, sensuality over against spirituality.[37]

Tudvad accurately describes characteristic tropes in Kierkegaard's discourse about Judaism, but the simple dichotomies of that rhetoric fail to capture the fundamental ambivalence of his relation to Judaism. In rashly charging anti-Semitism, Tudvad's own rhetoric falls into the trap of oversimplification. To gain a more nuanced sense of Kierkegaard's relation to Judaism, we need to find a way to understand how and why he could make such negative statements about Judaism despite the profoundly Jewish background of his own religious conceptions.

The key to such an understanding is the pagan-Jew-Christian triad that fundamentally structures Kierkegaard's thought about religions. When we read his statements through the lens of that triad, we see that the distinguishing feature of Judaism for Kierkegaard is its location *between* entirely natural paganism and entirely spiritually transformed Christianity. As between, Judaism is at one and the same time outside Christianity as a non-Christian religious Other and alongside Christianity as a common recipient of the God

---

36. Tudvad, *Stadier på Antisemitismens Vej*, p. 436.
37. Tudvad, *Stadier på Antisemitismens Vej*, p. 15.

of Israel's self-disclosures. Kierkegaard's readiness to think both thoughts at the same time is vividly illustrated by two consecutive journal entries, both commenting on Galatians and both made on May 2, 1835:

> Now it is certainly true that Paul, for example, in his letter to the Galatians (4:3) calls it [Judaism] στοιχεῖα του κόσμου and at that particular point it is by and large placed on the same level as paganism. But this does not help us greatly, for it only leads us to a contradiction, since it is clearly taught in other passages in the New Testament that Mosaism and Judaism were a divine revelation. (*JP* 2, 2207)

> For the Christian who now looks at Judaism it is apparent that Judaism was merely a point of transition. . . . For it is all very well that the law was given in order to prevent transgressions and consequently was a teacher (Galatians 3:21-23), but how do we account for its actually promising men salvation if they fulfill it. I can well understand that it could mean punishment for transgressions, but the divine (likewise now the Christian) certainly must have perceived that it would be impossible to fulfill it, and how then could it promise salvation on the basis of a condition which it recognized to be impossible. (*JP* 2, 2208)

While Kierkegaard resists a Gnostic or Marcionite temptation to cut Christianity loose from its Jewish roots, he also clearly distinguishes Christianity from Judaism on familiar Lutheran lines, identifying Judaism as the doomed project of fulfilling the law that is superseded by the Christian dispensation of salvation through grace. Kierkegaard states this supersessionist view in a distinctly Hegelian idiom in *The Concept of Irony*:

> Precisely because every particular historical actuality is continually but an element in the realization of the idea, it carries within itself the seeds of its own downfall. This appears very clearly particularly in Judaism, whose significance as a transitional element is especially remarkable. It was already a profound irony over the world when the law, after having declared the commandments, added the promise: If you obey these, you will be saved, since it turned out that people could not fulfill the law, and thus a salvation linked to this condition certainly became more than hypothetical. That Judaism destroyed itself by itself is expressly shown in its historical relation to Christianity. . . . [John the Baptist] destroyed [Juda-

ism] not by means of the new but by means of Judaism itself. He required of Judaism what Judaism wanted to give — justice, but this it was unable to give, and thereby it foundered. Consequently, he let Judaism continue to exist and at the same time developed the seeds of its own downfall within it. (*CI,* 262-63).

On this view, Judaism receives a key but incomplete revelation: God is a moral God, a God who demands justice. This revelation distinguishes Judaism from paganism, whose gods as presented by, for example, Greek and Roman mythology are hardly paragons of moral perfection. But by attempting and failing to fulfill the revealed moral demands embodied in the law, Judaism undoes itself and prepares the way for the fuller revelation of God delivered to Christianity. Assigning Judaism a transitional, preparatory role — the dominant model for Christian supersessionist understandings of Judaism since Irenaeus's *Against the Heretics* — gives Kierkegaard a way to affirm both a common source in divine revelation and a fundamental difference.

Kierkegaard's most distinctive trait as a thinker is arguably his penchant for "concrete universals," that is, for using specific literary figures to represent abstract ideas. In exploring Judaism's dual status as both Christianity's Other and brother, he invokes two symbolically charged figures: Ahasversus (the Wandering Jew), to represent Judaism's status as Christianity's religious Other; and Abraham (the father of faith), to represent Judaism as sharing a common relation to the God of Israel with Christians. By looking more closely at the significance of these two figures for Kierkegaard, we can gain a better sense of his deep and never resolved ambivalence about Judaism.

The Wandering Jew

Kierkegaard's earliest project as an aspiring author was gathering notes on "the three Great Ideas," Don Juan, Faust, and Ahasversus (the Wandering Jew), who together represent for him "life outside of religion" (*JP,* entry 795). While Kierkegaard never wrote the anticipated book, his reflections on the three great ideas are the basis of later published writings, most directly the first volume of *Either/Or,* depicting aesthetic existence as sensuality (Don Juan), doubt (Faust), and despair (Ahasverus). Additional echoes of his early engagement with the three figures reverberate through the whole authorship, notably in the analysis of despair in *The Sickness unto Death.* Of these three outsiders to Christian faith, two are culturally Christian. But Ahasverus, as an explicitly Jewish figure, plays a key symbolic role in representing the Jewish religious Other in the midst of European Christendom. As such, looking at how the Wandering Jew figures in Kierkegaard's thought gives us key though partial insight into his views of Jews and Judaism.

Focusing on this figure is undeniably problematic since Ahasverus is entirely a Christian construct, a vision of Judaism framed in medieval and early modern Europe by those intent on caricaturing, controlling, and excluding Jews. Further, twentieth-century uses of the figure of the Wandering Jew by murderous anti-Semites cast dark shadows back over Kierkegaard's fascination with him.[38] That said, the Wandering Jew exercises such power in Kierkegaard's mind because his haunting narrative is dense with multiple layers of significance. By excavating those layers, we can see how symbolically fraught Judaism is for Kierkegaard. But before turning to that analysis, it will be useful to review briefly the legend as Kierkegaard knew it.

There are an impressive number of literary and visual representations of the Wandering Jew, with significant variations among them.[39] George Pattison offers a succinct summary of the core narrative:

> The main features of the story are that Ahasverus, a cobbler in Jerusalem, having been part of the crowd which called for Christ's crucifixion, is standing by his front door on the road up to Golgotha when Christ arrives carrying his cross. Christ asks if he can sit down and rest, but Ahasverus rebuffs him, and is told that it is he, Ahasverus, who must now keep on walking until the end of the world.[40]

Doomed to an endless life that is a living death, Ahasverus opens matchless narrative possibilities. Storytellers trace his wanderings through all historical epochs and all lands. Ahasverus is there to witness the destruction of the temple in Jerusalem; he fights as a gladiator in Rome; he is an eyewitness to the Crusades; he endures to wander around Christian Europe. While the core narrative goes through many variations, the meanings of that narrative shift conspicuously from age to age: starting out in the Middle Ages as a heartless tormentor of Christ, Ahasverus becomes a romantic hero in

38. See George Pattison, "'Cosmopolitan Faces': The Presence of the Wandering Jew in *From the Papers of One Still Living*," in *International Kierkegaard Commentary*, vol. 1: *Early Polemical Writings*, ed. Robert F. Perkins (Macon, GA: Mercer University Press, 1999), pp. 128-29.

39. See *The Wandering Jew: Essays in the Interpretation of a Christian Legend*, ed. Galit Hasan-Rokem and Alan Dundes (Bloomington: Indiana University Press, 1986).

40. Pattison, "'Cosmopolitan Faces,'" p. 111.

Kierkegaard's own century before becoming an arch-villain in Nazi anti-Semitic propaganda in the twentieth century.

For Kierkegaard, the definitive version of the legend was given in Ludvig Auerbacher's folkbook, which he read at the Student Society in 1835 and purchased in 1836.[41] Within the narrow compass of the simple folktale gathered by Auerbacher, there are at least four distinct dimensions of significance for Kierkegaard: personal, psychological, political, and theological.

PERSONAL

Clearly, there is an autobiographical dimension to Kierkegaard's engagement with "the three great ideas" in the years 1835-38. This was the time when his relations to his father and his father's faith were most strained and when he felt himself most "outside religion." Of the three figures, Ahasverus has particular resonance: his despair parallels Kierkegaard's deep melancholy; his wanderings figure Kierkegaard's aimless studies; his survival of the deaths of all dear to him resonates with Kierkegaard's loss of most family members in a short time. During this time period, Kierkegaard clearly saw himself as a kindred spirit to the Wandering Jew. His father's belief that a divine curse rested over the Kierkegaard family, dooming the father to survive to see the deaths of all his children, bears a disturbing resemblance to the story of Ahasverus.[42] The notion of such a curse became moot when his father died in 1838, but well after these early years the Wandering Jew continues to play a role in Kierkegaard's self-understanding. Beyond specific references to the legend, Kierkegaard's romantic notion of himself as an isolated outsider aligns him with the figure of the Wandering Jew. If the Wandering Jew is an image of the religious Other for Kierkegaard, it is an image in which he sees his own visage reflected.[43]

PSYCHOLOGICAL

In "The Unhappiest One," of *Either/Or* 1, Kierkegaard's aesthete describes himself and his compatriots in the Symparanekromenoi as connoisseurs of

41. Tudvad, *Stadier på Antisemitismens Vej*, pp. 60, 64. Tudvad's chapter on Kierkegaard's engagement with the Wandering Jew is 110 pages long and offers extremely detailed summaries of many versions of the legend and of Kierkegaard's acquaintance with them.

42. See Tudvad, *Stadier på Antisemitismens Vej*, pp. 97-98.

43. Bruce Kirmmse writes, "[I]n Kierkegaard, antisemitism is a reflexive concept which recoils more upon Kierkegaard himself and upon the Christianity of his society than it does upon any actual Jews." Kirmmse, "Kierkegaard, Jews, and Judaism," p. 84.

suffering. In that regard, at least, Kierkegaard and A are entirely in line with one another. Throughout his authorship, Kierkegaard shows himself to be an unparalleled phenomenologist of the many forms of mental and spiritual distress. However varied the forms of suffering he recognizes, he views the reality of suffering as inevitable. Kierkegaard presents us with a Hobson's Choice: if one has faith, one will suffer as a believer; if one lacks faith, one will suffer despair. The former suffering is ideally realized in Christ, the latter suffering in the Wandering Jew, the icon of soul-sickness without end. Though there are no explicit references to the Wandering Jew in *The Sickness unto Death*, Kierkegaard's descriptions of despair as living death are direct developments from his engagement with him as a powerful symbol.[44] For Kierkegaard, the figure of the cursed Jew carries universal psychological significance, capturing imagistically experiences of alienation, guilt, and hopelessness.

POLITICAL

In the context of nineteenth-century European modernization, the Wandering Jew acquires a new and highly charged social and political symbolic significance. Condemned never to remain more than three days in any place, the Wandering Jew is a rootless cosmopolitan, at odds with the powerful currents of nationalism sweeping the continent. Nationalists aspired to organize political states in terms of historically rooted cultural, linguistic, and ethnic identity. During Kierkegaard's lifetime, for example, Denmark went from a kingdom incorporating territories in northern Germany to a smaller, more ethnically and linguistically uniform constitutional monarchy. But even as the ideology of nationalism reached its zenith, forces of modernization threatened to disrupt and dissolve homogeneous traditionalist communities in favor of heterogeneous cities celebrating novelty. George Pattison, who vividly places Kierkegaard in this context of social transformation and associated anxiety, notes that the Wandering Jew serves as a powerful symbol of Jewish cosmopolitanism.

> When the situation was conceived in this way, it took only one further small step to mark out a particular people as the bearers and agents of cos-

---

44. For a fuller discussion of despair as living death, see my essay, "Knights and Knaves of the Living Dead: Kierkegaard's Use of Living Death as a Metaphor for Despair," in *Kierkegaard and Death*, ed. Adam Buben and Patrick Stokes (Bloomington: Indiana University Press, 2011), pp. 21-43.

mopolitanism, namely, that people which had no geographically defined national homeland, but which, while preserving a sense of common identity among its members, was dispersed throughout Europe: the Jews. By this route, then, "cosmopolitan" and "cosmopolitanism" became key code words in the vocabulary of European anti-Semitism, words that marked out the Jew as the principal enemy of national historical identity and the harbinger of the new rootlessness.[45]

The prominent role of Jews in left-wing and reformist movements in Europe, notably "Young Germany," led Kierkegaard, following his teacher Poul Martin Møller, to see the Wandering Jew as charged with political and philosophical import. To quote Pattison again,

> [T]he Wandering Jew symbolizes for Kierkegaard the despair of the present age, a despair rooted in its separation from the substantial ground of religion and manifesting itself in both political reform movements and philosophical nihilism.[46]

THEOLOGICAL

Beneath all the other layers of meaning associated with the legend of the Wandering Jew lies a core theological meaning: the story of Ahasverus serves to explain the persistence and dispersion of Judaism despite its purported supersession by Christianity. Rather than seeing the persistence of Judaism as evidence of its continuing validity and vitality, the legend casts that persistence as a punishment for failing to acknowledge the Messiah. There are at least three key theological features of the legend:

1. The legend defines Judaism exclusively in terms of its relation to Christianity and not as a religious phenomenon in its own right.
2. The legend depicts Judaism as a decrepit, senescent religion that has survived long past the proper time of its passing.[47]
3. The legend explains the "unchoosing" of God's chosen people in terms of "punitive supersession": by failing to acknowledge and by playing a

45. George Pattison, *Kierkegaard, Religion and the Nineteenth-Century Crisis of Culture* (Cambridge: Cambridge University Press, 2002), pp. 72-73.

46. Pattison, *Kierkegaard, Religion and the Nineteenth-Century Crisis of Culture*, p. 76.

47. Kendall Soulen labels this view "economic supersessionism." Soulen, *The God of Israel and Christian Theology*, p. 29.

role in crucifying Christ, the Jews themselves cancel their status as God's chosen people, making room for the church to take that role.[48]

We find all three of these elements in Kierkegaard's statements on Judaism.

First, at no point in his career does Kierkegaard show significant interest in Judaism as a religious phenomenon in its own right. Rather, his interest is confined to Judaism as the historical background to Christianity and as a useful foil that serves to bring out the distinctiveness of Christianity. (As he puts it, *Opposita juxta se posita* [Opposites placed next to each other in close proximity; *JP* 2, 2225.) This is evident in the absence of works of Jewish theology from his library and in his talk of Judaism as a "point of transition" or "transitional element" on the way to Christianity. All elements of the story of the Wandering Jew depict him in relation to Christ and Christianity, but the subordinate relationship of Judaism to Christianity is most vividly symbolized in his role as a guide for Christian pilgrims:

> How beautifully the preparatory relationship of the Jews to Christianity is intimated in the legend of the Wandering Jew . . . which relates how in the latter part of his life he continually guides those who come from afar to visit the holy land. (*JP* 2, 2210)

Second, key to the horror of the Wandering Jew is the prospect of indefinitely prolonged aging, of life continuing when all the vigor of youth has long since departed. As T. S. Eliot writes in "The Wasteland," "I will show you fear in a handful of dust."[49] For Kierkegaard, not only is contemporary Judaism such a senescent reality, but the Judaism from which Jesus emerged was already exhausted and expired. In *Concluding Unscientific Postscript,* Johannes Climacus observes that "Upon its entrance into the world, Christianity was not proclaimed to children but to an outworn Jewish religiosity" (*CUP* 1:293). (To be fair, Climacus immediately says that his own generation is much more "sluggish" than were first-century Jews.) Given that he viewed Judaism as a spent force already at the time of Christ, it is not surprising that Kierkegaard, following Schleiermacher, viewed it as an anachronistic

---

48. Soulen, *The God of Israel and Christian Theology,* p. 30.

49. T. S. Eliot, *The Waste Land,* line 30. Among the variety of associations this line carries, one stands out as especially relevant to the Wandering Jew: in Ovid's *Metamorphoses* (book 14, lines 130-53), the Cumaean Sybil is granted by Apollo as many years of life as there are grains in a heap of sand. Unfortunately, Apollo did not also offer enduring youth, and so the Sybil lives on as a withered, wraith-like thing.

survival in his own day. The figure of the Wandering Jew serves to express and confirm that view.

Third, the most significant but also the most troubling aspect of the legend of the Wandering Jew is its symbolic representation of God's revocation of the covenant with the Jews. God cannot instigate such a revocation without betrayal and self-contradiction; rather, the Jews themselves purportedly cancel the special relationship through their guilt. In the legend of the Wandering Jew, the "blood libel" of Jewish culpability for the crucifixion is transposed into Ahasverus's refusal to let Christ rest on his way to Golgotha. In a journal entry from 1835, Kierkegaard compresses this whole line of thought into a terse observation: "The Wandering Jew seems to be modeled on the fig tree that Chr. bids wither away" (*KJN* 3, Notebook 2:13).[50]

In linking the legend to the "hard saying" from Matthew 21, Kierkegaard not only seeks to give biblical credentials to a story without any biblical basis, but he also appears to endorse "punitive supersessionism" and thereby to associate himself with a complex of ideas that have fueled Christian persecution of Jews over many centuries. If Kierkegaard does endorse the notion of a special Jewish guilt for the death of Christ that places Jews uniquely outside forgiveness, then he is properly judged to be anti-Semitic. But does he? Two passages from 1847-48, one published, one in the journals, seem to send different signals on this. A passage in Part Three of *Christian Discourses* endorses the idea of a revocation of the Jews' special status:

> [Peter] *left* the faith of his fathers and thereby *the people to whom he belonged, the fatherland, the love of which binds with the strongest bonds.* He no longer belonged to any people; he belonged only to the Lord Jesus. In faith he had to understand that God's chosen people, to whom he belonged by birth, was disowned, that there no longer existed a chosen people; in faith he had to understand that what once had certainly been his proudest thought, to belong to God's chosen people, from now on was hardness of heart and perdition in everyone who continued to hold fast to that thought. (*CD*, 184)

A journal entry from about the same time Kierkegaard wrote *Christian Discourses* sends a significantly different message: that culpability for Je-

---

50. Several years later, Kierkegaard comments on Romans 10 that the prophets had warned that if the Jews were not obedient, then the heathen could inherit their blessedness (*KJN* 2: KK 7).

sus' death belongs to universal human sinfulness rather than to the Jews in particular:

> The death of Xt is the result of two factors — the guilt of the Jews item the acknowledged evil of the larger world. Because Xt was the God-man, the significance of his crucifixion cannot be that the Jews of that period happened to be demoralized and that Xt's coming thus took place, if I may venture to put it so, at an awkward moment. No, the fate of Xt is an eternal one, indicating as it does the specific gravity of the hum. race; Xt's fate would be the same in any age. Xt can never express anything accidental. (*KJN* 4, Notebook 2:37)

The two passages, though contrasting, are not conflicting. The first asserts the revocation of the special status of the Jews; the second denies any special guilt on the part of the Jews. But if there is no special guilt, why would the status of the Jews as chosen people come to an end? A footnote from *The Book on Adler*, again from about the same time period, suggests an answer:

> To be Christian because one is born of Christian parents is the fundamental illusion from which a host of others is derived. One is a Jew by being born of Jewish parents; quite so, since Judaism is essentially connected to and bound in natural qualifications. But Christianity is a qualification of spirit, so that in it there is neither Jew nor pagan nor *born* Christians. It is fitting that from being a pagan, from being a Jew, from being born of Christian parents one *becomes* a Christian, since the qualification of spirit is higher than the qualification of nature. (*BA*, 135n.)

For Kierkegaard, the coming of Christ revokes the special status of the Jews as God's chosen people not because they bear some special guilt for his crucifixion but rather because Christ opens possibilities for relationship to God that are not determined by external, accidental factors, such as ethnicity, but rather by internal, individual, free responses to Christ as savior. Especially in the Climacus texts, Kierkegaard strains to show that when it comes to believing in the Absolute Paradox of the God in time, there are no advantages that go along with accidents of time and place. When confronted with the Paradox, all stand equally poised between possibilities of faith and offense. It is fundamentally this egalitarian impulse that lies behind Kierkegaard's conviction that Christianity supersedes Judaism.

Without a doubt, talk of the Jews as "disowned" by God is very dangerous. Such rhetoric is bloodstained by the terrible record of Christian persecution of Jews. But Kierkegaard's line of thought, whether we agree with it or not, is diametrically opposed to that of typical anti-Semites. Where anti-Semites invoke Jewish guilt to justify excluding an ethnic and religious group from a place in society, Kierkegaard advocates for Christian supersessionism in the name of inclusion.[51]

While this analysis of his supersessionism challenges the charge of anti-Semitism, it points up a supreme irony: everything that Kierkegaard says about Judaism as tied to accidents of birth can be and has been said about Christian emphasis on the unique significance of a particular person, Jesus, as the saving presence of God in time. Kierkegaard sharply criticizes Christian theologians who blur the significance of the historical particularity of Christ in order to see him as a symbol of something universally human and therefore equally accessible to all. But Kierkegaard's supersessionism is grounded in exactly the sort of universalist thinking he criticizes in others. While Kierkegaard maintains a dialectical balance between historical particularity and universal access in his discussions of Christianity, he brings no such nuance to bear in his overt statements about Judaism.

But perhaps those overt statements don't tell the whole story of Kierkegaard's relation to Judaism. While the Wandering Jew, sometimes for better but too often for worse, iconically captures his explicit negative judgments about Judaism, the figure of Abraham at least initially represents a more positive relation between Christianity and Judaism as understood by Kierkegaard.

Abraham

Given that he uses one Jewish figure, Ahasverus, as the epitome of life outside religion, it is striking that Kierkegaard singles out another Jewish figure, Abraham, as the ideal embodiment of religious faith. While a religious life-view is present only as an afterthought in *Either/Or*, Kierkegaard's next pseudonymous work, *Fear and Trembling*, focuses on the distinctiveness of religious

---

51. George Pattison reaches a similar conclusion by focusing on the Wandering Jew not as a specifically Jewish figure but as a universal symbol of modern dislocation: "Kierkegaard's concern with the Wandering Jew is not directed toward delineating and thereby facilitating the exclusion of the other, the one-who-we-are-not, but aims at articulating a condition that belongs to the inner destiny of all who inhabit the condition of modernity." Pattison, *Kierkegaard, Religion and the Nineteenth-Century Crisis of Culture*, p. 94.

existence. In this work, the pseudonym, Johannes de Silentio, uses the story of the binding of Isaac from Genesis 22 to raise fundamental questions about the nature of faith and especially about the relation between religious faith and ethical obligation. In contrast to Judge William, who describes a comfortable coincidence of religious piety and moral dutifulness, Silentio confronts readers with the terrible story of Abraham's trial, in which obedience to God requires transgression of fundamental ethical obligations. I will discuss *Fear and Trembling* in more detail in chapter 3, but as we assess Kierkegaard's view of Judaism, we have to take into account his choice of Abraham, the patriarch of the Jewish people, as the central, iconic figure in this text.

Johannes de Silentio nowhere discusses Abraham as Jewish. Abraham is presented simply as the father of faith without stipulating Jewish faith versus Christian faith. This can be taken in different ways. On the one hand, it implicitly acknowledges that the God of Israel is the same God worshiped by Christians and that the Hebrew Bible is an essential part of Christian scripture. Further, it recognizes Abraham's mode of relation to that God — trust and obedience even in the face of rational expectation — as the same sort of relation seen in paradigmatic Christian figures such as Mary and the Apostles (*FT,* 64-66). On the other hand, Silentio's silence about Abraham's Jewish identity can be taken as an act of appropriation. The Abraham we get in *Fear and Trembling* is often a very Pauline and even a very Lutheran Abraham. Nonetheless, Silentio's elevation of Abraham as the paradigmatic embodiment of faith carries several striking implications.

First, in highlighting the Akedah and focusing on the possibility of a "teleological suspension of the ethical," Silentio undercuts Kierkegaard's own tendency to associate Judaism with the ethical stage. As we have seen, Kierkegaard's Lutheran theological training made it very natural for him to assimilate Judaism to the ethical stage of existence, where relation to God is mediated entirely through the law. But in focusing on the Akedah, Silentio presents Abraham as relating to God as a single individual outside the universal. How striking that, for Kierkegaard, it is the founding father of Judaism who discovers that "up higher there winds a lonesome trail, steep and narrow" (*FT,* 76).

Second, Silentio's expressed intent in *Fear and Trembling* is to debunk the ambitions of modern speculative philosophers and theologians to "go beyond faith." Rather than seeing faith as a sort of immediacy that must "go to ground" in reflection and doubt as a preliminary to philosophical understanding, Silentio presents faith as "a task for a whole lifetime" (*FT,* 6). He makes his case by showing that "Abraham was the greatest of all, great by that power whose strength is powerlessness, great by that wisdom whose secret is foolishness, great by the hope whose form is madness, great by the love that is hatred to oneself" (*FT,* 16-17). That is, by presenting Abraham in his full paradoxical magnitude, Silentio seeks to show that there is no question of going beyond him, of superseding him. But what does that imply for Christian supersessionist views of Judaism? If one acknowledges the unsurpassable greatness of Abraham's faith, one cannot consistently maintain that Jewish relation to God is somehow per se inferior to Christian relation to God. Put another way, Jewish faith cannot be somehow inherently substandard when Abraham, the archetypal Jew, is himself the standard by which faith is measured.

Because Silentio never directly addresses Judaism or Christian-Jewish relations, these implications remain tacit in *Fear and Trembling* itself. It appears that, in later years, Kierkegaard himself became concerned about *Fear and Trembling's* implicit recognition of the authenticity and completeness of Jewish faith. In 1850, he drafts a response to a review of *Fear and Trembling* by "Theophilus Nicolaus" that significantly qualifies the presentation of Abraham as the paradigm of faith:

> Abraham is called the father of faith because he has the formal qualifications of faith, believing against the understanding, although it has never occurred to the Christian Church that Abraham's faith had the content of the Christian faith, which relates essentially to a later historical event. (*FT,* 260)

The form/content distinction Kierkegaard invokes here parallels the discussion of the fervent pagan in *Postscript.* Both Abraham and the pagan have the *how* of faith even though their faith lacks the decisive *what:* belief in Christ. I, for one, find no indication of such a distinction in the text of *Fear and Trembling.*

By 1853, Kierkegaard does not just qualify *Fear and Trembling's* presentation of Abraham; he utterly reverses it, retelling the tale of Abraham and Isaac in order to set Christianity and Judaism in opposition. In a startling journal entry titled "New 'Fear and Trembling,'" Kierkegaard offers a revised "Exordium" in which Abraham fails to hear God's command to halt and plunges the knife into Isaac. Kierkegaard concludes his retelling by writing:

> This is the relationship between Judaism and Christianity. In the Christian view Isaac actually is sacrificed — but then eternity. In Judaism it is only an ordeal [*Prøvelse*] and Abraham keeps Isaac, but then the whole episode still remains essentially within this life. (*FT,* 271; *JP* 2, 2223)

In *Fear and Trembling*, Johannes de Silentio stands in awe of Abraham not for being willing to sacrifice Isaac but for his ability to receive him back. For Silentio, faith differs from infinite resignation precisely in its capacity to reengage finite, worldly existence after having first disengaged from it in committing oneself absolutely to God. But the very traits for which Silentio praised Abraham become targets of critique in Kierkegaard's later journals. In his "New 'Fear and Trembling,'" he recasts Abraham's receiving Isaac back in this life as a symbol of worldliness, a trait he repeatedly associates with Judaism. In an entry from 1852, Kierkegaard contrasts Jewish worldliness with Christian hope for eternity by juxtaposing Abraham and Mary:

> Abraham draws the knife — then he gets Isaac again; it was not carried out in earnest; the highest earnestness was "the test [*Prøvelsen*]," but then once again it became the enjoyment of this life.
>
> It is different in the N.T. The sword did not hang by a horsehair over the Virgin Mary's head in order to "test" her to see if she would keep the obedience of faith in the [crucial] moment — no, it actually did penetrate her heart, stabbed her heart — but then she got a claim upon eternity, which Abraham did not get. (*JP* 2, 2222)

This association of Judaism with worldliness leads Kierkegaard into stark, harsh, and disturbing declarations of fundamental opposition between Christianity and Judaism:

> Here we see the striking contrast between Judaism and Christianity. Jewish piety always clings firmly to the world and construes essentially according to the ratio: the more pious one is, the better it goes for him on earth. . . .
>
> Judaism postulates a unity of the divine and this life — Christianity postulates a cleft. The life of the true Christian, therefore, is to be fashioned according to the paradigm which for the Jews is the very paradigm of the ungodly man. (*JP* 2, 2217)

Kierkegaard and Judaism?

Having surveyed Kierkegaard's complex, changing views of two idealized representatives of Judaism, Ahasverus and Abraham, what are we to conclude about Kierkegaard's attitudes toward and conceptions of Judaism?

Peter Tudvad hauls Kierkegaard before the bar of judgment and reads out a verdict of anti-Semitism. Undeniably, Kierkegaard said and wrote lamentable things about Judaism, and Tudvad has performed an important service by pressing us to confront them. But he fails to make a convincing case that Kierkegaard stands out from others of his time and place in this regard. Tudvad is surely correct that Kierkegaard's comments about Jews become harsher in his later years, but then his comments about most everyone are pretty shrill by then.

Bruce Kirmmse acknowledges the disturbing character of Kierkegaard's remarks on Jews and Judaism but argues that most of those comments are really directed at a very different target:

> Judaism is identified with everything Kierkegaard finds despicable in the established Christian religiosity of Golden Age Denmark . . . [so that] however offensive and objectionable his rhetoric is, it doesn't really have a great deal to do with Jews and Judaism, but is principally a part of Kierkegaard's battle against the lukewarm and flimsy Christendom of his times.[52]

Kirmmse is surely right to read many of Kierkegaard's comments about Jews as directed at Christian targets; how else can we make sense of his repeated assertions that N. F. S. Grundtvig, an ordained Lutheran pastor and Danish nationalist, is "altogether Jewish" (*M,* 566)? Just as Kierkegaard came to use "pagan" to describe the half-hearted cultural Christianity of his day, he also comes to use "Jew" for the same purpose. Kirmmse documents that Kierkegaard increasingly collapsed pagan and Jew into each other as an undifferentiated category comprising anything non-Christian.[53]

What emerges from our review of the two iconic figures, Ahasverus and Abraham, is the radical variability and even inconsistency of Kierkegaard's use of the terms "Jew" and "Jewish." One set of traits, associated with the Wandering Jew, emphasize exile, rootlessness, cosmopolitanism, and despair, while a contrasting set of traits, which come to be associated with Abraham,

---

52. Kirmmse, "Kierkegaard, Jews, and Judaism," pp. 88, 95.

53. "Kierkegaard ends up merging the category of Judaism entirely into that of paganism. He abolishes the difference between paganism and Judaism more or less unambiguously for the first time in 1850, when he writes: 'The possibility of offense is what is dialectically decisive; it is "the boundary" between paganism, Judaism — Christianity' [*JP* 3, 3035]. (Kierkegaard's punctuation makes it clear that he is assuming a dualism of which paganism and Judaism are seen as forming one side and Christianity the other." Kirmmse, "Kierkegaard, Jews, and Judaism," p. 88.

include feeling at home in the world, pursuit of temporal goods, a focus on family and procreation, and self-definition in terms of ethnic identity. It seems, then, that "Jew" and "Jewish" are free-floating signifiers to be pressed into polemical service as needed.[54]

I will close my consideration of Kierkegaard and Judaism by returning to the metaphor I used in opening the discussion: Judaism is the essential background to Kierkegaard's authorship, but Kierkegaard was prone to scrawl disfiguring graffiti across that background. Despite using a rhetoric of stark opposition between Judaism and Christianity, Kierkegaard's late writings can be read as a recovery of the "Jewish Christianity" associated with the Epistle of James. In reaction to Luther's overwhelming emphasis on Pauline Christianity and consequent disdain for James as "a right strawy epistle," Kierkegaard attempts to rethink the relation of grace and works along lines suggested by James.[55] Ironically, in his final years, just when his rhetoric is most negative about Jews, just when he most offensively asserts the utter opposition of Judaism and Christianity, the substance of his thought represents a reaffirmation of Christianity's fundamental and positive relation to Judaism.

54. Kirmmse notes that in 1855 Peter Christian Kierkegaard, who was aligned with Grundtvig, denounced his brother for promulgating a Jewish version of Christianity! Kirmmse, "Kierkegaard, Jews, and Judaism," p. 96.

55. See Timothy Polk, "'Heart Enough to Be Confident': Kierkegaard on Reading James," in *The Grammar of the Heart: New Essays in Moral Philosophy and Theology*, ed. Richard H. Bell (San Francisco: Harper & Row, 1988), pp. 206-33. In correspondence, C. Stephen Evans helpfully called my attention to the significance of Kierkegaard's fondness for the Epistle of James.

CHAPTER 2

Truth and Religious Pluralism

When Kwame Anthony Appiah spoke at Florida International University in spring of 2010, he gave a simple but striking bit of advice to students: "See one movie with subtitles a month."[1] Appiah's recommendation is a wonderfully concentrated version of his broader endorsement of cosmopolitanism, an open, informed, respectful stance toward diverse peoples and cultures.[2] Appiah's choice of film as a point of contact makes sense given the familiarity of today's college students with visual media, but he could as well have recommended experiencing the musics, literatures, or cuisines of other cultures.

In a similar vein, Robert McKim uses culinary imagery to make a plea for a "global approach" toward other religions that parallels Appiah's cosmopolitanism:

> The global approach requires that each of us sets out to see the point of view of others on matters of religious significance. It involves an open, exploratory, curious approach to others and an attempt to learn about them and their traditions, history, ideas, perspectives, insights, customs, experiences, sacred texts, and more. It asks why anyone should settle for the comparatively meager diet that is to be found within any single religious tradition — given global abundance of religious ideas, religious texts, religious experience, and so on.[3]

1. http://news.fiu.edu/2010/04/kwame-appiah-discusses-%E2%80%98world-citizenship%E2%80%99-at-fiu/13443.

2. Kwame Anthony Appiah, *Cosmopolitanism: Ethics in a World of Strangers* (New York: Norton, 2007).

3. Robert McKim, *On Religious Diversity* (Oxford: Oxford University Press, 2012),

As much as I find myself in sympathy with McKim's call for curiosity, openness, and empathetic understanding, his comparison between cuisine and religion raises troubling questions. Can we, should we, approach religious diversity in just the way we approach culinary diversity? To think of religions along the lines of cuisines is to invite, in Kierkegaardian terms, an aesthetic attitude. Because they constantly seek fresh, interesting experiences and fear above all else boredom born of monotony, Kierkegaard's aesthetes make diversity an overriding value. McKim, in invoking his culinary metaphor, similarly makes diversity an unambiguous good and exclusivity an unambiguous loss. Why, after all, would we want to eat standard American fare day after day if we are lucky enough to live in a city with a rich diversity of ethnic restaurants? But to apply this preference for diversity to religion ignores two key aspects of religious existence: commitment and conviction.

An exploratory stance implies absence of commitment. To consider various faiths as interesting alternatives is imaginatively to stand outside of them. One learns about them without being claimed by them. But when one moves from the stance of the curious spiritual epicure to the perspective of a committed adherent, McKim's culinary analogy breaks down. There is no breach of fidelity involved in trying out different cuisines, but many faiths, especially the Abrahamic monotheisms, conceive the relation of the believer and God along the lines of monogamy, in which fidelity requires exclusivity. If religious faith is like marriage, then the appropriateness of an "open, exploratory, curious" attitude is not so obvious.[4]

However widely cuisines differ (and however unfortunate it would be to place dishes from some of them together on a single plate), they don't make conflicting truth-claims in the ways that diverse religions do. People of faith persistently and pervasively understand religion to involve truth-claims. Accordingly, when people of different faiths encounter each other,

---

p. 155. John Hick similarly writes, "[W]hen we feed our minds and hearts by reading the scriptures and writings of great saints, we do not need to restrict ourselves to the Bible and to Christian writers." *A Christian Theology of Religions: The Rainbow of Faiths* (Louisville: Westminster John Knox, 1995), p. 136.

4. In *Either/Or*, Kierkegaard shows us what it would mean to elevate diversity to highest importance and to eliminate fidelity as a concern: one gets the aesthete's "Rotation Method" whereby one is advised to avoid all commitments and to practice arbitrariness in order to avoid boredom; one gets the sexual predator fictionally realized in "Diary of a Seducer." If Kierkegaard were writing *Either/Or* today, he might well have had his aesthete "rotating" among a variety of religions as a sort of spiritual tourist. (John Hick does compare exploring other faiths to international travel; see *A Christian Theology of Religions*, p. 136.)

they inevitably become aware of the places where their faiths contradict each other. And that poses a question. If different faiths make incompatible claims, the ordinary canons of thought require us to conclude that all those claims can't be true.[5] This raises the prospect either of asserting the superior truth of some religious convictions over others or else of despairing of the truth of religious convictions generally. Many, desperate to avoid grasping either handle of this dilemma, seek to modify the issue of truth in religion so as to open a third option of complementary, compatible diversity. And yet, for those who think of their faith as inextricably bound up with profoundly important truth-claims, claims that express their deepest sense of who they are, what the cosmos is like, how they should live, and who or what is the ultimate source of self, world, and duty, the reality of conflicting truth-claims remains an unavoidable, insistent issue as they come face to face with people of other faiths.

What resources does Kierkegaard offer us as we struggle with truth as a central problematic of religious diversity? Can he offer us a better, more genuinely religious basis for an open, appreciative, respectful relation to people of other faiths than an aesthetic appeal to the inherent value of diversity? Can he offer us ways to think about religious truth that will guide us as we live out our lives in a religiously diverse world? This chapter will look at three aspects of a Kierkegaardian perspective on conflicting religious truth-claims. In a first interpretive section, I will once again focus on the famous passage from *Concluding Unscientific Postscript* in which Johannes Climacus favorably compares a fervent pagan idolator to a nominal Christian; in a second constructive section, I will argue that Kierkegaard's "phenomenology of moods" offers a way to view afresh the fixed and overly familiar categories of exclusivism, inclusivism, and pluralism, used to stake out battle lines in debates over conflicting religious truth-claims; in a third section, I will present Kierkegaard's analysis of humor as suggesting a helpful way to think about differing religious truth-claims.

Truth, Subjectivity, and the Parable of the Fervent Pagan

In all of Kierkegaard's writings, no passage speaks more vividly — or more controversially — to the issue of truth and religious diversity than Johannes Climacus's parable of the fervent pagan:

5. His culinary analogy aside, McKim is quite clear on this implication, writing, "Actually to believe p and not to believe — when the subject arises — that those who believe not-p are mistaken, is, in effect, not to believe p at all." McKim, *On Religious Diversity,* p. 20.

> If someone who lives in the midst of Christianity enters, with knowledge of the true idea of God, the house of God, the house of the true God, and prays, but prays in untruth, and if someone lives in an idolatrous land but prays with all the passion of infinity, although his eyes are resting on an idol — where, then, is there more truth? The one prays in truth to God although he is worshiping an idol; the other prays in untruth to the true God and is therefore in truth worshiping an idol. (*CUP* 1:201)

Stripped out of context, the parable seems focused on our topic: how to think about religious diversity. Read in context, it is part of a large-scale attack proximally on Hegel but more broadly on post-Cartesian philosophy for so emphasizing theoretical knowing that the task of existing as an individual drops out of sight.[6] Against the existential absentmindedness of his age, Climacus advances his intentionally provocative definition of truth as subjectivity:

> When subjectivity is truth, the definition of truth must also contain in itself an expression of the antithesis to objectivity. . . . *An objective uncertainty, held fast through appropriation with the most passionate inwardness, is the truth,* the highest truth there is for an *existing* person. . . . [T]ruth is precisely the daring venture of choosing the objective uncertainty with the passion of the infinite. (*CUP* 1:203)

Climacus's parable brings this definition to life, favorably comparing the passionate pagan worshiper to the nonchalant Christian who enters church as if it were a university lecture hall, expecting to hear speculative insights and objective truths from the pulpit.

While Climacus's agenda here is not advancing a general theory of religious diversity, his provocative suggestion that a pagan idolator embodies "more truth" than his Christian counterpart inevitably raises such issues. In what direction does Climacus's parable point us?

Recent philosophical and theological discussions of religious diversity are overwhelmingly structured around a tripartite scheme of exclusivism, pluralism, and inclusivism.[7] Each of these terms designates a broad approach

---

6. See Rick Furtak's "The Kierkegaardian Ideal of 'Essential Knowing' and the Scandal of Modern Philosophy," in *Kierkegaard's "Concluding Unscientific Postscript": A Critical Guide,* ed. Rick Anthony Furtak (Cambridge: Cambridge University Press, 2010), pp. 87-110.

7. This schema was first proposed by Alan Race in *Christians and Religious Pluralism* (London: SCM Press, 1983).

to religious diversity rather than a specific position. Further, the terms are used to designate positions on questions both of truth and of salvation. For the purposes of this chapter, exclusivism asserts the unique truth and salvific power of a single faith; pluralism asserts that multiple faiths are equally true and redemptive; and inclusivism asserts that a particular faith is uniquely true but extends salvation beyond the confines of its own religious community.[8] As we set about appropriating Climacus's parable, it is almost inevitable that we try to place it in this familiar scheme. In doing so, we must ask not just where in the scheme Climacus's parable should be placed but also how well it ultimately fits into these categories.

It speaks to the ambiguity of Climacus's parable that it has been claimed by all three main approaches to religious diversity: pluralism, exclusivism, and inclusivism. On first reading, the passage seems to point toward pluralism. For Climacus urges readers to focus more on the *how* than on the *what* of devotion: "*Objectively the emphasis is on **what** is said; subjectively the emphasis is on **how** it is said.* . . . Ethically-religiously, the emphasis is again on: *how*" (*CUP* 1:202). If truth lies in praying truly, in fervently devoting oneself "with all the passion of infinity," then presumably all faiths can be loci of truth.

W. T. Jones draws from the parable a robustly pluralist implication: "[For Kierkegaard] the belief of a Hindu that Vishnu is God, the belief of a Mohammedan that Allah is God, the belief of a Nuer that *kwoth* is God — even the belief of an atheist that there is no God — all are true; providing only that in each of these beliefs an objective uncertainty is embraced with passionate intensity."[9] Jones's picture of Kierkegaard as a crude relativist is simplistic to

8. While many discussions take religious traditions as sets of propositional beliefs and evaluate truth and falsity at the level of particular tenets, this chapter will consider truth and falsity as global features of religious faiths. Kierkegaard insists that religion is an existence communication, guidance for living a life, rather than a set of discrete doctrinal propositions. While one can, no doubt, isolate individual propositions from overall religious worldviews, Kierkegaard and his pseudonyms tend not to do so. For example, in *Philosophical Fragments*, Climacus juxtaposes Socratic and Christian religious perspectives as comprehensive worldviews. Kierkegaard and his pseudonyms consistently ask not which propositions one should accept but which "life-view" one should adopt. In this respect, Kierkegaard's approach parallels George Lindbeck's assertion that, "As actually lived, a religion may be pictured as a single gigantic proposition." Lindbeck, *The Nature of Doctrine: Religion and Theology in a Post-Liberal Age* (Philadelphia: Westminster, 1984), p. 51. See also Joseph Runzo's discussion of faith as commitment to a "world-view" in "God, Commitment, and Other Faiths: Pluralism vs. Relativism," *Faith and Philosophy* 5, no. 4 (October 1988): 346.

9. W. T. Jones, *A History of Western Philosophy*, vol. 4: *Kant to Wittgenstein and Sartre*,

the point of caricature, making this passage a favorite quotation by opponents of subjectivist readings. But other interpreters with more nuanced grasps of Kierkegaard reach something like Jones's conclusion that Kierkegaard is a relativist and subjectivist and therefore a pluralist on matters of truth. In particular, some who interpret Kierkegaard as a postmodernist *avant la lettre* gladly take this and similar passages as suggesting that attempts to ground truth in mind-independent reality fail, so that whatever truth is available to us will be a function of closed circuits of subjectivity or intertextuality.[10]

In sharp contrast, Matthew Jacoby reads the passage as an "impossible hypothetical" that shows that "Kierkegaard must be understood as an exclusivist in every respect."[11] Drawing heavily on Climacus's earlier text, *Philosophical Fragments,* Jacoby argues that worshiping truly is only possible in relation to Christ as the objective reference of faith. Apart from a transformative encounter with the teacher as the god in time, humans are in untruth and so incapable of true devotion. "In the *Fragments,* Climacus has clearly expressed that *truth can only be had in relationship with this specific god who has done these specific things.* How can he then say that the object of the relation is a matter of indifference?"[12] The picture of the authentically worshiping pagan is, on this reading, a provocation, an "impossible hypothetical,"[13] designed to remind readers that genuine devotion is only possible when enabled by and directed toward its uniquely appropriate object, Christ. In

---

2nd ed. (New York: Harcourt Brace, 1969), p. 228. Cited from C. Stephen Evans, *Kierkegaard's "Fragments" and "Postscript": The Religious Philosophy of Johannes Climacus* (Atlantic Highlands: Humanities, 1983), p. 115.

10. Don Cupitt writes, "[For Kierkegaard,] everything is decided within the sphere of human subjectivity. All the different ways of life that he discusses . . . appear simply as various possible forms of consciousness, shapes that the human spiritual life may assume and worlds that it may construct around itself. None was assessed in terms of its correspondence with objective facts and structures out there; all were assessed from within, and in terms of their inner logic and movement." *Sea of Faith* (London: BBC, 1984), p. 153. Quoted from Steven Shakespeare, *Kierkegaard, Language and the Reality of God* (Aldershot: Ashgate, 2010), p. 13. A good example of a reading of Climacus's texts as endlessly intertextual is Louis Mackey's: "As an indirect communication, the *Fragments* is a system of signs that systematically severs its bond with any referent that it might be supposed to designate. The meaning of the text is therefore to be sought exclusively in the interrelations of the signifiers themselves, their reflection upon each other, and not in their allusion to any transcendent thought or thing." Mackey, "A Ram in the Afternoon: Kierkegaard's Discourse of the Other," in his *Points of View: Readings of Kierkegaard* (Tallahassee: Florida State University Press, 1986), p. 136.

11. Matthew Gerhard Jacoby, "Kierkegaard on Truth," *Religious Studies* 38 (2002): 32.

12. Jacoby, "Kierkegaard on Truth," p. 35.

13. Jacoby, "Kierkegaard on Truth," p. 39.

line with Jacoby's reading, Climacus writes in the same chapter as the parable that "[t]he direct relationship with God is simply paganism, and only when the break has taken place, only then can there be a true God-relationship" (*CUP* 1:243). For Jacoby, the fact that "his eyes are resting upon the image of an idol" (*CUP* 1:201) means that, however fervent, the pagan cannot be in a true relation to God and so cannot himself embody truth.

While rarely using the label, many close readings of Climacus's parable construe it as inclusivist in import. Inclusivism holds two ideas in tension: on the one hand, it stands by the robust claim of the unique correctness of one religion that characterizes exclusivism; on the other hand, it follows pluralism in acknowledging the authentic devotion of followers of other faiths. To reconcile these thoughts, inclusivism postulates ways in which genuine devotion can find its way to its appropriate object and salvific benefits can flow from that object of devotion to the devotee.

C. Stephen Evans is a prime example of a broadly inclusivist approach to these texts. He has repeatedly returned to Climacus's assertion that truth is subjectivity and the associated parable, consistently reading them as simultaneously affirming the objective truth of Christian belief and the subjective truth of the pagan's devotions.

> Kierkegaard asserts that even though a person's understanding may be faulty, if that understanding has permeated and transformed his existence in a quite definite manner, then that person will be in the truth. This does not mean that his beliefs are objectively true; they are still false to the extent that they are false. Nor does this imply that it is unimportant what a person believes. What it implies is that the primary concern of an existing individual should not be speculation about theological correctness, but rather concern over whether he is manifesting the truth in his acts. To say that it is possible for an individual to be in the truth while holding false beliefs about God does not imply that it is unimportant whether or not a person holds false beliefs about God.[14]

Evans's reading of the parable, with its apparently paradoxical assertion that a person may be "in the truth while holding false beliefs about God," highlights Climacus's distinctive dual theory of truth.

14. C. Stephen Evans, "Kierkegaard on Subjective Truth: Is God an Ethical Fiction?" *International Journal for Philosophy of Religion* 7 (1976): 294-95. See also Evans, *Kierkegaard's "Fragments" and "Postscript,"* p. 126.

When the question about truth is asked objectively, truth is reflected upon objectively as an object to which the knower relates himself. What is reflected upon is not the relation but what he relates himself to is the truth, the true. If only that to which he relates himself is the truth, the true, then the subject is in the truth. When the question about truth is asked subjectively, the individual's relation is reflected upon subjectively. If only the how of this relation is in truth, the individual is in truth, even if he in this way were to relate himself to untruth. (CUP 1:199)[15]

What Climacus says here about objective truth seems strikingly conventional, even traditionalist. Objective truth involves the mind accurately reflecting its object; it is correspondence of belief and its object; it is *adequatio intellectus ad rem*. Climacus does differentiate between empirical truth, where the known is an actually existing being, and ideal truth, where the known is abstract possibility. The former, because the knower and the known are both constantly changing, is endlessly elusive; the latter, because it remains confined within the mind's own realm of ideas, is tautological. But in both cases, truth is correspondence. If the mind accurately reflects its object, it is in truth.

So far, this seems entirely conventional. Though many of the ideas that motivate Nietzsche's radical writings about truth are already present in Climacus's texts (the world is in flux; the knower is existentially situated so that all knowing is perspectival; desire, emotion, and volition shape belief formation; accepted truths often serve ideological roles), he apparently accepts standard notions of objective truth, making his distinctive ideas about subjective truth stand out more vividly.[16]

As in the case of objective truth, subjective truth involves correspondence, but here the direction of the correspondence is reversed. In objective truth, ideas conform to the objects they reflect; in subjective truth, the

15. Such a dual conception of truth is already in evidence from the beginning of Kierkegaard's career as a writer: "This phrase ['know thyself'], somewhat like the word 'truth' in Christian terminology, unquestionably contains an ambiguity that serves precisely to recommend it, since it is just as applicable to a theoretical as to a practical position" (*CI*, 177).

16. "Kierkegaard seems to accept the kinds of epistemological premises that are often regarded as justifying antirealism, but he combines these epistemological views with a quite traditional acceptance of realism." C. Stephen Evans, "Realism and Antirealism in Kierkegaard's *Concluding Unscientific Postscript*," in *Cambridge Companion to Kierkegaard*, ed. Alasdair Hannay and Gordon D. Marino (Cambridge: Cambridge University Press, 1998), p. 161; see also p. 169.

knower changes her entire existence — thought, action, feeling, desire — to conform to an idea passionately embraced. When Climacus asserts that "truth is subjectivity," he isn't saying that we can make any proposition true simply by fervently believing it. Instead, he is saying that the most important form of truth, "essential truth," is something we are, something we live, rather than just something we know. As Rick Furtak puts it, "truth is found in a 'taking to heart' of beliefs that can transform a person — not in a neutral, unconcerned endorsement of a 'sum of propositions.'"[17] It is this understanding of Climacus's claim that "truth is subjectivity" that Evans has in mind when he writes, "even though a person's understanding may be faulty, if that understanding has permeated and transformed his existence in a quite definite manner, then that person will be in the truth."[18]

This reading of Climacus on subjective truth aligns with inclusivist approaches to religious diversity. Granted, Climacus's language is atypical of inclusivism in that inclusivists typically differentiate between truth and salvation whereas Climacus talks about two types of truth. But Climacus's "subjective truth" matches up well with what inclusivists mean by salvation. Both involve persons achieving their destiny, becoming what they, by nature, are meant to become.[19] By differentiating between objective truth and subjective truth, Climacus creates a framework for making just the sort of mixed assessment of religious Others characteristic of inclusivism: the pagan's god is pejoratively labeled an idol even as his devotion to that idol is recognized as genuine; the pagan's religious views are objectively false even though his life is subjectively true. Further, Climacus makes the characteristic inclusivist gesture of asserting that genuine worship reaches the true God despite the misguided beliefs of the worshiper about God. But Climacus goes a step beyond many inclusivists, asserting the corollary principle that inauthentic worship finds its way to false gods no matter how objectively correct the worshiper's doctrinal convictions: "The one prays in truth to God although he is worshiping an idol; the other prays in untruth to the true God and is therefore in truth worshiping an idol" (*CUP* 1:201).

Having surveyed pluralist, exclusivist, and inclusivist readings of Climacus's definition and parable, which reading is most convincing? If one is

---

17. Furtak, "The Kierkegaardian Ideal of 'Essential Knowing,'" p. 88.

18. Evans, "Kierkegaard on Subjective Truth," p. 294.

19. See Richard Schacht, "Kierkegaard on 'Truth Is Subjectivity' and 'The Leap of Faith,'" *Canadian Journal of Philosophy* 2, no. 3 (March 1973): 300.

choosing among these three options, there is compelling evidence in favor of an inclusivist reading.

First and foremost, the inclusivist reading is more faithful to all elements of the relevant texts. Both pluralist and exclusivist readings can point to supporting passages, but both seem to ignore key statements by Climacus. The pluralist disregards Climacus's labeling of the pagan's god as an idol, a false god; the exclusivist has to get around Climacus's assertion that the fervent pagan truly worships and worships the true God. Only the mixed judgment of the religious Other characteristic of inclusivism matches the dialectical complexity of Climacus's text.

Second, the rhetorical logic of the parable requires an inclusivist reading. Climacus doesn't address this text to pagan audiences but to Danish Christians. When he suggests that a *pagan* worships more truly than an orthodox Danish Lutheran, he intentionally shocks the sensibilities of those who feel comfortably superior to adherents of more "primitive" religions. But in shocking those sensibilities, he nowhere challenges the doctrinal superiority of Lutheran Christianity as compared to paganism. He simply makes the characteristic inclusivist point that an adherent of an objectively false religion can live in an authentic relation to the true God.

As noted in the previous chapter, Climacus's rhetorical strategy here is exactly parallel to that of Jesus' parable of the Good Samaritan. After two travelers with impeccable Jewish credentials pass by a man beaten and left for dead, a despised Samaritan intervenes with needed help. When Jesus rhetorically asks, "Which is the true neighbor?" he doesn't challenge but rather presupposes the superiority of Judaism as contrasted with Samaritan religion. Both Climacus and Jesus shame their orthodox audiences by presenting examples of superior lived faith on the part of people who are uncontroversially adherents of inferior religions. Only some sort of inclusivism can accommodate such a rhetorical strategy.

Third, both pluralist and exclusivist readings run into significant obstacles when one tries to fit them into the larger framework of Climacus's *Postscript*. Throughout the *Postscript*, Climacus derides Hegel and his Danish epigones for presuming to rise above the contradictions of existence to a speculative vantage point where all such contradictions are mediated. As a "poor, existing thinker," Climacus finds mediation beyond his capacity, and so he finds it necessary to guide his thoughts by "the principle of contradiction": the Aristotelian principle that two inconsistent propositions cannot be simultaneously true. However laudable its impulse to acknowledge the authenticity of multiple forms of religious life, pluralism often seems to seek a vantage point apart from and above any particular religion.[20] The judgment that each faith is true in its own way is a judgment not from a particular religious perspective but rather from some lofty height above the various faiths. Climacus would, I strongly suspect, detect more than a whiff of Hegelianism in many contemporary articulations of pluralism.[21]

Exclusivist readings of the *Postscript* will be left with the challenge of what to do with Socrates. While Socrates serves as a foil in *Philosophical Fragments,* representing the idea of immanent truth over against the Christian idea of transcendent, revealed truth, in *Postscript* Socrates is presented as the paradigmatic "existing thinker," as someone concerned above all else to reduplicate his ideas in his life.[22] He is, in short, a figure entirely parallel to Climacus's fervent pagan: both lack access to key truths made available through Christian revelation, but both live according to their own lights, passionately appropriating the truth as far as they know it. Climacus seems to think of Socrates along the lines of Dante's Virgil: a good and trusted guide up to but not beyond the point where specifically Christian truth is made known. But, beyond dispute, Socrates is presented by Climacus as an icon of subjective truth. Only a reading of Climacus that allows for a non-Christian, a pagan, to exist "in the truth" can accommodate this key feature of the text.

Finally, an inclusivist reading fits better not just with Climacus's parable and definition of subjective truth, and not just with the *Postscript* as a whole, but also with the larger Kierkegaardian authorship. In my Introduc-

20. At the opening of his *An Interpretation of Religion,* John Hick characterizes his project as religious but not confessional, that is, not "developed within the confines of a particular confessional conviction." Hick, *An Interpretation of Religion: Human Responses to the Transcendent* (New Haven: Yale University Press, 1989), p. 1.

21. It is useful to set descriptions of Hegelian mediation and pluralism side by side: "Hegel's dialectical method was supposed to enable the thinker to reach the standpoint of 'pure thought,' the exalted viewpoint of 'reason' that leaves behind the thinking of the understanding, which is tied to the traditional Aristotelian principle of noncontradiction. From this exalted viewpoint, the thinker can 'mediate' philosophical disagreements, seeing the truth contained in rival viewpoints and incorporating those truths in increasingly adequate and more comprehensive perspectives." Evans, "Realism and Antirealism," p. 163. "Someone who becomes a pluralist . . . steps out of his own antecedently held tradition in an important respect. . . . [The pluralist] subscribes to a deeper truth, a metalevel truth that other members of her own tradition, not to mention members of other traditions, may not be aware of. As a pluralist, therefore, she feels she understands the situation of others better than they themselves understand it." McKim, *On Religious Diversity,* p. 106.

22. See M. Jamie Ferreira, "The 'Socratic Secret': The Postscript to the *Philosophical Crumbs,*" in Furtak, ed., *Kierkegaard's "Concluding Unscientific Postscript": A Critical Guide,* pp. 6-24.

tion, I advanced the claim that all of Kierkegaard's thought about religion is structured by a dialectical tension between universalist and particularist impulses. Kierkegaard would no doubt find problems with most if not all actual articulations of inclusivism; but, like Kierkegaard, inclusivism stays with the tension between particularity and universality. In contrast, pluralism resolves the tension in favor of universality while exclusivism resolves the tension in favor of particularity.

So, the evidence, both textual and contextual, points toward something like an inclusivist reading of Climacus's parable. And yet, we ought to be leery of classifying Climacus's elusive, subversive text so readily in terms of our familiar categories. As Steven Shakespeare puts it, the offered interpretation "remains rather too neat."[23] Shakespeare asks whether Climacus can simply combine statements about objective truth and subjective truth without the two mutually complicating each other:

> It is as if adding together the objective existence of God and the subjective faith of the believer solved our problems. The real question is whether this language of subjective and objective is not placed under unbearable tension by the tasks it is asked to perform: accounting for the nature of human selfhood and divine reality. If we are no longer sure what the objective existence of God or the subjective inwardness of the individual might actually *mean,* then we would have to go somewhat deeper than this surface reflection.[24]

What, precisely, is the problem with combining an objective judgment about religious truth with a parallel emphasis on subjective appropriation? Why can't the two types of judgment complement rather than destabilize each other? For the inclusivist, the great virtue of Climacus's parable is precisely the way it manages to acknowledge simultaneously the objective truth of theological orthodoxy and the subjective truth of the genuine worshiper.

While such a reading is the most natural direct construal of what Climacus says, the parable becomes much more problematic when we turn Climacus's characteristic questions back on his own text. The overall project of the *Postscript* is to challenge pretensions to objective knowledge in matters of religion. Climacus relentlessly asks who is supposed to have such knowl-

---

23. Steven Shakespeare, *Kierkegaard, Language and the Reality of God* (Farnham, Surrey: Ashgate, 2002), p. 24.

24. Shakespeare, *Kierkegaard, Language and the Reality of God,* p. 24.

edge, how she came by it, and where she sits as she obtains it. It is only fair to ask Climacus how he comes by his knowledge that the Christian church is "the house of the true God" while the pagan worships an idol, a false god. Shakespeare writes, "Climacus talks of relating to 'untruth' (however 'truly' one might relate to it) in a way which implies that there is some ultimate standpoint from which it can be judged that some statements about reality are truer than others. However, no such standpoint seems available to us — so how can Climacus justify his language?"[25]

Shakespeare's point is that the parable doesn't have just the two obvious characters. Alongside the nominal Christian and the fervent pagan stands an observer, presumably Climacus himself, who takes the measure of the two. What precisely is the nature of Climacus's stance? When he judges that the nominal Christian worships "with knowledge of the true God" and "in the house of the true God," he seems to manifest exactly the objective stance toward religious truth he decries in the nominal Christian. Perhaps instead Climacus is actually a fervent Christian believer, humorously taking on the incognito of someone interested in Christianity without being a Christian. In that case, his judgments of the truth of Christianity issue from his passionate subjectivity. But then, why would he involve himself in comparative judgments about the religious lives of the two characters in the parable? The passionate believer, according to Climacus, is focused relentlessly on herself and her own appropriation of religious truth. Curiously peering into the souls of others has no place in that life. After all, Climacus opens the *Postscript* by making fun of Jacobi's impertinent interest in the condition of Lessing's spiritual life and by celebrating Lessing's use of irony to turn such intrusive inquiries away unsatisfied (*CUP* 1:70).[26]

And so, we are faced with a dilemma: Climacus can only self-consistently name the Christian God as true if he is speaking out of his own passionate commitment to that God; but if he speaks out of such a passionate commitment, he wouldn't be voyeuristically assessing the spiritual conditions of others but would be focused relentlessly on the authenticity of his own commitment.

---

25. Shakespeare, *Kierkegaard, Language and the Reality of God*, p. 164.

26. While Climacus takes a radical position on the distinctness of self-concern as contrasted with concern for others, Kierkegaard's own analysis of love in *Works of Love* describes our obligation to love others in ways that open for them possibilities of authentic God-relationship. Clearly, *indifference* to the salvation of others is incompatible with love. Still, speculating curiously about the salvation of others is just the sort of stance Climacus critiques as an evasion of one's own existential task.

Rather than fitting neatly into the inclusivist box in our classificatory scheme, Climacus's parable subverts the inclusivist stance. It calls into question an implicit objectivism in the inclusivist's judgment of the superior truth of her own faith. It simultaneously renders dubious the whole enterprise of speculating about whether people outside one's own faith are saved or not. My own salvation should be my agenda. If I were to relate with subjective truth to God, my own imperfect efforts to appropriate the truth I profess would give me more than enough to keep me busy without leaving me time to speculate about the spiritual condition of others. Inclusivism's tendency to feel secure about its own hold on the truth while worrying about the extension of salvation to others is profoundly at odds with the fundamental spirit of Climacus's thought. But exclusivism and pluralism are also, as we have seen, out of sync, though in different ways, with key elements of his thought. We are brought, then, to the conclusion that the parable just doesn't fit neatly into any of the categories of our familiar scheme.

Having used our familiar triadic scheme as a lens through which to view Climacus's familiar parable — and having noted that the view is somewhat fuzzy — I will next turn the tables, using Kierkegaard's "phenomenology of moods" as a lens through which to view our triadic scheme in hopes of seeing that scheme in new and suggestive ways.

Mood and Religious Diversity

> And my problem is this: when I become really aware of these other ways of looking at the world, these other ways of responding religiously to the world, what must or should I do? What is the right sort of attitude to take?[27]

From a Kierkegaardian point of view, Alvin Plantinga asks exactly the right question in this passage. But it isn't the question that most philosophers of religion ask when confronted with the reality of plural faiths. Philosophers, trained to attend to the truth or falsity of beliefs, focus primarily on

---

27. Alvin Plantinga, "Pluralism: A Defense of Religious Exclusivism," in *The Rationality of Belief and the Plurality of Faith,* ed. Thomas D. Senor (Ithaca: Cornell University Press, 1995), p. 192. Here, Plantinga uses "attitude" to connote one's overall stance toward the world as a whole and specifically toward the diverse faiths and believers one meets there, but in other texts he speaks much more narrowly of "propositional attitudes" as affirming, denying, or withholding in relation to a specific proposition; see, for example, p. 199.

the question of how to think about the incompatible truth-claims of various faiths. Plantinga himself is a prime example of this tendency. But Plantinga's question about what *attitude* to take toward "other ways of responding religiously to the world" turns the question back from the *object* (the person of another faith and her beliefs) to the *subject* of that awareness. It also moves the focus from a theoretical issue of logical consistency to a practical issue of response. And with those shifts, the question potentially changes profoundly. When I move from asking, "How should I assess the truth of conflicting beliefs promulgated by different religions?" to "What attitude is best for me to take toward the multiple faiths and diverse believers that I encounter?" then *I* become the object of my own scrutiny.

John Hick speaks of his encounter with multiple faiths as occasioning in him a sort of "Copernican Revolution."[28] What Hick has in mind is a transition from a Christocentric theology (which he regards as inherently exclusivistic) to a God-centered theology (which he thinks is much more accommodating of diversity). But the "Copernican Revolution" that is most relevant to the field of philosophy is Immanuel Kant's critical philosophy in which the knowing subject, not the known object, becomes the focus of attention.[29] In that Kantian spirit, I take up Plantinga's question about attitude and suggest a fundamental recasting of the question of religious diversity as a question of our own attitudinal stance toward people of other faiths rather than, initially, as a question about the truth or falsity of their beliefs.[30]

Martha Nussbaum makes a brief, suggestive comment along these lines in an article on religious intolerance. She writes,

Two ideas typically foster religious intolerance and disrespect. The first is that one's own religion is the only true religion and that other religions

28. John Hick, *God Has Many Names* (Louisville: Westminster John Knox Press, 1982), p. 36.

29. "Hitherto it has been assumed that all our knowledge must conform to objects. But all attempts to extend our knowledge of objects by establishing something in regard to them a priori, by means of concepts, have, on this assumption, ended in failure. We must therefore make trial whether we may not have more success in the tasks of metaphysics if we suppose that objects must conform to our knowledge. . . . We should then be proceeding precisely on the lines of Copernicus' primary hypothesis." Immanuel Kant, *The Critique of Pure Reason*, trans. Norman Kemp Smith (New York: St. Martin's, 1965), p. 22.

30. Robert McKim opens his *On Religious Diversity* by asking, "what attitude should such a person take toward the beliefs and salvific prospects of members of other traditions?" but McKim makes his case for "a spirit of mutual respect" via a detailed analysis of standard approaches to the conflicting truth claims of diverse religious faiths. *On Religious Diversity*, pp. 4-5.

are false or morally incorrect. But people possessed of this view can also believe that others deserve respect for their committed beliefs, so long as they do no harm. Much more dangerous is the second idea, that the state and private citizens should coerce people into adhering to the "correct" religious approach.[31]

Pluralists have focused primarily on the first, exclusivist belief as the source of religious intolerance and oppression. They have laid the blame on exclusivism for bloody centuries of religious violence and have argued that until truth-claims are effectively abandoned we can't hope to get along with each other. But Nussbaum says that exclusivism per se is not necessarily violent or oppressive.[32] History is on her side in this. Though the Muslim majority in the Ottoman Empire were supremely confident in the superior truth of Islam, they coexisted peacefully with Christian and Jewish neighbors for long periods. One could cite many similar examples. What concerns Nussbaum is the attitude one assumes toward those one takes to hold false religious beliefs: it is when adherents of one faith come to view the adherents of another as an offense, as unendurable, as an abomination, as needing to be coerced, that religious violence is close at hand. What matters crucially is the attitude of those interacting with adherents of the other faith, and that attitude isn't simply a function of agreement or disagreement with their truth-claims.

Kierkegaard, by developing mood as a central category in his writings, can serve to facilitate such a "Copernican Revolution" in reflection on religious diversity. But what, precisely, is mood for Kierkegaard, and how does mood relate to the neighboring concept of emotion?

Throughout the history of philosophy, emotions have been assigned a decidedly inferior role, far behind cognitions and volitions in attention and prestige. Philosophers have tended to view emotions as too subjective, ephemeral, irrational, and ineffable either to warrant or to bear systematic scrutiny. That bias has come under challenge recently, notably in Nussbaum's *Upheavals of Thought*, which forcefully argues for the integral role of the

31. Martha Nussbaum, "Religious Intolerance," *Foreign Policy*, September/October 2004, p. 44. For a later, fuller development of these views, see Martha Nussbaum, *The New Religious Intolerance: Overcoming the Politics of Fear in an Anxious Age* (Cambridge, MA: Harvard University Press, 2012).

32. See also Merold Westphal, "The Politics of Religious Pluralism," in *Proceedings of the Twentieth World Congress of Philosophy*, vol. 4 (Bowling Green: Philosophy Documentation Center, 1999), pp. 1-8.

emotions in both cognition and action. But even Nussbaum finds it hard to say anything positive about mood. In her typically massive volume, she manages only a short section on moods, and there she tellingly refers to them as "mere moods."[33] Why the disregard? Central to Nussbaum's brief on behalf of emotions is their intentionality. That is, emotions manifest the same *aboutness* that characterizes beliefs. (I believed *that* the check I wrote would clear the bank. I am angry *that* it didn't.) But moods don't.

> Emotions always have an object, even if it is a vague object; they always invest the object with value and involve the acceptance of beliefs about the object. . . . Moods such as irritation, gloom, elation and equanimity lack these characteristics.[34]

Nussbaum's purely negative characterization of mood as an affective state lacking intentionality leads her to view it as nothing more than a subjective coloring of our psychological life (ironically repeating the dismissive gesture she is at such pains to correct).

But another philosophical tradition, begun by Kierkegaard and brought to full theoretical development by Heidegger, locates the fundamental significance of mood precisely in its non-intentionality. Mood is not about any particular aspect of the world. Rather, mood is the way the world as a whole reveals itself. To speak Heideggerese for a moment:

> Moods are not sensuous states that belong to the lower irrational and "appetitive" faculty of the soul, and which often lead "rational man" astray from his calm intellectual contemplation and deliberate conduct. Rather, they are [a] fundamental way in which Dasein is aware of its Being-in-the-world, and which are more *ontologically* primordial than the rational thematization of being as something that lies "at-hand" *(vorhanden)* before the contemplative intellect. It is not "reason" that gives Dasein its basic access to being, but *moods*.[35]

33. Martha Nussbaum, *Upheavals of Thought: The Intelligence of Emotions* (Cambridge: Cambridge University Press, 2001), p. 133.

34. Nussbaum, *Upheavals of Thought,* p. 133. At least some theorists of mood dispute this point by arguing that *the entire world* is the generalized intentional object of the mood. Eric Lormand discusses but doesn't endorse this view (which he calls "fishy") in his "Toward a Theory of Moods," *Philosophical Studies* 47 (1985): 392-93.

35. Quentin Smith, "On Heidegger's Theory of Moods," *Modern Schoolman* 58 (May 1981): 213.

Alphonso Lingis makes the same point in a more poetic idiom:

> The world extends resplendent or desolate and oppressive, laughing and full of promise or menacing and evil. Mood is how we are tuned in to the layout, or how the layout reverberates and resonates in us. The world, which extends far about us and whose forms our practical look surveys, is felt to affect us, its materiality matters to us. The world is grasped formally in the practical looking about and looking for and is sensed materially in mood.[36]

What Heidegger explicates in turgid German, replete with hyphens and neologisms, Kierkegaard realizes in literary form. While Kierkegaard approaches mood theoretically in several books (especially *The Concept of Anxiety* and *The Sickness unto Death*), that is not his exclusive way of engaging mood. In addition, he creates a variety of pseudonyms, each ideally representing a life-view, a particular "stage on life's way," who write books from their own distinctive perspectives. Kierkegaard exercises a fascination over many readers in no small part because of his ability to change style radically as he moves from pseudonym to pseudonym. Here, style is philosophically significant. Each of his pseudonyms' styles captures not just a distinctive set of beliefs or values; it captures the way the world appears to that person. That is to say, the style of each book captures the mood of each archetypal character. Thus, in his pseudonymous authorship, Kierkegaard offers what Vincent McCarthy aptly terms a "phenomenology of moods," that is, a philosophical engagement with a variety of fundamental moods that attends as closely to how the world looks and feels to the pseudonyms as it does to what they believe and do.[37]

Since that world includes the religious Other, the mood that structures our being-in-the-world determines the way that religious Other appears to us: as threat or irrelevancy or fellow-seeker or child of God to be loved. In discussing the motto "Truth is subjectivity," we saw that Kierkegaard and key pseudonyms, notably Climacus, try to move us toward practically oriented self-reflection and away from an externally directed objective attitude. In keeping with that subjective, existential turn, Kierkegaard's "phenomenology

---

36. Alphonso Lingis, "The World as a Whole," *Research in Phenomenology* 25 (1995): 150-51.

37. Vincent McCarthy, *The Phenomenology of Moods in Kierkegaard* (Boston: Martinus Nijhoff, 1978).

of moods" prompts us to ask how we view and respond to the other. Rather than an objective curiosity about the beliefs represented by other religions, we instead face the interesting ethical question of how we should encounter our neighbors of various faiths.

Kierkegaard's usefulness to the question of religious pluralism is more specific than such a general encouragement to self-consciously attend to mood: he offers specific analyses and literary realizations of three moods — seriousness, irony, and humor — that are of particular significance to this study.

Kierkegaard investigates irony, first in its Socratic and then in its German Romantic modes, in his thesis *The Concept of Irony*. In the first volume of his next work, *Either/Or*, he brings irony to life in the person of a young aesthete, who studiously avoids taking anything seriously. The second volume of *Either/Or*, chiefly composed of two interminable letters to the aesthete by a lower court judge, is ponderously serious. Kierkegaard's core philosophical writings, *Philosophical Fragments* and *Concluding Unscientific Postscript*, are penned by Johannes Climacus, a self-described humorist. These three moods — seriousness, irony, and humor — correlate to and give new perspective on the three main theoretical approaches to religious diversity: exclusivism, pluralism, and inclusivism.

Exclusivism and Seriousness

On initial encounter, exclusivism appears as an unexceptional extension of a logical truism to the domain of religious claims. Merold Westphal writes,

> I shall use the term "logical exclusivism" to signify the view 1) that the truth of any particular statement excludes the truth of all statements logically incompatible with it and 2) that those who believe any particular statement are obliged to consider false all statements logically incompatible with it. . . . I shall use the term "theological exclusivism" to signify the inclusion of statements and beliefs about the Divine within the domain of logical exclusivism.[38]

But, as Westphal vividly illustrates, what one does with this truism is open to a range of choices. In his *God, Guilt, and Death: An Existential Phenomenol-*

---

38. Westphal, "The Politics of Religious Pluralism," p. 4.

ogy of Religion, Westphal brackets questions of truth, seeking to understand empathetically a wide range of faiths without ever asking which gets it right and which gets it wrong.[39] By placing questions of truth "in *epoche*," Westphal finds deep similarities among the existential concerns that differing religions seek to address.

In contrast, exclusivism as a developed position begins and ends with the truism, making the logical exclusion of incompatible beliefs the guiding principle for thinking about religious diversity. That overriding emphasis on contradiction as the basic mode of interreligious contact both comes from and helps establish a distinctive perspective, tone, and style characteristic of exclusivism. Viewed through a Kierkegaardian lens, exclusivism manifests a pervasive mood: seriousness.

Seriousness is hard to describe succinctly, in part because it is a complex, multidimensional mood, and in part because we are pervasively ambivalent about it. The complex character of the mood comes across in the diverse ways we speak of someone or something as being serious. It can designate honesty versus imposture (as when someone makes a surprising assertion and we ask, "Are you serious?"), concern versus indifference (as when we appeal to someone to take a matter seriously), authenticity versus inauthenticity (as when we differentiate between a serious scholar or musician and a dilettante), commitment versus experimentation (as when we ask whether a relationship is serious), and significance versus meaninglessness (as when we ask whether some activity is serious or not). While each of these uses of "serious" is positive, another range of uses is perjorative. The serious person can come across as pompous and pedantic, smug and self-content, pretentious and pharisaical, fatuous and finicky. Think of Shakespeare's Polonius and the Marx brothers' Margaret Dumont. Oscar Wilde exploits to the full the comic potential of seriousness in *The Importance of Being Earnest.*[40]

Kierkegaard's aesthete, A, gives us a derisive view of seriousness in *Either/Or* 1, where he mocks the busy burghers of Copenhagen; but in *Either/Or* 2, through the letters of Judge William, Kierkegaard takes us into the world of the serious man. For Judge William, life is about making choices: one must make the right choices, in the right way, and then stand by those

39. Merold Westphal, *God, Guilt, and Death: An Existential Phenomenology of Religion* (Bloomington: Indiana University Press, 1987).

40. I discuss Kierkegaard's take on seriousness at greater length in "The Importance of Being Earnest: Coming to Terms with Judge William's Seriousness," in *International Kierkegaard Commentary,* vol. 11: *Stages on Life's Way,* ed. Robert Perkins (Macon, GA: Mercer University Press, 2000).

choices through thick and thin. In pleading with A to leave aside his dissolute, experimental life based on taking nothing seriously, Judge William encourages A to marry, that is, to undertake a life-long, irreversible commitment with profound implications, aesthetically, ethically, and religiously. Just as the decision to marry is a decision "not to be entered into lightly," so Judge William approaches his life as a whole as a "solemn and momentous matter" (*EO* 2:157). Having approached his own life with requisite seriousness, Judge William enjoys the satisfaction of moral self-approval.

Just as Kierkegaard presents seriousness through the writings of a single paradigm, we can see seriousness as the prevailing mood of exclusivism by focusing on Alvin Plantinga's "Pluralism: A Defense of Religious Exclusivism" as well as the slightly amended version of that essay included in *Warranted Christian Belief*. At first glance, Plantinga's texts seem very distant from Judge William's letters; their topics are different, and the analytic style of Plantinga's writings, characterized by explicit definitions and rigorous arguments, couldn't contrast more sharply with Judge William's diffuse, windy style. But underlying both Judge William's and Plantinga's texts are many common features: the same deep earnestness; the same overwhelming sense of the life-and-death importance of choosing rightly in conditions of uncertainty; the same tendency to see all issues from an ethical perspective; and ultimately the same sort of defensiveness over against alternative perspectives.

A first indication that Plantinga speaks out of a mood of seriousness is his persistent positive use of the term. The authentic adherent of a faith is "a serious believer";[41] one fulfills one's epistemic duty by giving "serious and responsible consideration" to a contested claim;[42] one encounters a potential defeater for one's beliefs when one meets "people of great intelligence and seriousness" who have incompatible beliefs.[43]

Plantinga endorses seriousness because he sees it as the uniquely appropriate attitude to take toward belief formation. When forming beliefs, especially about ethical and religious questions, "the stakes are, indeed, very high (it matters greatly whether you believe the truth). . . . I realize I can be seriously, dreadfully, fatally wrong, and wrong about what it is enormously important to be right."[44] The reference here to getting belief right points to the intimate connection between Plantinga's realism and the prevailing

---

41. Alvin Plantinga, *Warranted Christian Belief* (Oxford: Oxford University Press, 2000), p. 454.

42. Plantinga, "Pluralism: A Defense of Religious Exclusivism," p. 205.

43. Plantinga, *Warranted Christian Belief*, p. 437.

44. Plantinga, *Warranted Christian Belief*, pp. 436-37.

mood of seriousness. Joel Kupperman writes, "When people think and speak seriously, this seriousness usually appears to be guided by the ideal of capturing definitive truth, getting the world just right."[45] That ideal is a key feature of Plantinga's thought: "One of our most fundamental and basic ideas is that there is such a thing as *the way things are* . . . the existence of truth is intimately connected with there being a way things really are, a way the world is."[46] Plantinga specifically affirms that such robust realism is an integral component of Christianity: "[I]t is certainly crucial to Christian belief to suppose that there *is* a way things are, and that it includes the great things of the gospel."[47] For Plantinga, getting one's beliefs about these "great things" right is maximally, eternally important, and so only a maximally serious attitude toward such questions can be appropriate.

As with Judge William, Plantinga's seriousness is pervasively ethical in character. In making his case that one can be justified in holding a realist belief in the face of alternative views, Plantinga invariably appeals to examples of despicable moral behavior: an employer discriminating on the basis of race, an employee lying about a colleague to advance one's career, David's seduction of Bathsheba, and a counselor seducing a client.[48] While a pluralist such as Hick draws on ethically neutral examples, such as Jastrow's duck-rabbit or wave-particle models of light, where diverse ways of seeing things can coexist peacefully, Plantinga's ethically charged examples solicit black-and-white, unequivocal, realist judgments.

In stating his case for such judgments, Plantinga gives expression to the fundamental orientation, the mood, that pervades his writings on religious diversity:

> I am dead sure that it is wrong to try to advance my career by telling lies about my colleagues; I realize there are those who disagree; I also realize that in all likelihood there is no way I can find to show them that they *are* wrong; nonetheless, I think they are wrong. If I think this after careful reflection — if I consider the claims of those who disagree as sympathetically as I can, if I try my level best to ascertain the truth here — and it *still* seems to me sleazy, wrong, and despicable to lie about my colleagues

---

45. Joel Kupperman, *Classic Asian Philosophy,* 2nd ed. (Oxford: Oxford University Press, 2006), p. 116.

46. Plantinga, *Warranted Christian Belief,* p. 425.

47. Plantinga, *Warranted Christian Belief,* p. 425.

48. Plantinga, "Pluralism: A Defense of Religious Exclusivism," pp. 199, 201, 204, 214.

to advance my career, could I really be doing something immoral in continuing to believe as before? I can't see how.[49]

Plantinga "stands his ground," to use the colloquial, or, as William Alston puts it, he "sits tight." He chooses to continue to inhabit his beliefs unreservedly, to feel at home in them, even after encountering alternative beliefs. This isn't just an act of cognitive assent. It reveals a mood, a way of encountering the world as full of different beliefs that I mustn't let throw me off course. It is the experiential mode that correlates to a certain epistemic doggedness.[50] Nowhere is this attitude more explicit and self-conscious than in Plantinga's diagnosis of postmodernism as a "failure of nerve." In contrast to postmodernist wobbliness, Plantinga lauds Christian thinkers — Pascal, Kierkegaard, Kuyper — who boldly affirm their faith commitments full in the knowledge that there are no foundations, no guarantees, no certainties:

> This is a stance that requires a certain epistemic hardihood: there is, indeed, such a thing as truth; the stakes are, indeed, very high (it matters greatly whether you believe the truth); but there is no way to be sure that you have the truth; there is no sure and certain method of attaining truth by starting from beliefs about which you can't be mistaken and moving infallibly to the rest of your beliefs. Furthermore, many others reject what seems to you to be most important. This is life under uncertainty, life under epistemic risk, and fallibility. I believe a thousand things, and many of them are things that others — others of great acuity and seriousness — do not believe. I realize I can be seriously, dreadfully, fatally wrong, and wrong about what it is enormously important to be right. This is simply the human condition: my response must be finally: "Here I stand; this is the way the world looks to me."[51]

This is undoubtedly stirring, especially to readers of Kierkegaardian sensibility. Plantinga boldly transposes Luther's "Here I stand" into an exis-

---

49. Plantinga, "Pluralism: A Defense of Religious Exclusivism," p. 201.

50. This doggedness is reflected in Julian Hartt's statement, "When we are seriously and affirmatively engaged with the Christian faith we not only *believe* the Gospel is true, we *claim* it is true, and we assert its truth." Quoted in Ronald F. Thiemann, *Revelation and Theology: The Gospel as Narrated Promise* (Eugene: Wipf & Stock, 2005), p. 93. This mood predominates in Thomas Oden's *The Rebirth of Orthodoxy* (New York: Harper, 2002), the second chapter of which is entitled "Serious Jews, Serious Christians."

51. Plantinga, *Warranted Christian Belief,* pp. 436-37.

tentialist key. But what does such an attitude mean for religious diversity? How does the religious Other appear when disclosed through the mood of Plantingian seriousness?

In the first analysis, Plantinga describes the presence of multiple faiths as disorienting: "the world displays a bewildering and kaleidoscopic variety of religious and antireligious ways of thinking"; the welter of faiths represents "a buzzing, blooming confusion."[52] After one adjusts to the cacophony of religious messages, the existence of other faiths emerges for Plantinga as a challenge or even a threat. Plantinga categorizes religious diversity as a possible defeater of Christian belief, that is, as evidence that potentially undercuts the warrant of Christian belief. He consistently discusses other faiths as competitors, as rival alternatives to Christian belief, not as complementary experiences of the sacred from which Christians might learn. And this is what we should expect when the guiding principle of an approach to diversity is the logical truism that contradictory beliefs can't both be true: "Think, for a moment, about disagreement. Disagreement, fundamentally, is a matter of conflicting attitudes with respect to a given proposition."[53] Viewed through the lens of seriousness, the pervasive mood of exclusivism, other religions appear first and foremost as rivals.

In both versions of his essay on exclusivism, Plantinga begins on an autobiographical note, describing his initial encounter with ideological diversity when he went to Yale for graduate training. He closes both versions on a similarly if implicitly autobiographical note. Whereas "for at least some Christian believers, an awareness of the enormous variety of human religious experience does seem to reduce the level of confidence in their own Christian belief,"[54] such an awareness can have the opposite effect on other believers.

> A fresh or heightened awareness of the facts of religious pluralism could bring about a reappraisal of one's religious life, a reawakening, a new or renewed and deepened grasp and apprehension of [the basic tenets of Christian belief]. . . . In this way knowledge of the fact of pluralism could initially serve as a defeater; in the long run, however, it can have precisely the opposite effect.[55]

52. Plantinga, *Warranted Christian Belief,* pp. 437, 438.
53. Plantinga, *Warranted Christian Belief,* p. 445.
54. Plantinga, *Warranted Christian Belief,* p. 456.
55. Plantinga, *Warranted Christian Belief,* p. 457.

This passage succinctly captures the main thrust of Plantinga's career: a dogged, determined, uncompromising defense of the rational warrant of Christian belief in the face of challenges, both religious and secular. Plantinga's response to disagreement, his unqualified identification of himself with what he understands as orthodox Christian belief, vividly embodies the mood of seriousness.

Pluralism and Irony

Just as Plantinga prefaces his discussion of religious diversity with an auto-biographical sketch, so John Hick opens his *God Has Many Names* by describing his movement from being "a Christian of a strongly evangelical and indeed fundamentalist kind" to becoming a dedicated advocate of religious pluralism: the view that all major faiths are equally well situated in relation to both truth and salvation.[56] After working and worshiping with Muslim, Sikh, Hindu, and Jewish communities in Birmingham, England, and then studying for a year in India and Sri Lanka, Hick became powerfully convinced that "essentially the same kind of thing is taking place in [mosque, temple, synagogue, and gurdwara] as in a Christian church — namely human beings opening their minds to a higher Divine Reality."[57]

Trained as a philosopher, Hick faced the challenge of reconciling his compelling intuition that all major faiths are equally authentic responses to the divine with the basic logical principle that contradictory beliefs cannot both be true. Much of Hick's philosophical career was devoted to resolving that challenge by articulating a pluralist philosophy of religion along broadly Kantian lines. Drawing on Kant's distinction between the noumenal and the phenomenal, Hick argues that "the great post-axial faiths constitute different ways of experiencing, conceiving and living in relation to an ultimate divine reality which transcends all our varied versions of it."[58] That is, "we . . . have to distinguish between the Real *an sich* and the Real as variously experienced-and-thought by different human communities."[59] By opening

---

56. Hick, *God Has Many Names*, p. 14.

57. Hick, *God Has Many Names*, p. 18.

58. Hick, *An Interpretation of Religion*, pp. 235-36.

59. Hick, *An Interpretation of Religion*, p. 236. In another essay, Hick makes this point especially vividly: "The religious tradition of which we are a part, with its history and ethos and its great exemplars, its scriptures feeding our thoughts and emotions, and perhaps above all its devotional and meditational practices, constitutes a uniquely shaped and colored 'lens'

a space between the Real as it is in itself and the Real as humanly experienced, Hick looks to defuse the problem of apparently contradictory truth-claims: different faiths are not making contradictory statements about the Real *an sich* (since the Real *an sich* is beyond our categories, we can't make statements about it at all), but they are instead making compatible and even complementary assertions about different phenomenal manifestations of the Real. "Such varying appearances of the Real within different collective and individual consciousnesses are no more mutually incompatible than are the larger cultural complexes to which they are integral."[60]

While the different faiths use "various religious languages"[61] to articulate their distinct experiences of the Real, pragmatically and soteriologically they are really all about the same project: reorienting selves from egocentric lives toward Reality-centered lives. In one of his early writings on religious pluralism, Hick extends the concept of truth to include such personal transformation. In a manner parallel to Climacus's idea of subjective truth, Hick describes "personalistic truth" as "the moral truthfulness of a person's life."[62] Sumner Twiss describes such truthfulness as "the existential coherence between propositional beliefs and the sort of life and character developed in light of those beliefs."[63]

The tone of Hick's writings is every bit as serious as Plantinga's. If anything, it is even more so. For Plantinga sprinkles his deeply serious defense of Christianity with facetious examples, many involving Frisians. Such playfulness is absent from Hick, who brings the missionary impulse of his evangelical days to his advocacy of pluralism. Where Plantinga simply aims to defend Chris-

---

through which we are concretely aware of the Real *as* the personal Adonai, or as the Heavenly Father, or as Allah, or Vishnu or Shiva . . . or again as the non-personal Brahman, or Dharmakaya, or the Void or the Ground. . . . Thus, one who uses the forms of Christian prayer and sacrament is thereby led to experience the Real as the divine Thou, whereas one who practices advaitic yoga or Buddhist zazen is thereby brought to experience the Real as the infinite being-consciousness-bliss of Brahman, or as the limitless emptiness of *sunyata* which is at the same time the infinite fullness of immediate reality as 'wondrous being.'" John Hick, "Religious Pluralism and Salvation," in *The Philosophical Challenge of Religious Pluralism*, ed. Phillip L. Quinn and Kevin Meeker (Oxford: Oxford University Press, 2000), pp. 59-60.

60. Hick, *An Interpretation of Religion*, p. 375.

61. Hick, *An Interpretation of Religion*, p. 246.

62. John Hick, "The Outcome: Dialogue into Truth," in *Truth and Dialogue in World Religions*, ed. John Hick (Philadelphia: Westminster, 1974), p. 144. Quoted by Sumner Twiss, "The Philosophy of Religious Pluralism: A Critical Appraisal of Hick and His Critics," in Quinn and Meeker, eds., *The Philosophical Challenge of Religious Pluralism*, p. 93.

63. Twiss, "The Philosophy of Religious Pluralism," p. 93.

tianity against challenges — to provide "defeater defeaters" — Hick undertakes a reformist project: he doesn't just want to change the way philosophers think about religious truth-claims; he aims for a fundamental revision of how the Christian church thinks about itself in relation to other faiths.[64]

While Hick makes his case in a relentlessly direct and utterly earnest way, when viewed through the lens of Kierkegaard's theory of moods Hick's pluralism reveals itself as irony. According to Kierkegaard, the "quality that permeates all irony [is] . . . that the phenomenon is not the essence but the opposite of the essence" (*CI*, 247). In its most basic form as a rhetorical trope, irony is a discrepancy between what is said (the phenomenon) and what is actually meant (the essence). But in the person of Socrates, Kierkegaard discerns a broader, more profound irony. In Socrates, irony is a "qualification of personality," an existential viewpoint that skeptically surveys the beliefs and practices of a given society as phenomena that lack essence, as currencies that lack any real assets to back them up. Socrates continues to live in Athens, as an Athenian. But the ideas and practices of Athens have lost their unquestioned and unquestionable authority for him. He inhabits his Athenian identity differently, diffidently, as a light, loose cloak. Further, Socrates enacts and disseminates his ironic stance through his life of questioning his fellow Athenians: "By means of his questions, he quietly sawed through for toppling the primeval forest of substantial consciousness" (*CI*, 190).

The parallel to Hick's basic idea is evident: the gap between the Real *an sich* (the noumenon) and the Real as-thought-and-experienced (the phenomenon) allows Hick to dissipate the appearance of contradiction between the beliefs of different faiths. Each faith authentically describes the Real as it is manifest to it. But that accommodation comes at a price: no faith knows or names the Real as it is in itself. And so, on Hick's construal, all language about the Real needs to be placed in "scare-quotes." As Hick puts it, "the different doctrinal systems are downgraded from conflicting universal and absolute truth-claims to local truths valid only within a given tradition."[65]

But what does it mean to a believer to "downgrade" her beliefs in this way, to shift from regarding the tenets of her religious faith in a straightforwardly realist way to viewing them as one among many culturally relative ways of talking about an inaccessibly remote divine reality? While seriousness is marked by a complete identification of the believer and her beliefs, Hick's pluralism opens an ironic distance between the two. Just as Socrates

---

64. See ch. 6 of Hick, *A Christian Theology of Religions*.
65. Hick, *A Christian Theology of Religions*, p. 42.

sought to waken Athenians from an uncritical, unexamined assumption that existing ideas and practices are legitimate, Hick challenges the unreflective realism, absolutism, and exclusivism of religious believers. Just as Socrates remained an Athenian, Hick remains a Christian, but in a different, diffident, loose-fitting way.

The ironic character of Hick's pluralism comes more clearly into focus when we call to mind Richard Rorty's definition of an ironist:

> I shall define an 'ironist' as someone who fulfills three conditions: (1) She has radical and continuing doubts about the final vocabulary she currently uses, because she has been impressed by other vocabularies, vocabularies taken as final by people or books she has encountered; (2) she realizes that argument phrased in her present vocabulary can neither underwrite nor dissolve these doubts; (3) insofar as she philosophizes about her situation, she does not think that her vocabulary is closer to reality than others, that it is in touch with a power not herself.[66]

There is an uncanny parallelism between Rorty's characterization of irony as an encompassing perspective and Hick's philosophical and theological development. Hick's encounter with devout people from a variety of faiths shook him to the core, causing him not only to doubt but to reject the exclusivist understanding of Christianity he had been taught. When Hick concluded that the central Christian doctrine of Christ's unique status as incarnate God is inextricably linked to such exclusivist understandings, he undertook to revise that doctrine radically, construing talk of Jesus' divinity as mythical or metaphorical. Far from calling on argument to support one final vocabulary over all others, Hick spent his career using argument to challenge any such priority. And, in regard to Rorty's third condition, the main thrust of Hick's pluralism is to insist that no religious final vocabulary is "closer to reality" than are the others: all are infinitely distant in that no vocabulary captures the ineffable Real; all are infinitely close in that they each can help "soteriologically align" believers with the Real so as to effect personal transformation.

Despite these parallels, there is a fundamental difference between Rorty's irony and Hick's pluralism: where Rorty's ironist denies any contact with or closeness to "a power not herself," Hick insists that such contact and close-

---

66. Richard Rorty, *Contingency, Irony, Solidarity* (Cambridge: Cambridge University Press, 1989), p. 73.

ness are universal features of the human condition. Rortean irony dwells in a world cut loose from all transcendent moorings, while Hick's pluralism presupposes a noumenal Real that lies behind and manifests itself in all the different particular religions.

But if Hick isn't a Rortean ironist, neither is he a metaphysician as Rorty uses the term. For Rorty, metaphysicians are those who believe that "the vocabulary they have inherited, their common sense, provides them with a picture of knowledge as a relation between human beings and 'reality.'"[67] But that is just what Hick is at such pains to deny, because such commonsensical realism drives exclusivist, absolutist tendencies in religion. Where Rorty's ironist "knows of no power of the same size as the one with which the metaphysician claims acquaintance," Hick's pluralist does.[68] Better, Hick's pluralist knows *of* such a power without knowing anything *about* that power. And this is where the parallelism between Hick's pluralism and Socratic irony as described by Kierkegaard comes into view.

In *Concept of Irony*, Kierkegaard uses Xenophon, Plato, and Aristophanes to triangulate Socrates' identity as ironist. Where Xenophon gives us a banal, earth-bound figure and Plato gives us a speculative metaphysician in the making, Aristophanes gives us a Socrates who hovers in his Thoughtery, midway between heaven and earth. This hovering captures for Kierkegaard Socrates' purely negative relationship to transcendent ideality. As aware of that ideality, Socrates is no longer earthbound, no longer fully identified with the realities of his time and place; but neither does he ascend into the heavens as the speculative philosopher aspires to do. Rather, Socrates' purely negative relation to the ideal takes shape as ignorance.

> [Socrates'] ignorance is by no means an empirical ignorance; on the contrary, he was a very well informed person. . . . In a philosophical sense, however, he was ignorant. He was ignorant of the ground of being, the eternal, the divine — that is, he knew that it was, but he did not know what it was. He was conscious of it, and yet he was not conscious of it, inasmuch as the only thing he could say about it was that he did not know anything about it. . . . Socrates had the idea as boundary. (*CI*, 169)

Just as Hick's Real *an sich* remains an utterly indefinite, ineffable ultimate object of religious devotion, beyond all particular phenomenal religious

---

67. Rorty, *Contingency, Irony, Solidarity*, p. 75.
68. Rorty, *Contingency, Irony, Solidarity*, p. 90.

manifestations, so Socrates' daimonion represents "something abstract, something divine, something that precisely in its abstraction is above definition, is unutterable and indescribable" (*CI*, 158). While neither Hick nor Kierkegaard's Socrates knows anything positive and substantive about this Real *an sich,* their awareness of it relativizes all particular attempts to name and know that reality. Just as that awareness places Socrates at an ironic distance from the civic gods of Athens, so Hick's notion of a noumenal divine reality leads him to describe all particular doctrinal characterizations of that reality as myths, as accounts to be taken with an ironic grain of salt.

Kierkegaard himself confirms this reading of Hick as ironist. In discussing the attitude toward religion characteristic of the German Romantics, Kierkegaard describes Lessing's *Nathan the Wise,* an unmistakable forerunner of Hick's pluralism, as ironic.

> One religion or another was momentarily the absolute for [Romantic irony], but it also was very well aware that the reason it was the absolute was that irony itself wanted it so — period. In the next moment, it wanted something else. Therefore it taught, just as it is taught in *Nathan der Weise,* that all religions are equally good. (*CI,* 278)

Despite the formal parallelism between Socrates' irony and Hick's pluralism, the unnamable, unknowable ideal serves different roles for the two thinkers. As Kierkegaard presents him in *The Concept of Irony,* Socrates is a subversive, polemically oriented toward an Athenian society that correctly viewed him as an existential threat: "For the ironic subject, the given actuality has lost its validity entirely; it has become for him an imperfect form that is a hindrance everywhere" (*CI,* 261). In contrast, Hick's agenda is basically conservative: if the various religions will moderate their absolutist claims, they all are able to carry on pretty much as before, just with less antagonism.

> Each tradition will continue in its concrete particularity as its own unique response to the Real. As the sense of rivalry between them diminishes and they participate increasingly in inter-faith dialogue they will increasingly affect one another. . . . But nevertheless within this growing interaction each will remain basically itself. In this respect, the pluralistic hypothesis makes comparatively little difference to the existing traditions.[69]

69. Hick, *A Christian Theology of Religions,* p. 30.

While Hick's stance toward the status quo is less ascerbic than Kierkegaard's, the prevailing mood of his pluralism, when viewed through a Kierkegaardian lens, is ironic.

This becomes much more evident when we turn from Hick to John Caputo, whose "religion without religion" makes a similar appeal to a divine reality that ultimately escapes our linguistic and conceptual nets, that is always other than any of our attempts to name it. Caputo writes,

> [T]he great monotheistic religions are all ways of giving determinate positive content to our desire for God, and even more fundamentally to our desire *tout court*. The great philosophical systems . . . do the same thing. But in my view . . . , the positive programs of both the philosophies and the theologies must be regarded with a certain ironic distance. These are beautiful and powerful constructions, but they are, as such, deconstructible.[70]

Any failure to remember this, any lapse into seriousness and its attendant realism, any succumbing to a "fundamentalism" whose belief is "direct, non-ironic and reactionary," unleashes unacceptable risks.[71] And so, for Caputo, the challenge is to figure out how to maintain ironic distance even as we call upon those traditions to make sense of our lives.

> When we cease to understand the contingency of our traditions *vis a vis* competing traditions, they become dangerous. Now the thing is, and I always ask myself this — is it possible to inhabit a construction, understanding that it's a construction? Can you inhabit a tradition with ironic distance?[72]

Pluralism as developed by Hick is an attempt to answer Caputo's question in the affirmative.

Inclusivism and Humor

In exploring exclusivism and pluralism, we have seen two approaches to religious diversity, each of which seems one-sided. Exclusivism, as the the-

---

70. John D. Caputo and Gianni Vattimo, *After the Death of God,* ed. Jeffrey W. Robbins (New York: Columbia University Press, 2007), pp. 118-19.

71. Caputo and Vattimo, *After the Death of God,* p. 154.

72. Caputo and Vattimo, *After the Death of God,* p. 155.

oretical correlate of seriousness, so identifies itself with its religious commitments that it sees the religious Other primarily in terms of disagreement. By coinciding so completely with itself, by resolutely committing itself to viewing the world from its own religious vantage point, it closes itself off from imaginative identification with the religious Other. Pluralism, eager to acknowledge the religious Other, so loosens its ties to its own beliefs that an ironic distance opens up. In imaginatively identifying with many different religious possibilities, pluralism can become homeless, nomadic, displaced, *khoric* (as Caputo puts it).

Inclusivism, as the third main option on the issue of religious diversity, takes up the right challenge: to remain fully committed, yet to take full account of other faiths; to have a religious home but to open one's doors in hospitality to the religious Other.[73] But how to pull that off? To insist, as inclusivists characteristically do, that one's own faith is the true one while allowing others some sort of honorary membership isn't really to move away from seriousness. Another more internally complex mood is needed, one that can accommodate the two distinct stances of commitment and openness. Humor is a plausible candidate for that role.[74]

Conrad Hyers describes religious humor (or, as he puts it, "holy laughter") as a complex dialectic of seriousness and playfulness. He writes, "The comic is fundamentally a certain attitude toward and perspective on life. The essential element in relation to the sacred is the periodic suspension of seriousness and sacrality (the comic spirit) and the realization of the playful, gamelike comic perspective."[75] But this suspension of seriousness is, paradoxically, grounded in seriousness. Hyers later writes, "Seriousness is the prerequisite and ground of humor; it is the precondition apart from which humor would be reduced to cynical contempt. . . . Humor as the profanation

---

73. Joseph Runzo characterizes the problem of religious pluralism thus: "how can we remain fully committed to our most basic truth-claims about God, and yet take full account of the claims of other world religious traditions?" Runzo, "God, Commitment, and Other Faiths," p. 343.

74. Simon Critchley discusses Helmuth Plessner's assertion that laughter reveals the eccentric character of humans, where eccentricity designates non-coincidence with self. "While animals are *zentrisch*" (they are what they are, they simply live and experience), "humans are *exzentrisch*" (they are reflective and thus "liv[e] outside themselves"). Simon Critchley, *On Humour: Thinking in Action* (London: Routledge, 2002), p. 28. This eccentricity, this "non-coincidence with self," is formally what we are looking for in seeking a way to combine commitment with openness, to hold together disagreement and approval.

75. Conrad Hyers, *Holy Laughter* (New York: Seabury, 1969), p. 7.

of the sacred . . . is to be differentiated from that which has no basis in the sacred, from that which is not grounded in faith."[76]

This paradoxical vision of a seriousness that checks and even suspends itself and of a playfulness that is deeply rooted in serious commitment is promising but in need of conceptual articulation. I propose that Kierkegaard's analysis of humor goes a long way toward such an articulation.

Kierkegaard's Analysis of Humor

Kierkegaard's most significant published statements on humor are found in his 1846 work, *The Concluding Unscientific Postscript,* attributed to the pseudonym Johannes Climacus. This text lives up to its self-description: it is highly "unscientific" in that its statements about humor are widely scattered throughout the text (often in footnotes), and they are so fragmentary, oblique, and even contradictory as to require considerable work on the part of the interpreter. Thankfully, several scholars, notably Robert Roberts, C. Stephen Evans, and John Lippitt, have set themselves the task of piecing together Climacus's tantalizing remarks on humor.[77] I will highlight just a few main points.

First, Climacus is no ordinary language philosopher, reconstructing standard usage of the term "humor." He refers to Christianity as the most humorous worldview and says that the humorist, like the religious individual, has an essential conception of suffering, by which he means that suffering is rooted in the essential structures of human existence, not in accidental features of particular lives (*CUP* 1:447). (To use Heideggerian terminology, suffering is ontological, not ontic.)

Second, Climacus aligns himself with the tradition that relates humor and contradiction. That is, some sort of incongruity, some contrastive juxtaposition, is essential to humor. This helps us to understand Climacus's

---

76. Hyers, *Holy Laughter,* p. 24.

77. Robert Roberts, "Smiling with God: Reflections on Christianity and the Psychology of Humor," and C. Stephen Evans, "Kierkegaard's View of Humor: Must Christians Always Be Solemn?" both appear in *Faith and Philosophy* 4, no. 2 (April 1987). Chapter 10 of Evans's *Kierkegaard's* Fragments *and* Postscript: *The Religious Philosophy of Johannes Climacus* is also very helpful. John Lippitt's *Humor and Irony in Kierkegaard's Thought* (London: Macmillan, 2000), is the fullest treatment of the topic. See also his "A Funny Thing Happened to Me on the Way to Salvation: Climacus as Humorist in Kierkegaard's *Concluding Unscientific Postscript,*" *Religious Studies* 33 (1997): 181-202.

surprising linkage of humor and religion: "The humorist continually . . . joins the conception of God together with something else and brings out the contradiction" (*CUP* 1:505). The greatness of God, set over against the smallness of all we do, know, and are, renders us more than a bit funny from the divine perspective. The humorist has enough of a sense of that perspective that humor becomes her life-view, her fundamental mood, and not just an episodic diversion.

Third, humor involves not just contradiction but, as Climacus puts it, a "way out," a resolution of or escape from the contradiction (*CUP* 1:520). Inescapable, irresolvable contradiction is tragic; an unrelieved sense of our smallness and insignificance leads to nihilism. True humor differs from both in finding a way to rise above the contradiction to a higher, reconciling perspective. Again, we see why Climacus tends to associate humor and Christianity, which does not simply offer a higher perspective but also promises grace and redemption as "ways out" of the tragic contradictions in which we mire ourselves.

Fourth, humor as mood orients the subject toward the world in a manner that qualifies and moderates the sense of urgency that naturally attends to ultimate issues. As John Lippitt puts it, the humorist is "laid back."[78] A sense of the disproportion between God and ourselves inoculates (at least it should) against hubris and inflated self-image. And that, in turn, should save us from an undue sense of how much is ultimately up to us, allowing us to take things with a grain of salt.[79]

While these themes are all clearly present in the *Postscript*, it isn't evident precisely how Climacus wants us to put them together to form a coherent overall conception of humor. He variously describes humor as an alternative perspective to Christianity, as the incognito (that is, the ambiguous external appearance that hides the internal subjective reality) of religious existence, and as a component aspect of Christianity. Different interpreters emphasize different aspects: Lippitt tends to emphasize the view that humor is an existence-form distinct from and inferior to Christianity; Evans and Roberts tend to emphasize humor as integral to Christian existence. All of these interpreters point to passages that support their views.

Sorting out Kierkegaard's full conception of humor is clearly beyond the scope of this chapter, but by focusing on several journal entries from 1837 we

78. Lippitt, "A Funny Thing Happened," p. 194.

79. Robert Roberts discusses the way Christianity can encourage taking even weighty moral matters with a "light touch." "Smiling with God," p. 172.

can see that he is working toward an idiosyncratic conception of humor that is highly suggestive for our consideration of religious diversity. The first of these entries, reflecting on Colossians 1:26, describes humor as an integral feature of Christianity:

> The humorous, which is implicit in general in Xnty is expressed in a fundamental principle which says that the truth is hidden in the mystery (ἐν μυστεριω ἀποχρυφη), which teaches not just that the truth is found here in a mystery (an assertion which the world on the whole has been more willing to hear since mysteries have arisen often enough in spite of the fact that those initiated into these mysteries promptly apprehended the rest of the world in a humorous light), but even that it is *hidden* in the mystery, which makes it precisely the life-view that sees the most humor in worldly wisdom; otherwise the truth is usually *revealed* in the mystery. (*KJN* 1: DD, 6)

Kierkegaard here specifically contrasts the Christian teaching that truth is *hidden* in mystery with the alternative religious notion of truth as *revealed* in mystery. When truth is viewed as revealed, a view the world is ready to hear, those granted the revelation know better and are able to laugh at those who aren't in the know. As he puts it, they "promptly apprehended the rest of the world in a humorous light." But when, as in Christianity, truth is hidden *in mystery,* all such pretension is blocked. In the next paragraph he writes, "no matter how much Christian knowledge increases, it will still always remember its origin and therefore *knows* everything εν μυστεριω [in mystery]."

Kierkegaard offers here a complex concept of revelation that asserts both genuine knowledge of the divine — he speaks of the increase of Christian knowledge — and God's ultimate hiddenness. (In a later appended note to this entry, he writes, "the concept of revelation can in itself very well include the concept of the hidden" [*KJN* 1: DD, 6c].) The mindset appropriate to such a concept of revelation is exactly the divided, complex attitude needed to respond authentically to the presence of the religious Other. The believer needs both a real sense that through her faith she has received an authentic disclosure of the divine (the dimension of seriousness) and an equally strong sense of the partial, provisional, and flawed character of that disclosure (the dimension of irony). Just as Conrad Hyers suggests in his discussion of holy laughter, Christian humor for Kierkegaard involves both seriousness and its ironic suspension.

On this distinctive notion of humor, the polemical dimension of the divine — the way the absolute relativizes all before it — applies as much to believers as to nonbelievers. That is, the superiority dimension of humor, the sense of knowing better than the butt of the joke, isn't claimed for oneself but is reserved for God. Kierkegaard turns to this self-reflexive dimension of humor in an undated passage from 1837 where he writes, "The ironical position is essentially: *nil admirari;* but irony, when it slays itself, has *disdained* everything with humor, itself included" (*SKP* II A 627; *JP* 2, 1688).[80]

This requirement that humor be self-reflexive comes through in an entry on Hamann from August 1837. There, Kierkegaard contrasts Hamann, a real Christian humorist, with many in Christian Europe who achieve no more than Christian irony. He writes, "They therefore either seek a resting-place in the church where the entire concord of individuals develops as a Christian irony in a humor against the world . . . , or, where religiousness has not been set in motion, form a club" (*KJN* 1: DD, 36). The thought here is that when individuals group together mutually to congratulate each other on their superior insight, they remain at the level of irony and their humor is incompletely realized. Hamann, in contrast, checks himself: what he knows of God as a Christian constantly reminds him how little and how provisionally he knows.

Kierkegaard did not himself work out the implications of his view of humor for the question of religious diversity. No doubt Kierkegaard's own position on religious diversity more closely resembled Plantinga's seriousness than either of the other alternatives I've sketched out. Like Plantinga, Kierkegaard describes faith as full, unqualified commitment (subjective certainty) to a belief that is acknowledged as objectively uncertain. But a framework for what I've described as a humorous stance toward religious diversity is already implicit in his distinctive, suggestive ideas. Most obviously, the element of epistemic humility, the emphasis on truth as hidden in mystery, checks imperialist, triumphalist impulses that are so frequently sources of interreligious conflict. So far, this parallels Hick's pluralism. But where Hick checks religious hubris by relativizing particular, positive religions in relation to a philosophically constructed idea of an ultimate noumenal reality, Kierkegaard looks within his own particular religious tradition in order to find grounds for humility and self-criticism. We see this in the early journal entries on humor quoted above, but the use of specifically Christian religious resources to critique Christian actuality is the dominant motif of

---

80. Simon Critchley writes, "In my view, true humor does not wound a specific victim and always contains self-mockery. The object of laughter is the subject who laughs." *On Humour,* p. 14.

Kierkegaard's "second authorship." As such, it isn't a long stretch to appeal to such resources of self-critique as the basis of a Kierkegaardian stance toward religious diversity.

This contrast points up a crucial strategic difference between various approaches to achieving healthy religious coexistence. Since the Enlightenment, many philosophers and theologians have looked to achieve harmony within pluralistic societies by asking various groups, especially religious groups, to subordinate their particular convictions to some set of broader, more generic principles that are accepted universally. A good example of this strategy for consensus and cooperation is John Rawls's *A Theory of Justice*. As Richard Mouw and Sander Griffioen put it,

> How can we deal justly with a diversity of perspectives on the meaning, value, and purpose of human existence? We can only do so, Rawls argues, if we operate with a thin notion of the good. For Rawls this means that we will be able to achieve consensus in the public realm only if we set up our deliberations in such a way that the thick contents of various religious, philosophical, and moral doctrines are not allowed to play a decisive role in public discussions about what is just and fair.[81]

What Rawls proposes as a political philosophy, Hick advocates as a philosophical and theological self-understanding. Where Rawls theorizes a liberal society organized in reference to a thin conception of the good, Hick points the way "towards thinner theologies"[82] when he argues for a move from highly particular Christocentric theology toward a much more generic theocentrism.

In sharp contrast, Kierkegaard calls upon the full resources of the Christian religious tradition, in all its scriptural thickness, to counter tendencies toward religious hubris. It is symbolically and substantively important that he developed his distinctive notion of humor specifically in reflecting on a particular biblical text, Colossians 1:26. Whereas much modern philosophy of religion takes as its subject generic monotheism, what William Rowe calls "revised standard theism," Kierkegaard, throughout his authorship, again and again takes richly specific texts as his point of departure. His exploration

---

81. Richard J. Mouw and Sander Griffioen, *Pluralism and Horizons: An Essay in Christian Social Philosophy* (Grand Rapids: Eerdmans, 1993), p. 21.

82. Philip L. Quinn, "Towards Thinner Theologies: Hick and Alston on Religious Diversity," in Quinn and Meeker, eds., *The Philosophical Challenge of Religious Diversity*, pp. 226-43.

of Genesis 22 in *Fear and Trembling*, the topic of the next chapter, is a case in point. Rather than checking religious hubris by thinning out, by attenuating, his theology, Kierkegaard with his idea of humor suggests going deeper into the rich particularity of faith traditions to find reasons for religious humility. Miroslav Volf lays out a specifically Christian case for Christian humility in a manner exactly parallel to Kierkegaard's notion of humor. In what he calls a "protective disclaimer," Volf writes,

> The first thing we need to remember as we seek to learn anything from Jesus Christ is that *we are not Jesus Christ.* Applied to the question of truth this means that, unlike Jesus Christ, we are *not* the truth and we are *not* self-effacing witnesses to the truth. This is why we believe in Jesus Christ — to help us see that we are not what we ought to be and to help us become what we ought to be. Our commitment to Jesus Christ who is the truth does not therefore translate into the claim that we possess the absolute truth. If we know the truth, we know it in our human and corrupted way; as the Apostle Paul puts it, we "know in part," we see "in a mirror, dimly" (1 Corinthians 13:12f).[83]

While Kierkegaard and Volf are entirely on the same page in finding resources internal to Christian faith to check religious imperialism, Volf goes beyond this negative moment in ways that Kierkegaard does not. For Volf, acknowledging our epistemic limitation, having a robust sense of our partial, biased, fallen view of things, opens the way for a "double vision" in which we *"step outside ourselves"* and *"move into the world of the other* to inhabit it temporarily,"* in order finally to *"take the other into our world."*[84] In his recent book *Allah: A Christian Response,* that other is specifically a religious Other, a follower of another faith. Volf's specific Christian commitment leads him to an open, respectful engagement with faithful Muslims, who, like Volf, enter conversation on the basis of their own particular faith, calling on the internal resources of that faith to sponsor authentic, constructive encounter with one not of their own faith.[85]

83. Miroslav Volf, *Exclusion and Embrace: A Theological Exploration of Identity, Otherness, and Reconciliation* (Nashville: Abingdon, 1996), p. 271.

84. Volf, *Exclusion and Embrace,* pp. 251-52.

85. Ronald Thiemann writes, "Communities of faith must come to recognize the compatibility between deep and abiding commitment to the truth claims of one's tradition and an openness and respect for the claims of another tradition." *Revelation and Theology* (Eugene: Wipf & Stock, 2005), p. 161.

While his analysis of Christian humor opens the door to the sort of "double vision" that Volf advocates, Kierkegaard himself didn't go through it. We look in vain in Kierkegaard for the sort of open, empathetic encounter with contemporary religious Others that Volf describes (though Kierkegaard does imaginatively engage with Socrates on something like these terms). Kierkegaard's own outlook, especially in his later writings, is closer in spirit to what I have described as seriousness. Like Plantinga, Kierkegaard acknowledges the *objective* uncertainty of his Christian faith, but he speaks of faith as embracing those uncertainties with *subjective* certainty, with unqualified conviction. "The understanding counts and counts, calculates and calculates, but it never arrives at the certainty faith possesses" (*WL*, 105).[86] To put it in terms of Pascal's wager, Kierkegaard sees faith as going "all in." That totality of commitment corresponds to a mood of seriousness that is very much in evidence in Kierkegaard's late religious writings. And from that totality of commitment and corresponding seriousness issue a number of statements with rather clear exclusivist import.

That acknowledged, Kierkegaard's scattered, unsystematic sketch of humor suggests ways in which religious faith can be "self-delimiting," ways in which it can check its own tendencies toward arrogant self-assertion. Beyond the potential narrowness of a seriousness that utterly identifies itself with its own convictions and a free-floating irony that inhabits viewpoints only provisionally and playfully, Kierkegaardian humor points toward a deep fidelity to one's own faith that itself motivates respectful, humble openness to those of other faiths by reminding us of our own tentative, incomplete, fallible hold on the very truth we acknowledge.

86. Stephen Evans called my attention to this passage in urging me to acknowledge fully affinities between Kierkegaard's and Plantinga's ideas of faith as objective uncertainties held with subjective certainty.

CHAPTER 3

Transposing Transgression:
Reading *Fear and Trembling* through Danish Film

In late September of 2001, with smoke still rising from the ruins at Ground Zero, I reluctantly followed my syllabus and took up the task of reading Kierkegaard's *Fear and Trembling* with a group of students.[1] Prior to 9/11, Kierkegaard's choice of the Akedah, Abraham's sacrifice of his long-awaited son, Isaac, as the paradigmatic example of religious faith was disturbing. In the immediate aftermath of real, cataclysmic religious violence, it was well-nigh unbearable. Kierkegaard wrote his disturbing text to shake up a complacent Europe in which religious faith was viewed as a blend of civic rectitude and popularized philosophy. But how are we to read it given our changed circumstances?

Troels Nørager argues that, in our new context, "all people of good faith" within the three Western monotheisms need to "take leave of" their shared patriarch, Abraham:

> [I]n our current world marred by acts of terror which is [*sic*] at least partly motivated by religious concerns, the story of Abraham and Isaac

---

1. Throughout this chapter, I will speak of Kierkegaard as the author of *Fear and Trembling*, but it should be noted that the stated author of the text is a Kierkegaardian pseudonym, Johannes de Silentio. Kierkegaard stresses that the writings of his pseudonyms are not to be attributed to him. Further, there is strong reason to believe that there are important differences of perspective between Silentio, who says he is not a Christian, and Kierkegaard, who writes as a Christian believer in his non-pseudonymous works. As important as the issue of pseudonymity is in coming to an adequate understanding of Kierkegaard's texts, it is not an issue I will take on in this chapter. For a recent discussion of differences between Johannes de Silentio and Kierkegaard, see ch. 3 of C. Stephen Evans's *Kierkegaard's Ethic of Love: Divine Commands and Moral Obligations* (Oxford: Oxford University Press, 2004).

has gained acute relevance. For even a superficial reading of Genesis 22 should prompt the reader to think of contemporary acts of terror where individuals see themselves as acting on God's command. In other words, a Biblical story that was always disturbing has become even more disturbing, to the point that it is time that we must ask ourselves whether it is time to be "taking leave of Abraham."[2]

Nørager boldly links the Genesis 22 account of the Akedah and contemporary acts of terrorism:

> Today, we cannot help drawing a parallel to the Palestinian suicide bomber (or Mohammed Atta in the plane on 9/11) who is en route to his target and waiting to enter the pearly gates of Paradise. Obviously, we have no way of knowing whether Kierkegaard, had he been writing F&T, would have been inclined to demand a less passionate version of faith, but it is certainly a question one cannot help asking.[3]

However Kierkegaard might have responded to contemporary events, Nørager declares *Fear and Trembling* a brilliant failure. As Nørager reads it, in *Fear and Trembling* Kierkegaard fundamentally seeks to give us an Abraham relevant to modernity, an Abraham who can retain his position as "the father of faith." But for Nørager, Abraham stands ineluctably as a symbol of blind, amoral obedience to absolute authority. And so, as he puts it, the time has come for people of faith to "take leave of Abraham." Though Kierkegaard sought to present Abraham as a paradigm of authentic faith, Nørager reads *Fear and Trembling* instead as a devastating exposé of the unacceptably authoritarian roots of Abrahamic religion, an exposé that demands that people of faith reflect self-critically and fundamentally adapt their faith to the circumstances of modernity, specifically to the democratic political order in which private religious convictions are not allowed to trump public secular determinations of policy and law. While Nørager's book has much to say about the appropriate place of religion within secular modernity and very little to say about the roots of religious violence, the figure of the religious terrorist is central to his argument. He repeatedly brandishes the case of Mohammed Atta to warn readers of the unacceptable implications of fol-

---

2. Troels Nørager, *Taking Leave of Abraham: An Essay on Religion and Democracy* (Aarhus: Aarhus University Press, 2008), p. 10.

3. Nørager, *Taking Leave of Abraham*, p. 52.

lowing Kierkegaard in trying to hold on to Abraham. And so, the cogency of his parallelism between Kierkegaard's Abraham and contemporary religious extremists is crucial to the success of his argument.

Contrary to Nørager, I am convinced that a careful reading of *Fear and Trembling* rules out viewing it as an apology either for violent religious fanaticism or for absolute amoral divine authoritarianism. At the root of our disagreement is the question of how to read Kierkegaard's disturbing text. Nørager insists that we read *Fear and Trembling* "straight" rather than construing the commanded sacrifice of Isaac in any metaphorical way.[4] Finding fault with many commentators on *Fear and Trembling* who try to get both Abraham and Kierkegaard "off the hook" by taking the Akedah as a metaphoric expression of one or another more palatable message, he insists on a literal reading. Nørager correctly notes that Kierkegaard himself decried evasive, comfortable readings of this text. In order to awaken his readers to the "fear and trembling" of Abraham's situation, Kierkegaard remorselessly reimagines the Akedah in all its terror, forcing us to walk with Abraham on the way to Moriah, to see him gather the wood and draw the knife. Nørager insists that we read *Fear and Trembling* in the same spirit that Kierkegaard read Genesis 22. The God of Genesis 22 commands that Abraham kill his innocent son; the Abraham of Genesis 22 obediently answers that command. To try to "hold on to" Abraham as "the father of faith" means, for Nørager, both accepting an absolutist vision of God and endorsing Abraham's resolution to obey. This in turn sets up his comparison of Abraham and contemporary religious terrorists.

Against Nørager's literalist reading of the text, I align myself with many other interpreters of *Fear and Trembling* who find it both more plausible and more interesting to read the text metaphorically, to approach it as asking subtler (if equally disturbing) questions than whether we ought to obey purportedly divine orders to go out and kill someone. Nørager is well aware of these other readings, reviewing a number of them in his book before dismissing them as evasions. Rather than rehearsing those other readings, I will approach *Fear and Trembling* obliquely in this chapter by viewing it through two Danish films, Carl Dreyer's *Ordet* (The Word) and Lars von Trier's *Breaking the Waves*. What I have found in years of teaching Kierkegaard is that the two films help my students achieve a much deeper sense of what is centrally at issue in *Fear and Trembling*. The presentation of abstract ideas in a visual format and through a narrative arc grabs college students in a way that texts

---

4. Nørager, *Taking Leave of Abraham*, p. 87.

(especially older texts) seldom do. Certainly, the shocking conclusion of *Ordet* and the wrenching horror of *Breaking the Waves* capture much of the "fear and trembling" that Kierkegaard set out both to describe and to evoke. But the key value of coming at *Fear and Trembling* via the two films is that transposing the transgression at the heart of Kierkegaard's text into different registers breaks the spell by which Abraham's raised knife freezes our gaze, allowing us to see aspects of Kierkegaard's text that we otherwise miss.

In what follows, I will first sketch out a reading of *Fear and Trembling* that brings issues of singularity and hope beyond all rational expectation to the fore, rather than divine command meta-ethics and the authentication of purported divine commands. Then I will discuss the two Danish films, von Trier's *Breaking the Waves* and its inspiration, Dreyer's *Ordet,* so as to emphasize several key themes in *Fear and Trembling* that are too easily missed. By bringing the text and the two films into dialog, I will both make a case for metaphoric rather than literalist readings of the text and highlight how fundamentally different Kierkegaard's Abraham is from the religious terrorists who have seized the spotlight in recent years.

Beyond "Pure and Holy Murder": A Different Way of Reading *Fear and Trembling*

Kierkegaard distills the troubling essence of the Abraham and Isaac story in his concept of a "teleological suspension of the ethical." In raising the question of whether there can be such a suspension, Kierkegaard asks whether ethical obligation is absolute or whether some non-ethical concern could override and therefore suspend our ethical obligations. We are familiar with the general idea of "suspension" from our experience of one ethical obligation overriding another, as when we "suspend" our duty to tell the truth in order to fulfill our duty to save innocent life. Kierkegaard asks in *Fear and Trembling* whether a non-ethical concern could similarly override and therefore suspend our highest ethical obligation. An example of a potential "teleological suspension" is Paul Gaugin's (in)famous decision to put the imperatives of artistic creation ahead of his ethical duties to his family by leaving France for Tahiti. For one who values aesthetic good over moral good, such a choice is presumably warranted. For Kierkegaard, the ostensive question is whether a primary religious good (obedience to God) could trump a primary ethical good (care for one's child).

As noted above, Kierkegaard's analysis naturally strikes us as profoundly dangerous in today's world of rampant religious violence. Not only does *Fear and Trembling* lift up an appalling story of intended violence as a paradigm of faith, but it also seems to provide a ready rationale for programs of religious violence. Insofar as the promotion of the True Faith is an ultimate concern, the requirements of that promotion presumably trump all merely ethical concerns, such as respecting the safety of noncombatants.

To resist such a reading of *Fear and Trembling,* we need to ask about Kierkegaard's agenda in writing the book. As it turns out, Kierkegaard has multiple agendas and the text is accordingly multilayered. But at the heart of his motivation in writing this text is a concern that his age has lost all sense of what it is to have faith, of what it is to exist as a Christian believer. This loss of understanding has two primary aspects: (1) the idea, associated with Hegel, that the content of faith (its "what") is reducible without remainder to the rational insights of philosophy; and (2) the understanding, operative in Christendom, that being a Christian (its "how") is reducible without remainder to fulfilling ethical obligations.

Kierkegaard focuses on God's command to Abraham that he must sacrifice Isaac, precisely because it isn't rationally explicable. The issuance of such a command is "indigestible" within Hegel's system, and resistant to philosophical explanation in general. Abraham has waited decades for the son promised as part of his covenant with God. When that promise is finally fulfilled (after all rational expectation had evaporated), it is incomprehensible that God would ask Abraham to sacrifice its fruits. Accordingly, Abraham is considered to be the father of faith for believing in that which transcends his capacity for rational comprehension and for humbling himself before the rational opacity of what he is asked to do.

Further, Abraham challenges the idea that faith is equivalent to moral rectitude. In ethical terms, he has to be classified as someone who was about to commit murder. If we are to hold on to him as "the father of faith," it must be by using a fundamentally different evaluative scheme than that used by moral and legal consciousness. As Kant notes, the mark of a law, whether natural or moral, is universality and necessity. Thus, moral imperatives are non-arbitrary (necessary) and general (universal). A moral requirement applies either to all humans *qua* humans (e.g., to respect innocent life) or to all members of a certain class of humans (e.g., the duty of parents to care for their children). But the command to sacrifice Isaac is neither necessary nor universal. There is no suggestion that God somehow *had* to command this sacrifice. It appears to be an entirely contingent trial that God imposes on Abraham. Further, the command is addressed to Abraham individually, not to Abraham as a token of a type. God commands Abraham to kill Isaac; God does not command all fathers over 100 to kill all their sons between the ages of 15 and 20.

The individual address of God's command to Abraham is crucial to Kierkegaard's project in *Fear and Trembling*. Fundamentally, Kierkegaard wants to ask whether faith (an individual's relation to God as an individual) is possible, or whether all relation to God is mediated by ethics and thus involves assuming (and disappearing into) generic roles. To function in society, all of us learn to disappear into generic roles by effacing our particularity. When one checks in at an airport to go on a trip, one assumes the role of generic passenger, just as airline staff play their roles generically (thus the uniforms). Such self-effacement obviously contributes to smooth, efficient functioning. But if ethical selfhood is the highest human goal, then self-effacement is a universal requirement. As Kierkegaard sums up this view, "The single individual . . . is the individual who has his τέλος in the universal, and it is his ethical task continually to express himself in this, to annul his singularity in order to become the universal. As soon as the single individual asserts himself in his single individuality before the universal, he sins" (*FT*, 54). Against this view, Kierkegaard presents Abraham as a case study of a man with an essentially individual (if terrible) vocation. Much of *Fear and Trembling* describes in excruciating detail how terrible such starkly individual existence can be: how such an individual cannot possibly communicate with others about that particular vocation and how such an individual is necessarily viewed as mad or immoral or both by his or her society.

While Kierkegaard's discussion of the teleological suspension of the ethical introduces the key theme of radical particularity, it doesn't capture all that is essential in the story of Abraham and Isaac. As Kierkegaard repeatedly stresses, it isn't Abraham's willingness to sacrifice Isaac that makes Abraham the father of faith. Rather, it is Abraham's unwavering expectation that Isaac will not ultimately be taken from him and his ability to accept back the son he was prepared to sacrifice that marks him as God's chosen. In contrast to "infinite resignation," which involves willingness to give up what is dearest to one in this life and to accept instead the consolation of an other-worldly communion with God, Abraham's paradoxical faith expects fulfillment in the here and now. "Abraham had faith. He did not have faith that he would be blessed in a future life but that he would be blessed here in the world. God could give him a new Isaac, could restore to life the one sacrificed. He had faith by virtue of the absurd, for all human calculation had ceased long ago" (*FT*, 36).

Kierkegaardian Themes in Lars von Trier's *Breaking the Waves* and Carl Dreyer's *Ordet* (The Word)

While a careful reader can see in Kierkegaard's text these motifs of singularity and hope beyond rational expectation for recovery of what is lost, the horrifying spectacle of Abraham lifting the knife over his son so transfixes our gaze that we have real difficulty in getting past typical, less illuminating readings of the text. This is where the two Danish films can help. Speaking generally, both von Trier's and Dreyer's films belong, with Kierkegaard's *Fear and Trembling,* to a tradition of presenting religious faith as paradoxical, as involving contact with an incomprehensible divine Other that, at least initially, plunges one into isolated anguish by alienating one from the values and ways of thinking of one's society. But the real value of the films emerges only at the level of specific details. To provide a framework for discussing those details, I offer a brief synopsis of the films, starting with von Trier's more recent (and familiar) *Breaking the Waves,* then moving on to Dreyer's classic, *Ordet.*

As *Breaking the Waves* opens, Bess, a good-hearted but apparently simple-minded girl from a severe Calvinist community in an isolated Scottish coastal village, weds Jan, a rough-hewn North Sea oil worker. (Significantly, Jan descends from the sky by helicopter for the wedding.) The wedding celebration brings two worlds into collision: the somber, puritanical world of Bess's church and the exuberant, profane world of the oil workers.[5] Great-hearted Bess is at home in both worlds because she unreservedly combines their disparate loves: she shows her love of God by spending hours cleaning the church where she engages God in constant, familiar conversation; her love of rock music and her frankly carnal delight in sex with Jan shows a love of worldly pleasures to match that of the oil

---

5. Kyle Keefer and Tod Linafelt write, "The coming together of Bess and Jan physically mirrors and depends upon the overcoming of the communal borders set up by Bess's church and embodied by the elders. Jan and his friends from the oil rig are patently presented as outsiders, whom Bess is introducing into this place in which they seem so foreign. The character of Bess embodies the erotic impulse toward border-crossing and the mixing of realms." Keefer and Linafelt, "The End of Desire: Theologies of Eros in the Song of Songs and *Breaking the Waves,"* in *Imag(in)ing Otherness* ed. S. Brent Plate and David Jasper (Atlanta: American Academy of Religion, 1999), pp. 55-56. Cited from Todd Penner and Caroline Vander Stichele, "The Tyranny of the Martyr: Violence and Victimization in the Martyrdom Discourse and the Movies of Lars von Trier," in *Sanctified Aggression: Legacies of Biblical and Post-Biblical Vocabularies of Violence,* ed. Jonnecke Bekkenkamp and Yvonne Sherwood (London: T&T Clark, 2003), p. 186.

workers.[6] After a short, blissful time together, Jan must return to work on the oil rig. Bess is distraught and prays to God to bring him home. As if in horrible fulfillment of her prayer, Jan suffers a devastating head injury on the rig and returns to shore for medical care. Much of the rest of the film traces the gradual deterioration of Jan's condition, both physical and mental. The doctors regard permanent paralysis as a given, and only repeated surgeries keep him alive. Whereas Jan had formerly been the self-confident, powerful partner and Bess childlike in her dependency, the tables are turned now, and Jan relies entirely on the care of others while Bess throws herself selflessly into caring for him. Diminished to a damaged mind in an unresponsive body, Jan makes a terrible request of Bess: to remind him of what it is to love, he asks that she have sex with other men and then narrate the events to him. Bess is appalled and initially walks away, hurling insults, but she quickly decides that it is her divinely ordained duty as a wife to obey Jan's request. Further, she is convinced that obeying can save Jan.

Though her attempts at fornication are excruciatingly awkward, she redoubles her efforts every time Jan's condition deteriorates. Cast out by both church and family, and dressed as a harlot, Bess makes the ultimate sacrifice to save Jan: she returns to a ship shunned by prostitutes as too dangerous, knowing she will be horribly treated. Indeed, she dies from the injuries she suffers there. Though Bess never learns of it before her death, Jan not only survives but recovers the use of his limbs (a minor miracle). Jan and his friends steal Bess's body from the church that formally consigns her to hell so that she may be surreptitiously buried at sea (thus an empty grave). In the final scene, the sound of church bells (beloved by Bess but forbidden by her church) echoes inexplicably over the empty North Sea (a major miracle).

While *Breaking the Waves* stands on its own both as a film and as a supplement to *Fear and Trembling,* a full understanding of the film requires awareness of its debt to Carl Dreyer's *Ordet.*[7]

As is the case with most of his films, Dreyer's *Ordet* works from a preexisting literary text, Kaj Munk's 1925 play of the same title. Munk, a Lutheran

---

6. According to von Trier, the original impulse behind *Breaking the Waves* was to make an erotic film. That impulse survives in a single explicit sex scene between Bess and Jan, a scene that is somewhat tamed in the American version of the film. Jack Stevenson, *Lars von Trier* (London: British Film Institute, 2002), pp. 90, 99.

7. In an interview with Ole Michelsen, von Trier says, "As I see it, the great masters cannot be plagiarized." Ole Michelsen, "Passion Is the Lifeblood of Cinema," in *Lars von Trier Interviews,* ed. Jan Lumholt (Jackson: University Presses of Mississippi, 2003), p. 7.

pastor as well as a playwright, was martyred by the Nazis during their occupation of Denmark. (Given that Dreyer produced his film within a decade of the war, the Munk connection lends a particular resonance to the film.) In the second year of his pastorate in an austere west Jutland parish, Vedersø, Munk was shaken by the deaths of a young woman and her child in childbirth. Shortly thereafter, the director of the Royal Theater in Copenhagen encouraged Munk to write a play that took the experience of farmers seriously.[8] The resulting play and film are set on a family farm, Borgensgaard, where an aging patriarch, Morten Borgen, presides over a household of three sons (Mikkel, Johannes, Anders), a daughter-in-law (Inger), and two granddaughters. Better, Borgen attempts to preside over his household but finds his grand ambitions slipping away. As a younger farmer, Borgen had orchestrated a Grundtvigian religious movement from the farm, but his hopes to see his sons carry on his efforts are coming to naught. His oldest son, Mikkel, expresses disbelief; his youngest son, Anders, wants to marry Anne, a girl from a sharply opposed religious movement; and Johannes, whom he had sent off to Copenhagen to study theology, has gone mad from reading Søren Kierkegaard and now believes himself to be Jesus Christ.[9]

The initial drama of the film turns on the Romeo and Juliet motif of Anders's and Anne's love. These star-crossed lovers try to bridge the yawning abyss that separates two varieties of Lutheranism: the life-affirming Grundtvigianism of Morten Borgen and the dour Inner Mission faith of Peter the Tailor (Anne's father) that emphasizes contrition and personal conversion. (There is a significant class dimension to this conflict. Borgen's Grundtvigianism is the ideology of affluent farm owners while Peter's Inner Mission faith is avowedly that of the poor and socially marginal.) But midway through the film, just as the romantic drama seems to be moving toward climactic conflict, the focus veers off to a health crisis. Inger, Mikkel's wife, has been a bright and sunny presence though the first half of the film, ex-

---

8. Kaj Munk, *Mindeudgave*, ed. Knud Bruun-Rasmussen and Niels Nøjgaard (Copenhagen: Nyt Nordisk Forlag, 1948-59), 1:8.

9. Dreyer's film departs from Munk's play at this point. In the play, when Mikkel explains Johannes's madness to the pastor, he traces the madness to reading Bjørnson and Kierkegaard. At first, Mikkel says that the two authors "filled his mind with doubt," but he goes on to explain that Johannes had been so "carried away" by a Bjørnson play that he had seen with his fiancée that he stepped out in front of a car. His fiancée pushed Johannes to safety, but she was killed in the process. Munk's version makes guilt the cause of Johannes's madness. Dreyer makes the extremity of Kierkegaard's thought the cause. Kaj Munk, *Five Plays*, trans. R. P. Keigwin (New York: The American-Scandinavian Foundation, 1953), pp. 103-5.

pressing radiant love and quiet faith, while cleverly working to win consent for Anne and Ander's marriage.[10] Suddenly, this most sympathetic character goes into labor with her third child. The labor goes badly, and the doctor is forced to dismember the child in order to save the life of the mother. After initial optimism that Inger is out of danger, she suddenly dies, plunging the household, especially her husband, into despair. The film concludes with her funeral. But it is no ordinary funeral. First, the chastened patriarchs agree to the marriage of Anne and Anders (a minor miracle). Then, Johannes, who has wandered in and out throughout the film, declaiming portentous biblical passages, appears just before the lid is placed on Inger's coffin and bids her rise from the dead in Jesus' name, which she does (a major miracle).

Below is a list of some of the key parallels between the two films:

1. Fools of God as main characters: At the center of both films are characters (Johannes and Bess) who exist in immediate communication with God and are regarded by their communities as either insane or "simple."[11] Further, both not only speak with but ventriloquize for God.

2. Isolated North Sea settings: Both films are set in bleak, wind-swept, sparsely populated communities along the North Sea. The sound of howling wind is a common element in both, and the color palette of *Breaking the Waves* is almost as gray as that of its black-and-white predecessor.[12]

3. Romantic attachments across social/religious divides: Both films turn on proposed marriages between members of radically different communities where religion plays a major role in community identity in one or both communities.

4. Pastors and doctors: Both films prominently feature doctors and pastors as iconic symbols of institutional science and religion. In *Ordet*, the doctor and pastor, the only two university-educated members of the rural community, play around a bit with science versus religion ri-

---

10. Inger's maiden name is Kjær. The Danish word for love is Kærlighed (formerly spelled Kjærlighed).

11. The parallelism of Johannes and Bess is not perfect because von Trier has combined elements of two different characters from *Ordet* in Bess. As noted, Bess is like Johannes in being a "fool of God," but she also has many elements of Inger. Both female protagonists express pure love in all their actions, and both face gruesome deaths.

12. In 1988, von Trier, working from a never-realized screen play by Dreyer, directed *Medea*, which sets the Greek tragedy in a Viking context. The howling wind of the Danish west coast is one of the most prominent aspects of that film.

valry. But as they complacently smoke cigars together, we see two similar urban-culture authority figures. In *Breaking the Waves,* the doctor and the pastor are again prominent, but the former is humane and sympathetic while the former is rigid and judgmental.[13] (Von Trier restages the parable of the good Samaritan as he has the pastor walk away from Bess after she has collapsed by the path to the church.)

5. Health crises: Life-threatening illnesses are at the center of both films. In both cases, the crisis is a bolt from the blue. Both set the stage for a contention between science and religion as to which is the appropriate framework within which to think about and respond to the health crisis. The life-or-death stakes impart to each film an emotional intensity otherwise unattainable.

6. Miracles: Both films are thematically fixated on the idea of miracles. The topic comes up repeatedly in *Ordet,* primarily in reference to the restoration of a character (Johannes) to sanity, but then in reference to another character's (Inger's) apparent survival of a disastrous delivery. Her eventual death seems to achieve the minor, subtle miracle of reconciling two feuding families who have kept young lovers from marrying. But just as we think that this rather trite "miracle" is the film's resolution, Dreyer hits us over the head with a shocking scene in which Inger rises from the dead at the command of Johannes. In *Breaking the Waves,* Bess lives in a world of magical thinking, believing implicitly in the power of prayer. She blames herself for Jan's injury, believing that it was caused by her prayer that he return home. She extracts a promise to pray for Jan's recovery from her skeptical but loving sister-in-law, Dodo. When told of Bess's request, the doctor says, "That would be a miracle, indeed." Following Bess's death, Jan not only survives but recovers use of his limbs. As in *Ordet,* this ambiguous miracle (an event not expected but not beyond potential natural explanation) is followed by an unambiguous miracle: everyone on the ship hears the joyous peal of church bells, even while the radar shows an utterly empty sea around them.[14]

13. In another mid-1990s production, *The Kingdom,* von Trier again stages a confrontation between the scientific worldview of modern medicine and believers in the supernatural, but in *The Kingdom* the doctors come off worse in the comparison.

14. In his 1982 interview with Ole Michelsen, von Trier complains that Danish cinema has become "boring" and "insipid" because of its aversion to including the miraculous ("Passion Is the Lifeblood of Cinema," in Lumholt, ed., *Lars von Trier Interviews,* p. 8). In a very informative 1996 interview with Christian Braad Thomsen, von Trier says, "I wanted [*Breaking the Waves*] to include a real miracle, and it had to be credible." When Thomsen states that the

7. Reversal: The final shocking miracles retroactively challenge the condescending views of the mad and/or simple central characters that viewers
naturally share with the "normal" characters in the films. Not only is our
confident sense that we can distinguish sane from insane destabilized,
but our sense that we know how the "real world" operates is shaken.[15]

These parallels, together with von Trier's statements and actions (such
as frequently wearing Dreyer's tuxedo), point to a linkage of the two films,
a linkage that has not been sufficiently acknowledged. What is even less appreciated is the shared Kierkegaardian background of the two films. I won't
focus on pathways of influence (though Kierkegaard was a major figure in
the intellectual development of the playwright Kaj Munk, whose play is the
basis of Dreyer's film).[16] Rather, my experience over years of showing these
films to students confirms that viewing the films against the backdrop of
Kierkegaard's *Fear and Trembling* allows us to appreciate the films more

---

miracle at the end of *Ordet* is not credible, von Trier replies, "I don't think I agree with you
on that." Von Trier explains that the credibility he is aiming for is in the context of the film
rather than in relation to reality. Earlier in the interview, von Trier says, "I regard religion
as I do miracles in that I don't believe in them but I hope for them to occur" ("Control and
Chaos," in Lumholt, ed., *Lars von Trier Interviews,* pp. 109, 110). This passage signals an ironic
and ambivalent attitude that is evident throughout von Trier's films. It is also interesting to
note that one of von Trier's earliest films, the seven-minute *Why Try to Escape That Which You
Know You Can't Escape From? Because You Are a Coward,* a boy killed by a truck rises from
the dead. Similarly, von Trier's 1982 student film, *Images of a Relief,* ends with a miraculous
ascension of a violently killed German soldier. Von Trier was raised in a rigorously secular and
unsentimental family setting, so his cinematic fixation on the miraculous and supernatural as
well as his involvement with Catholicism has the character of radical rebellion. Jack Stevenson
writes, "The final 'miracle scene' with the heavenly church bells clanging in the sky, was not,
so to speak (no pun intended), pulled from out of the blue. Von Trier had placed 'miraculous'
scenes in other films. . . . As corny as it sounds, he believed in miracles, at least in the movies.
And he wanted the film to be corny, to both brutally realistic and to be a children's fable at the
same time" (Stevenson, *Lars von Trier,* pp. 12, 28, 91-92).

15. In von Trier's *The Kingdom,* two hospital dishwashers with Down syndrome are presented as having deeper insights into the strange goings-on in Rigshospitalet than the so-called
normal personnel and patients.

16. Von Trier cites the Marquis de Sade's *Justine* as the direct inspiration of *Breaking
the Waves* (Stevenson, *Lars von Trier,* pp. 89-90). While the theme of suffering goodness is
central to *Breaking the Waves,* de Sade's heroine remains conventionally ethical while Bess
does not. I have found no interviews or statements indicating a self-conscious reliance on
Fear and Trembling by von Trier. Accordingly, I point out illuminating parallelisms between
his film and Kierkegaard's book while maintaining an agnostic attitude toward the causes of
these parallelisms.

profoundly, just as the films make vivid several elusive and troubling aspects of Kierkegaard's text.

Despite their many parallels, the two films transpose the transgression at the heart of *Fear and Trembling* differently. Dreyer's film completely transfers the transgression of law from the moral to the natural realm. Miracles have exactly the same structural features as teleological suspensions of the ethical: in both instances, a divine command authorizes a particular exception to a universal principle. While such miracles represent an offense to reason, they don't offend moral judgment. Rather, the miracles at issue in *Ordet* are all morally laudable (restoration of sanity, of peaceful relations between adversaries, and of life).

While von Trier's film follows Dreyer's in including miracles both subtle and overt (to offend our sense of how the natural order works), he follows Kierkegaard much more closely in offending our moral sensibilities by presenting the horrifying image of command and obedience at odds with universal moral principle. Following his injury and resulting paralysis, Jan asks Bess to have sex with other men and then narrate the events to him. He initially presents the idea as a concession to Bess, but when she expresses revulsion he asks her to do it for him as a way of reminding him what love is. Asserting that "Love is a powerful force" and that it is the only thing that can keep him alive, Jan's request is tantamount to a command. (Further, Bess's church stresses the absolute duty of the wife to obey her husband.) Thus, Jan's prurient request takes on the force of God's terrible command to Abraham. In both cases, an absolute authority figure issues a command that contravenes moral principles. This command is addressed to a specific person in specific circumstances in contrast to the universality of moral commands.

The idea of faith as an individualized relation between lovers rather than as a relationship mediated by generic rules comes through clearly in the aftermath of Bess's first sexual encounter with another man. Rushing off the bus where the encounter occurred, she vomits and cries out, "Forgive me, Father, for I have sinned." She closes her eyes, lowers her head, and switches into a deep brogue, signaling God speaking, and replies, "Mary Magdalene was a sinner and yet she was among my dearest."[17]

Her community, in contrast, can only imagine relation to God as mediated by rules and doctrines that are universal. In a telling scene, Bess enters her church, dressed as a prostitute, during a service. A member of the congregation declares, "There is only one thing for us, sinners that we are,

---

17. *Breaking the Waves* 1:35.

to achieve perfection in the eyes of God: through unconditional love for the word that is written, through unconditional love for the law."[18] Though the church forbids women to speak in church, Bess asks, "How can you love a word?" She answers her own question, "You can love another human being. That is perfection." And, of course, she is immediately cast out.

The theme of social ostracism is a central part of both *Fear and Trembling* and *Breaking the Waves*. By obeying their individually addressed commands, both Abraham and Bess are isolated from their communities. They can't explain themselves, and their actions are necessarily viewed by their communities as immoral, insane, or both. Kierkegaard employs all his literary powers to make us feel the terrible isolation of Abraham, but the images of Bess cast out from her church, locked out of her home, stoned by jeering children, left unconscious by the path to the church, and, finally, mortally beaten by sadistic sailors are fully as harrowing.

Von Trier is stunningly successful in bringing Kierkegaard's idea of a teleological suspension of the ethical to life on the screen. The theological implications of his cinematic adaptation are, however, quite troubling. Initially, Jan is a benevolent, even paternal presence who descends from the gray skies to wed Bess and to live with her in rapturous love. But the Jan who issues terrible commands is paralyzed, semi-conscious, barely alive, and, in his own words, "evil in the head."[19] While God's motivation for ordering the sacrifice of Isaac is left deeply mysterious, Jan's motivation for ordering Bess to commit adultery is sexual voyeurism caused by physical impotence.[20] It is as if von Trier has combined Kierkegaard's idea of the teleological suspension of the ethical with Nietzsche's idea of the death of God: a God on "life-support" makes arbitrary, perverse, destructive demands on believers who are willing to do anything to keep their failing beloved alive. Jan is aware of and disturbed by his descent into pathological imaginings and desires. He asks Bess, "You think we turn into different people when we get close to the edge, that we turn bad when we are going to die?" Bess doesn't answer his question but insists, "You are not going to die, I promise you."[21] Jan does indeed die shortly thereafter — his heart stops during surgery — but

18. *Breaking the Waves* 2:05.

19. *Breaking the Waves*, 1:47.

20. The line between Jan and God blurs in Bess's mind. Throughout the film, when Bess speaks to God, she ventriloquizes for God, lowering her head, closing her eyes, and deepening her voice. When the injured Jan lies unconscious, Bess similarly ventriloquizes for him, saying in an altered voice, "I love you too, Bess. You are the love of my life." *Breaking the Waves*, 1:06.

21. *Breaking the Waves*, 1:37.

he is brought back to life, whether by the doctors' defibrillator or by Bess's simultaneous fornication we are left to wonder. When Jan sees Bess again, he hands her a shaky note reading, "Let me die, I'm sick in the head." Bess's response is, "I love you no matter what is in your head."[22] Her response raises troubling questions about religious devotion that is not based on moral regard, questions that are near at hand in Kierkegaard's idea of a teleological suspension of the ethical.

If we attend only to Jan's perverse commands and Bess's willingness to obey them, *Breaking the Waves* looks like a warning against religious devotion in the age of the death of God.[23] But when we focus on another key theme from *Fear and Trembling,* Abraham's expectation that he will get Isaac back, the film seems to vindicate Bess's faith. Kierkegaard distinguishes a "knight of faith" from a "knight of infinite resignation" in terms of the former's expectation of restoration or recovery of a cherished good that has been lost or sacrificed. Knights of infinite resignation, by contrast, give up all hope of happiness in this life and turn instead to the otherworldly consolation of an atemporal god-relationship.

Bess is surrounded by knights of infinite resignation who call on her to surrender hope as well. The doctors tell Bess that perhaps death is better for Jan than a life of paralysis. Jan himself says that he has no hope and wants to die. Bess's mother speaks to her of learning to endure loneliness and isolation. Most vividly, Bess's widowed sister-in-law, Dodo, trudges through life in a grim, determined way, with no suggestion that she still hopes for happiness. Against Dodo's resigned widowhood, von Trier sets Bess's fierce refusal to give up hope of Jan's recovery. Where calculative reason sees no prospect of Jan's recovery, Bess conceives the situation in terms of obedience, sacrifice, and miracle: if she obeys Jan's request, distasteful as it is to her, then Jan will be cured. When Dodo discovers Bess's strange sense of mission, she calls Bess stupid and accuses her of "disappearing into a world of make-believe."[24] Nonetheless, she honors Bess's request that she pray for

---

22. *Breaking the Waves,* 1:47.

23. At the conclusion of *Medea,* von Trier also appears to refer to the divine as non-moral in a closing epigram (it looks like text for a silent film, no doubt a Dreyer reference): "A human life is a journey into the darkness where only a god can find the way, for what no man dares believe, God can bring about" (*Medea* 1:15). Here, the suggestion is that God brings about inconceivably awful things, not that God brings about unexpected restorations of life and hope. This places the idea of a non-moral God in a premodern context (classical Greek and Viking) in contrast to the postmodern context of *Breaking the Waves.*

24. *Breaking the Waves,* 1:40.

Jan's recovery. (Learning of this, the doctor says that such a recovery would be a miracle, indeed.)[25] When Bess makes the ultimate sacrifice, returning to a ship to face certain brutality and death, Jan not only survives but recovers use of his limbs. As if this vindication of Bess's faith isn't enough, von Trier ends the film with a divine endorsement, with the sound of bells miraculously tolling over the empty North Sea.

Reading *Fear and Trembling* after 9/11

Having taken a detour through two Danish films, I return to the question of reading *Fear and Trembling* after the terrible events of 9/11 and in the larger context of a world that has seen a significant increase in religiously motivated violence over the past several decades.[26] Specifically, what do these films suggest in regard to Nørager's argument in *Taking Leave of Abraham* that, after 9/11, we ought to read *Fear and Trembling* as exposing Abrahamic faith as fundamentally untenable? As I view them, the two films bear significantly on three key claims Nørager advances: (1) that we ought to read *Fear and Trembling* "straight," that is, to keep central the divine command to kill an innocent and Abraham's willingness to obey that command; (2) that there are significant similarities between Kierkegaard's Abraham and contemporary terrorists who claim religious warrant for their acts;[27] and (3) that absolute divine authority is integral to Abrahamic faith in a way that renders it fundamentally unsuited to modernity generally and secular democracy specifically.[28] The two films "speak" forcefully against the first two claims but deliver mixed messages on the third.

---

25. *Breaking the Waves*, 2:16.

26. William T. Cavanaugh mounts a forceful challenge to cogency of the concept of "religious violence" in his *The Myth of Religious Violence* (Oxford: Oxford University Press, 2009), but Mark Juergensmeyer documents that between 1980 and 1998, the U.S. State Department's list of terrorist organizations went from almost no religiously associated movements to more than half having such links. Mark Juergensmeyer, *Terror in the Mind of God: The Rise of Global Religious Violence* (Berkeley: University of California Press, 1998), p. 6.

27. "[F]rom a contemporary perspective, [Abraham] still looks suspiciously like a religious fanatic or a suicide bomber." Nørager, *Taking Leave of Abraham*, p. 225.

28. "[W]e need to finally distance ourselves from the uncomfortable implication of Abraham's intended sacrifice, namely that the model (i.e. Abraham as the 'father of faith') we are called to emulate is one where what is perceived as God's commands should be unquestioningly obeyed, always." Nørager, *Taking Leave of Abraham*, p. 221.

Separability

Breaking the Waves, like its inspiration, *Ordet*, succeeds marvelously in giving dramatic expression to key themes in Kierkegaard's *Fear and Trembling*. That success argues against Nørager's insistence on reading the text "straight." Von Trier and Dreyer demonstrate in their films that key themes from Kierkegaard's text can be "transposed" into contexts very different from the Akedah and utterly removed from a command to kill an innocent. Their successes point toward both the legitimacy and the fecundity of metaphoric readings of *Fear and Trembling*.

Disanalogy

The Abraham surrogates in the two films, Bess in *Breaking the Waves* and Johannes in *Ordet*, help us to see more clearly how misguided Nørager's claim is that Abraham is significantly like contemporary religious extremists. Nørager makes his claim seem plausible only by ignoring every aspect of Kierkegaard's Abraham other than willingness to kill in obedience to a purported divine command. But Kierkegaard insists that Abraham is the father of faith *not* because of his willingness to kill his son but because of his expectancy beyond reason that Isaac will be restored to him. Bess and Johannes embody radical hope, a hope for miraculously restored life and health that they maintain against the "knights of infinite resignation" who surround them. Nørager repeatedly mentions suicide bombers as his paradigm for a religious extremist, but clearly the most apt Kierkegaardian label for such figures is "knights of infinite resignation." Von Trier's and Dreyer's "knights of faith" highlight the implausibility of Nørager's claim by isolating what Kierkegaard describes as Abraham's key feature — radical hope for this life — from his nondistinctive feature — willingness to kill.

If there is any feature of Abraham that Kierkegaard stresses even more than radical hope, it is existing as a single individual before God. In a "teleological suspension of the ethical," one relates one-on-one to God rather than through the mediation of the universal rules of ethics and the shared meanings of language. Bess and Johannes render vivid the isolation, misunderstanding, and opprobrium that Kierkegaard describes as Abraham's. As Kierkegaard highlights in Problema III, Abraham *cannot* explain himself. The singularity of his situation — like that of Bess and Johannes — renders him incomprehensible to others in his community. In sharp contrast, as

Mark Juergensmeyer notes, "[Religious] terrorism is seldom a lone act. . . . It takes a community of support and, in many cases, a large organizational network for an act of terrorism to succeed."[29] These networks don't just supply logistical support and training; more fundamentally, they provide "ideologies of validation."[30] In his chapter entitled "The Theater of Terror," Juergensmeyer stresses the symbolic nature of "performative violence."[31] Where Kierkegaard's Abraham exists in stark isolation, unable to explain himself to others, contemporary religious terrorists communicate in a symbolic vocabulary that is understandable both within their supporting communities (where it is lauded) and without (where it is condemned). There are many other characteristic features of religious terrorists that Juergensmeyer identifies which fail to match at all with Kierkegaard's Abraham, but the features of radical hope and radical singularity suffice to put paid to Nørager's charge.

Authority

Explaining his title, Nørager writes, "I see no alternative to *taking leave of Abraham*. From him we can learn nothing. If anything, he is an early warning of the contemporary dangers of absolute faith and listening to the alleged commands of a 'strong' and commanding God."[32] What comes across in this statement is Nørager's concern that a God who can "teleologically suspend" ethical demands is one who is "beyond good and evil," an absolute, arbitrary authority. As I discussed earlier, von Trier gives us a nightmarish realization of that fear in the figure of Jan, who commands perverse and self-destructive acts on the part of his wife. In sharp contrast, *Ordet* presents a God who disrupts the normal order of things only in the service of life. Which film best captures the spirit of Kierkegaard's *Fear and Trembling*?

Undoubtedly, Kierkegaard's choice of Genesis 22 is deeply disturbing. God commands and Abraham obeys without explanation, leaving a dire suspicion of divine authority unguided by moral goodness. But the whole corpus of Kierkegaard's writings cries out his profound belief in the goodness of God. Kierkegaard's God is a God of love, not a God of arbitrary, amoral authority. But what to make of the command to kill Isaac?

29. Juergensmeyer, *Terror in the Mind of God*, pp. 10-11.
30. Juergensmeyer, *Terror in the Mind of God*, p. 11.
31. Juergensmeyer, *Terror in the Mind of God*, p. 124.
32. Nørager, *Taking Leave of Abraham*, p. 97.

In the Prelude to *Fear and Trembling*, Kierkegaard repeatedly returns to the image of a mother who blackens her breast as part of the process of weaning her child. Clearly, Kierkegaard invokes this image to suggest that loving motivations may lie behind apparently unloving actions. This suggestion is poignantly relevant to his own recent broken engagement with Regine Olsen, an action that he understood as motivated, at least in part, by his love for her even though it seemed not just unloving but an immoral breach of his commitment to her. However disturbing Kierkegaard's use of Genesis 22 to explore the nature of faith, nothing in the entire corpus of his writings suggests anything other than a profound confidence in the goodness of God.

That observation, however, doesn't fully address Nørager's concern regarding religion and authority. His most fully developed concern isn't that divine authority is amoral but that it stands outside the political process of modern secular polities. What worries him most about Kierkegaard's Abraham is the vision of an individual who puts his or her personal religious convictions above the collective determinations of a secular political order. While Nørager's concern has merit, his resolution of it is disturbing in its own right. For in proposing that "democracy" must trump religious conviction lest we fall prey to religious violence and fanaticism, he runs the risk of absolutizing the nation-state, which gets, in very large measure, to determine what it is that "democracy" has backed. William Cavanaugh's *The Myth of Religious Violence* shows in detail and in depth that just the sort of concerns Nørager expresses over the dangers of religious violence and fanaticism have served as the ideological justification for the authority of the nation-state. As Cavanaugh compellingly argues, that ideology is as capable — or even more capable — of legitimating violence as any religious ideology. Rather than "taking leave of Abraham," perhaps we need to hold on to him, as does Merold Westphal, as an iconic outsider able to critique the prevailing social and ideological order.[33]

Filming the Numinous: Ambiguity and Overtness in Cinematic Presentations of the Divine

As great as is my appreciation of the two films discussed in this chapter, I confess that I find their conclusions radically out of step with Kierkegaard.

33. Merold Westphal, *Kierkegaard's Critique of Reason and Society* (University Park: Penn State University Press, 1992).

Kierkegaard stresses throughout his writings that certainty is unavailable to us in this life, especially on matters of ultimate concern. For him, faith is a passionate, risky commitment to an objective uncertainty. But both *Breaking the Waves* and its forerunner, *Ordet,* end with blatant miracles that apparently dispel uncertainty.[34] Inger's resurrection from the dead instantly converts her skeptical husband, who says, "Now I have found your faith." Similarly, the empty radar screen on the ship gives a scientific/technological validation to the miracle of the bells at the end of *Breaking the Waves.* While Kierkegaard no doubt would have appreciated the shock value of these final miracles, he would have been troubled by their unambiguous verification of religious faith.

This concluding unambiguity of the two films seems especially strange given that the most striking contribution of these films to the tricky matter of representing the divine on film is ingeniously ambiguous. The three great monotheistic faiths all depict God as relating to humans primarily through the mode of speech. But how can one present the divine as speaking in a film without falling into the camp bombast of a Cecil B. Demille film such as *The Ten Commandments*? A film such as Kubrick's *2001: A Space Odyssey,* which presents the numinous object as ineffable and silent, is much more moving cinema. But in these two films, Dreyer and von Trier use ventriloquism by mentally suspect protagonists to bring divine speech into the film. Purportedly divine words echo throughout both films, but other characters in the films (and we as viewers of the films) can never confidently take them as unambiguously the real article. On the contrary, we have every reason to dismiss them as symptoms of psychopathology. And yet, the films themselves force us to hesitate in our rush to judgment. There is a subtle prescience to the purported words of God in both films that leaves us just a bit uneasy in our dismissive attitudes, until the final miracles completely shake our sense of who is mad and what is real. The way the films present the purported voice of the divine but leave it shimmering in uncertainty impresses me as their greatest contribution to the cinematic representation of the religious. It is also the place at which the Kierkegaardian affiliation of Dreyer and von Trier is most evident.

---

34. There is no hint of skeptical response in the film version of *Ordet,* but after Inger's resurrection in Kaj Munk's play the script reads, "DOCTOR *(decisively):* These amateur death-certificates must be done away with." Munk, *Five Plays,* p. 148.

CHAPTER 4

Religion and Religions:
Kierkegaard and the Concept of Religion

Given the variety and indirection of his authorship, saying anything about Kierkegaard that is genuinely beyond dispute is challenging. That said, a prime candidate for such an uncontroversial claim is that Kierkegaard is a *religious thinker,* meaning both that he writes persistently *about* religious life and that he does so *from* religious concerns and convictions.[1] The project of this book — viewing religious diversity through the lens of his thought and writings — reinforces and broadens that identification of Kierkegaard as a religious thinker, but it also problematizes it.

For Kierkegaard and for his pseudonyms, "the religious" is a term of great richness, but their uses of it appear, at least initially, relatively straightforward and conventional. In Kierkegaard's authorship and journals, "the religious" designates an appropriately devoted relationship between humans and the divine. As Silentio puts it, to exist religiously is to stand in an absolute relation to the absolute, a relation he associates with worship (*FT,* 70). Further, the range of his applications of the term is relatively limited. When reaching for examples to illustrate discussions of "the religious," Kierkegaard and his pseudonyms draw almost exclusively on Jewish and Christian traditions, with references to classical Greece and Rome as typically their furthest forays into religious diversity.

---

1. In *The Point of View for My Work as an Author,* Kierkegaard writes, "The contents of this little book affirm, then, that I am and was a religious author" (*PV,* 5). As David Gouwens notes, even if, with Henning Fenger, one has doubts about Kierkegaard's self-characterization of his writings, "one can still read the literature on its own as religious." David Gouwens, *Kierkegaard as Religious Thinker* (Cambridge: Cambridge University Press, 1996), p. 8.

As we read Kierkegaard's texts in the context of our greatly expanded sense of the range of human spiritual life, "the religious" becomes problematic in at least two ways.[2] First, given that Kierkegaard framed his own thinking about religious existence within quite circumscribed boundaries, we must ask how well his characterizations of religion hold up when applied to traditions beyond his ken. For example, how relevant is Kierkegaard's thought when brought into conversation with the nontheistic religious traditions of Asia? The next chapter on Kierkegaard and comparative philosophy will take up that issue directly, but this chapter will focus on a second, more fundamental issue: the problematic character of the very idea of religion as the genus to which particular religions belong as species. As we look more closely at Kierkegaardian explorations of "the religious," we find a striking ambivalence: on the one hand, the category is an indispensable element in Kierkegaard's endeavors to map the contours of human existence; on the other hand, the idea of religion as a genus to which Christianity belongs as a species undercuts his core message about the uniqueness and absoluteness of Christian faith. Behind this ambivalence lies the fundamental dialectical tension in Kierkegaard between a universalist impulse that insists that all humans must have equal opportunities for ethical and religious fulfillment and a particularist impulse that insists that Christianity is *sui generis,* without parallel or analogy.

To make Kierkegaard's ambivalence apparent, I set side by side two sharply contrasting journal entries from late in his life, the first from 1855 and the second from 1851:

Religious Statistics

If one takes the population of the entire world, this is the situation: Among the many millions in every generation there are always only some very few individuals who actually have religion, whether it be the Christian,

---

2. In his survey essay "Religious Diversity: Familiar Problems, Novel Opportunities," Phillip Quinn notes that what seemed plausible definitions of religion in earlier times have been rendered obsolete as our horizons have expanded. For Quinn, this represents a "novel opportunity" for philosophy of religion: "As a result of this expanded knowledge, we have many more examples . . . that can serve as data against which to test a proposed definition of religion. Framing definitional proposals and testing them against such data might be regarded as one of the main tasks of comparative philosophy of religion." In *The Oxford Handbook of Philosophy of Religion,* ed. William J. Wainwright (Oxford: Oxford University Press, 2005), p. 406. As noted earlier, I am taking Quinn's "familiar problems" and "novel opportunities" as the organizing framework for this study.

the Jewish, the Mohammedan, or a pagan religion, but always only some very few individuals who actually have religion.

On the other hand, in similar fashion, among the many millions in every generation there are also some very few individuals who in fact live among the Christians or Mohammedans or Chinese — in short, in any religious society whatever — but always only some very few individuals who actually have no religion.

The rest are to be viewed as male and female members of the *corps de ballet:* Born in China, they have the Chinese religion; in a Christian country, the Christian; in an evangelical Lutheran country, the evangelical Lutheran religion — in short, they do not actually have any religion, but still with this infinite difference from the very few who actually have no religion: That they imagine that they have religion, that they allow the priests to let them imagine it, the priests who — as the Devil's Ballet Masters and disguised as the "Servants of the Lord" — deceptively arrange the matter with these battalions of male and female ballet dancers, who in turn beget children, who, continuing what has already taken place, have the same religion and whom the ballet masters immediately list as having religion.

The formula, expressed by Christianity, for having religion is essentially the same for every religion: First God's Kingdom. This is the formula for the relationship to the Unconditioned, and all religion, even that which is most untrue, has the property that the person who in truth has this religion expresses this "First," in which lies the break with everything else and the most complete isolation. (*SKP* XI 3 B 161)

Freedom of Religion

Our times' notions concerning freedom of religion are indeed so far from being an expression of Xnty's victory that, on the contrary, they express that Xnty has abandoned hope of victory over the world, is willing to be satisfied with being permitted to look after itself. Truly, if that had been Xnty's original view, Xnty would never have come into the world. It came into the world through its need to suffer unto death for the faith; that was precisely why it conquered the world. This need for martyrdom was its "suffering" intolerance. Now it has lost the desire and the need to suffer, lost the intolerance of martyrdom, and is well satisfied with being a religion like other religions, on an equal footing with Judaism, paganism, and irreligion.

Wanting to kill others because of their faith is the intolerance that is repugnant to Xnty. But for oneself to be willing to be put to death for the sake of one's faith — yes, let us not overlook it — this is also intolerance, it is the suffering intolerance. Modernity is indifferentism inasmuch as it does not so much express that Xnty has abandoned the world as that Xnty has abandoned itself — or more correctly, that Xndom has abandoned Xnty. (*SKP* X, 4 A 10)[3]

The first thing to note about the two entries is their shared dismissal of religion as an empirical sociological phenomenon: the 1855 passage asserts that *real* religious people, like *real* atheists, are rare, while most people simply follow the religious customs of their time and place; the 1851 passage contrasts the *real* Christians of the age of martyrdom with the indifferent participants in contemporary Christendom.

What is it that distinguishes *real* religiousness from mere social conformity? In both passages, it is an absolute relation to God, a prioritizing of the divine that utterly subordinates all other agendas. In the first passage, this is put in relatively abstract terms as "relationship to the Unconditioned [*den Ubetingede*]" and "First God's Kingdom." In the second passage, it is put in more existential terms as willingness to die (but not to kill) for one's faith.

If the theme of absolute devotion is common to both, the implications for how we think about religion as a general category could not be more discrepant. In the 1855 passage, Kierkegaard sees absolute devotion to the divine not just as *possible* in all religions but as the *essential character of religion qua religion*. After naming an unusual variety of religions — Christian, Jewish, Muslim, Chinese, and pagan *(afgudisk Religion)* — Kierkegaard says directly that "having religion is essentially the same for every religion" and that for "any religious society whatever [*hvilketsomhelst religioust Samfund*]" one has in mind, the "formula" for real faith is the same.[4] In noting that real nonbelievers are as rare as real believers, Kierkegaard comes close to affirming the paradox that genuine atheists are more authentically religious than are conventional believers. Here, people of true faith are quite rare, but their locations cut utterly across confessional lines.

3. Thanks to Bruce Kirmmse for providing provisional translations of these two entries prior to their publication in *Kierkegaard's Journals and Notebooks*.

4. While asserting the essential sameness of all religions *qua* absolute devotion, Kierkegaard still differentiates between religions when he says that the formula holds "even [for] that which is most untrue [*selv den usandeste*]." Thus, this passage echoes the parable of the fervent pagan in *Postscript*, which recognized the authentic devotion of the idolator even while judging idol worship as false religion.

In contrast, the 1851 passage wraps Christianity in the mantle of "suffering intolerance" and regards social guarantees of religious freedom as evidence of loss of faith and indifferentism. The true believer, the person of real faith, burns with a "need to suffer unto death for the faith," presumably as a result both of stridently confessing that belief to unreceptive listeners and of living out the radical, countercultural implications of that faith. Strikingly, Kierkegaard explicitly castigates the idea that Christianity is "satisfied with being a religion like other religions, on an equal footing," as itself a betrayal of faith, as evidence of loss of real conviction.

What are we to make of these two sharply contrasting passages, one of which uses "religion" as a general honorific term for genuine human devotion to the divine, the other of which sees "religion" as pernicious leveling, as a category that surreptitiously undercuts the absoluteness of Christianity by making it one faith among many? Placed side by side, the passages seem simply contradictory. But Kierkegaard, a self-styled dialectical thinker, articulates a framework for thinking about human existence that combines, though never fully integrates, these two discrepant views. A cleft runs throughout Kierkegaard's writings, setting "infinite resignation" over against "faith," Socrates over against Jesus, "Religiousness A" over against "Religiousness B," "the upbuilding" over against the "decisively Christian." In each of these pairs, a natural, universal religious capacity, which Kierkegaard labels "immanent religion," is juxtaposed with a miraculous, historically specific divine self-disclosure that utterly transforms its recipient, which he labels "transcendent religion." Of the two journal entries quoted above, the 1855 passage speaks distinctly out of the perspective of immanent religion while the 1851 passage speaks the language of decisive Christianity in its unmediated transcendence.

What seems simply incompatible in abstract statement becomes co-involved in the richness, complexity, and ongoing development of human existence. By placing these two modalities of religious existence within his theory of the stages, Kierkegaard finds a way to bring together his universalist and particularist impulses so that they become complementary insights within an unfolding human life.

While each of the two modes of religious existence is itself vividly, distinctively, and even (as in *Fragments*) algebraically presented, how they stand to each other within an encompassing category of "the religious" is highly problematic. Are immanent religion and transcendent religion two subsets of a general category of religion? Is immanent religion itself the general category and transcendent religion a specification of it? Or is the relation between the two dialectical, a Hegelian *Aufhebung,* where one modality of religious existence is simultaneously supplanted by and retained in the other? Each of these views has supporters, and in the next three sections of this chapter we will look at interpreters of the Climacus texts who propose these three distinctive ways of understanding the relationship between immanent and transcendent religion. What will emerge as we work through those three interpretations is that each implies a characteristic stance on the question of relations between Christianity (the one faith Kierkegaard regards as genuinely transcendent) and other faiths (all of which Kierkegaard regards as immanent).

"Good Fences Make Good Neighbors": Robert Roberts on the "Utter Contrast" of Immanent and Transcendent Religion

While the contrast between immanent and transcendent religion runs throughout Kierkegaard's writings, the clearest and most developed comparisons of the two are offered in *Philosophical Fragments* and its "sequel," *Concluding Unscientific Postscript to the Philosophical Fragments,* the two published works by the pseudonym Johannes Climacus. Despite their common authorship and shared concerns, the two texts are a study in contrast: where *Fragments* is terse and algebraic, *Postscript* rambles on at length; where *Fragments* develops the idea of transcendent religion as a thought-experiment, scrupulously avoiding explicit reference to Christianity, *Postscript* clothes the problem of *Fragments* in "historical costume" (*CUP* 1:10), identifying Christianity as the unique transcendent faith.[5] Both texts take their point of departure in answering the questions posed cryptically on the title page of *Fragments* and quoted at the beginning of the *Postscript:*

> *Can an eternal consciousness have an historical starting-point? How can such a starting-point have more than historical interest? Can one build one's eternal happiness on historical knowledge?* (*PF,* 1; *CUP* 1:15)

Climacus condenses these three questions into one as he opens Chapter One of *Fragments: "Can the truth be learned?"* Out of bare "No" and "Yes"

---

5. "As is well known, Christianity is the only historical phenomenon that despite the historical — indeed, precisely by means of the historical — has wanted to be the single individual's point of departure for his eternal consciousness" (*PF,* 109; *CUP* 1:15).

answers to this question, Climacus purports to draw forth immanent religion (identified with Socrates and specifically with the doctrine of recollection that lay behind his maieutic method of teaching) and transcendent religion (which Climacus coyly presents as his own imaginary creation despite protests of plagiarism from an unnamed interlocutor). At the heart of immanent religion, according to Climacus, is the belief that a relation to God and a capacity to develop that relation are always already part of every human's fundamental identity. As universally, eternally, inseparably present in each person, this *truth* — here used to name a saving relation to the divine — *cannot* be "learned" (that is, acquired) in time. In contrast, Climacus develops as a "B hypothesis" the idea that truth can be learned, that a saving relation to the eternal might commence in time through a relation to something itself historical, namely a teacher who is the saving truth.[6]

In *Faith, Reason, and History*, Robert Roberts restages — in his words, "rethinks" — *Philosophical Fragments*'s development of the fundamental conceptions of immanent and transcendent religion, but without succumbing to Climacus's conceit that he is simply conducting a thought experiment. Behind Climacus's Cheshire Cat grin, Roberts perceives a serious agenda: making unmistakably apparent the "utter contrast" and "abysmal disanalogy" between Christianity, as the unique transcendent faith, and all the other faiths, which, despite their differences, ultimately represent immanent religion.[7]

> Climacus's serious purpose is not to produce valid deductions, but to point out some pertinent incompatibilities. His real, as opposed to ostensible, program is to begin with the historically given basic Christian understanding of Christ and to compare it with another paradigm of religious teacher. The Socratic paradigm is of interest because it is one in terms of which theologians and philosophers, as well as ordinary people, are strongly and perennially inclined to think of Christ — with the result that their Christianity is fundamentally distorted. The Christ-disciple relationship has some grammatical features that are incompatible with some features characterizing any relationship between a merely human religious teacher and his disciple. It is Climacus's purpose to impress these incompatibilities upon his reader. The point of Climacus's discourse, then,

6. I adopt the terminology of a "B hypothesis" from Stephen Evans, *Passionate Reason: Making Sense of Kierkegaard's "Philosophical Fragments"* (Bloomington: Indiana University Press, 1992), p. 28.

7. Robert C. Roberts, *Faith, Reason, and History: Rethinking Kierkegaard's "Philosophical Fragments"* (Macon, GA: Mercer University Press, 1986), pp. 25, 26.

is to force upon his reader some fundamental exclusive disjunctions ("either/or's") that will inoculate him against a certain kind of heretical understanding of Jesus and thus free him to come into the correct kind of relationship with Christ.[8]

On Roberts's reading, Climacus's fundamental agenda is one of differentiation: he lays out the two forms of religious existence, not to identify what they share as religion, but to correct a pernicious tendency to conflate what is fundamentally distinct. As the epigram for *Fragments* puts it, "Better well hanged than ill wed." Climacus undertakes his work of differentiation specifically to counter efforts of Hegelian theologians to assimilate Christian faith to speculative philosophy, but Roberts sees such a tendency to conflate Christian and non-Christian religion as a pervasive, persistent problem. Using Climacus's distinction between the fundamental logics of immanent and transcendent religion, Roberts subjects Friedrich Scheiermacher, Rudolf Bultmann, and John Cobb, significant modern Christian theologians, to critical evaluation and finds them all guilty of basic confusion: "some of the greatest theological thinkers of an age have been gibbering ungrammatical theology."[9]

The specific confusion Roberts targets relates to the distinctive roles of teachers in the two modes of religion. In immanent religion, because each potential learner already has the truth within herself, the teacher is only an occasion, a dispensable, forgettable, inessential prompt for recollecting the truth. Climacus's model for this sort of teacher is Socrates, but we find similar deflationary comments about the importance of teachers in many different world religions that locate the truth within the depths of each potential convert. For example, Lin Chi (the Chan Buddhist teacher notorious for recommending that if you meet the Buddha, you should kill him) writes,

> Followers of the Way, if you want to be the same as the Buddha and the Patriarchs, then don't seek outside yourself. The nondiscriminating light of your mind at this instant becomes the essence-body of the Buddha inside you. . . . [Y]ou can only come to this vision when you cease searching for anything outside yourself.[10]

8. Roberts, *Faith, Reason, and History,* pp. 23-24.

9. Roberts, *Faith, Reason, and History,* p. 27.

10. *Zen Sourcebook: Traditional Documents from China, Korea, and Japan,* ed. Stephen Addiss, with Stanley Lombardo and Judith Roitman (Indianapolis: Hackett, 2008), p. 48.

In stark contrast, the teacher of transcendent religion is essential. Not only does this teacher bring truth to a learner who had previously lacked it; this teacher *is* the truth. Within Christianity, Jesus' role as savior is so disanalogous to the roles of teachers within immanent religions that Roberts questions the appropriateness of treating them as parallel: "The primary work of Jesus and the primary work of the [Socratic religious teacher] are indeed so different that one might wonder how it could occur to Climacus to compare them." And that, according to Roberts, is the real point of *Fragments*: "The form of the book is entirely unstable: the reader who takes seriously the project of comparing Socrates and Jesus as teachers ends up staring at the abysmal disanalogy between the two. . . . [T]he upshot of the 'comparison' is that no comparison is possible."[11]

While Roberts does not explicitly draw this conclusion, his emphasis on utter difference between immanent and transcendent faiths drains the significance from labeling both as religion. How useful, after all, is a general category if the particulars that fall under it are so utterly, incomparably discrepant? And so, Roberts's analysis leads us right up to the judgment Kierkegaard issues in the 1851 journal entry quoted above: even to classify Christianity as a religion among other religions is inherently leveling. It is entirely in the spirit of Climacus's confessedly disingenuous "thought experiment" that *Fragments* might subvert a key concept in its own framing of the issues.

Beyond Roberts's analysis, there are additional reasons to be cautious in embracing the very idea of religion as a genus to which Christianity and other determinate religious traditions belong as species. So familiar is the concept of religion to us that it is hard for us to realize how recent its provenance is. In *Beyond Anthropology: Society and the Other*, Bernard McGrane argues that the very idea of religion emerges during the Enlightenment as a direct result of Christianity's displacement as the West's reigning ideological framework.[12]

McGrane draws on Foucault's notion of "epistemes" to argue that, since the Renaissance, the West has moved through multiple fundamentally different paradigms for thinking about "the Other," specifically the anthropological (i.e., non-European) Other. Foucauldian epistemes are the tectonic plates of intellectual history; they are the ubiquitous and therefore invisible

---

11. Roberts, *Faith, Reason, and History,* pp. 25-26, 26n.

12. Bernard McGrane, *Beyond Anthropology: Society and the Other* (New York: Columbia University Press, 1989).

classificatory orders, the "historical *a prioris*," that define not only the true and the false in a given age but also the thinkable and the sayable.[13] For Foucault, these "plates" remain as stable, unnoticed frameworks of thought for indeterminate periods, until, abruptly, ruptures occur and all is shaken, clearing a space for a new paradigm to take its predecessor's place.

The episteme in terms of which Europeans conceptualized their first contact with non-European Others maps the world in terms of Christianity. Thus, non-European Others were conceived first and foremost as non-Christian, that is, as pagans. "The Other in the sixteenth century is, precisely, the non-Christian, dwelling entirely in the hollow of absence, the inscribed inhabitant of an inverted space."[14] Since Christianity is the social space ordered by God, paganism is the space beyond divine grace and guidance; it is the domain of the infernal and demonic. McGrane backs up his claim about the mental geography of pre-Enlightenment Europeans with shocking statements from the travel writings of Oviedo and de Acosta as they encountered non-Christian indigenous peoples:

> Satan has now been expelled from the island . . . his influence has disappeared now that most of the Indians are dead. . . . Who can deny that the use of gunpowder against pagans is burning incense to Our Lord?[15]

> [F]or the Prince of darkness being the head of all Infidelite, it is no new thing to find among Infidells, cruelties, filthiness and follies fit for such a master.[16]

Clearly, not all Europeans demonized the non-European Others they encountered, but "the massive and ceaseless task of conversion," which McGrane describes as "the fundamental European response to the alien Other," supports his claim that Europeans of this time period organized the world in terms of a fundamental Christian/non-Christian divide.[17]

In the eighteenth century, with the coming of the Enlightenment, knowledge versus ignorance/superstition becomes the fundamental organizational grid in terms of which the religious Other is placed:

13. Michel Foucault, *The Archaelogy of Knowledge*, trans. Rupert Swyer (New York: Pantheon, 1972), p. 144.

14. McGrane, *Beyond Anthropology*, p. 10.

15. McGrane, *Beyond Anthropology*, p. 10.

16. McGrane, *Beyond Anthropology*, p. 11.

17. McGrane, *Beyond Anthropology*, pp. 13-14.

It is at this juncture that we can locate a radical transformation of the West's self-understanding: the European-Christians-and-Jews-as-opposed-to-the-savage-idolatrous-non-Christians became the civilized-Europeans-as opposed-to-the-superstitious-ignorant-primitive. It was in the Enlightenment, at this epistemological moment, that the European *became civilized* (and since then, on the most primitive level, the West's self-understanding has been absolutely interwoven around its conception of itself as "civilized").[18]

In the pre-Enlightenment paradigm, the common feature of pagans ancient and modern was their non-Christianity; the Enlightenment paradigm locates the shared feature of paganism in its ignorance of hidden but entirely natural causes of phenomena. Paganism is, in short, pre-scientific; it is ignorant and superstitious rather than heterodox. The eighteenth-century project of natural religion and coordinate movements to rationalize Christian religion are attempts to establish modes of religious consciousness that belong, with science, on the enlightened side of the knowledge versus ignorance/superstition fault line.

Once deposed from its status as the fundamental ordering principle, Christianity itself needs to be classified, and thus the concept "religion" is born as the genus under which particular religious species are ordered. McGrane writes,

Christianity drastically contracted from being the all pervasive general intellectual horizon upon which difference was experienced and interpreted, and became one element in a more complex general configuration termed "Religion." It was not in the grey dawn of Paleolithic man but in the Enlightenment that "religion" first emerged. In the Enlightenment "religion" was first constituted as a general category, i.e., "religion" became a concept detached from Christianity and from Christianism, and, in an oedipal-like operation, usurped its place.[19]

18. McGrane, *Beyond Anthropology,* p. 56.

19. McGrane, *Beyond Anthropology,* pp. 56-57. For a parallel account of the rise of the idea of religion out of the Enlightenment idea of natural religion, see Peter Byrne, *Natural Religion and the Nature of Religion: The Legacy of Deism* (London: Routledge, 1989). Paul Tillich sketched out a version of this argument decades earlier: "A symptom of [Enlightenment Universalism] is the rise of philosophies of religion, the very term implying that Christianity has been subsumed under the universal category of religion. This seems harmless enough, but it is not . . . [because it puts in danger] a unique claim for Christianity by contrasting revelation

McGrane's narrative of the development of religion as a general category forms a fascinating backdrop against which to read Roberts's interpretation of *Fragments*. As Roberts sees it, the fundamental project of *Fragments* is to "inoculate" readers from inappropriately assimilating Jesus to the general model of religious teacher. But what makes that inappropriate assimilation so common, so endemic, that inoculation is called for? Why is it, Roberts asks, that Christian believers are "strongly and perennially inclined" to conflate the two types of teachers? Why do the greatest modern theological minds persistently succumb to "gibbering ungrammatical theology"?[20] If, in modernity, Christianity is seen as a religion like other religions, a token of the general type, then one would naturally expect the founding teacher of Christianity also to fit the general model of religious teacher. McGrane's analysis suggests that this conflation is not some incidental mistake but is rooted in our very notion of religion, which, in turn, is rooted in fundamental ways we understand and organize the world. In challenging the assimilation of Socrates and Jesus, Climacus (and Roberts with him) is resisting the dominant paradigm and implicitly challenging the cogency of the category of religion itself.[21]

So, what does this discussion imply for a Kierkegaardian view of religious diversity? In what direction does Roberts's interpretation of *Fragments* point us as we live out our lives in the globalized, pluralistic present? Roberts's Kierkegaard, with his overriding zeal for keeping separate things separate, calls to mind Robert Frost's famous if ironically intended line: "Good fences make good neighbors." Rather than playing down distinctiveness so as to find

---

— restricted to Christianity — with religion as designating every non-Christian religion." Paul Tillich, *Christianity and the Encounter of the World Religions* (New York: Columbia University Press, 1963), pp. 41-42. More recently, William Cavanaugh has traced the rise of the concept of religion within the context of the emergence and legitimation of the nation-state. See especially ch. 2, "The Invention of Religion," in *The Myth of Religious Violence* (Oxford: Oxford University Press, 2009), pp. 57-122.

20. Roberts, *Faith, Reason, and History*, p. 27.

21. Stephen Evans's analysis of Climacus's critique of mediation is useful to note here. As Evans reads him, by "mediation" Climacus means treating goods as qualitatively similar and therefore comparable and substitutable. When Climacus rejects the appropriateness of mediation in regard to one's relation to the absolute, Evans interprets him as saying "there is some good that simply cannot be considered as one good among others." *Kierkegaard: An Introduction* (Cambridge: Cambridge University Press, 2009), p. 127. Evans is not here discussing the issue of religious diversity, but his analysis suggests that considering one's own faith as simply one religion among others, qualitatively like those others, is to have entered into mediation and to have abandoned an absolute relation to it.

common ground in a generic spirituality, Roberts's Kierkegaard would counsel people of faith to claim boldly their various religious particularities, to maintain conceptual fences between their various fundamental convictions.

But there is more to *Fragments* than assertive distinctiveness. Throughout *Fragments,* Climacus manifests deep respect toward *both* models of religious existence he juxtaposes, the Socratic and the Christian. At no point in the text does he suggest that disagreement entails disrespect. Rather, Climacus saves his contempt for those who muddle up fundamentally different views as if they amounted to the same thing. Climacus's model of respect for differing religious perspectives together with his profound sense of human epistemic fallibility should "inoculate" (to use Roberts's metaphor) against arrogant religious assertiveness as much as against muddled religious syncretism.

Common Ground: M. Jamie Ferreira on Climacus's "Socratic Secret"

As Robert Roberts effectively argues, the main thrust of *Fragments* is the distinctiveness of Socrates and Jesus as teachers. Wielding a very sharp scalpel serves Climacus's stated agenda in *Fragments* — challenging the Hegelian theological establishment's assimilationist predilections — but an unrelenting emphasis on difference obscures equally real commonalities. Why does Climacus choose to compare Jesus and Socrates rather than, say, Jesus and Johannes the Seducer or Jesus and Judge William (both of whom, after all, style themselves as teachers of sorts)? Why does Climacus (and, for that matter, Kierkegaard himself) set Socrates on a pedestal as the ideal fulfillment of natural human potentiality? Implicit in Climacus's attention to and respect for Socrates is recognition of him as an authentic religious figure. And so, in the spirit of Freud's return of the repressed, religion as a category encompassing the non-Christian as well as the Christian haunts the pages of *Fragments.*

What is largely implicit in *Fragments,* Climacus makes explicit in *Concluding Unscientific Postscript.* In "The 'Socratic Secret': The Postscript to *Philosophical Crumbs,*" Jamie Ferreira argues that *Postscript* really is a postscript and not just a sequel. That is, it represents an addition that fundamentally alters as well as repeating and enlarging upon the message of *Fragments.*

> [H]owever successful *Philosophical Crumbs* may have been on its own terms, Kierkegaard later judged that it could not be allowed to stand as it was. . . . [I]t needed to be importantly qualified. . . . *Postscript* was to provide something new. This supplement involved not only a more

appreciative take on Socratic subjectivity . . . but more radically the presentation of Socratic subjectivity as a *necessary* preliminary to genuine Christianity. I suggest that whereas in *Crumbs* Socratic subjectivity was presented as an alternative to the non-Socratic (Christian) position, the *Concluding Unscientific Postscript* reveals them in a positive relation. That is, the "postscript" within *Postscript* corrects the "either-or" presentation of *Crumbs* by introducing the importance of a specific sort of "both-and" (which nonetheless differs from "mediation").[22]

At the most obvious level, Ferreira is noting that the name "Socrates" is used in very different ways in *Fragments* and in *Postscript*. In order to make the immanent/transcendent religion contrast as sharp as possible, Climacus throws nuance overboard in *Fragments,* using Socrates as the iconic symbol for *all* philosophies and religions that see truth as within us. The very distinction between Socratic irony and Platonic speculation at the center of Kierkegaard's dissertation, *The Concept of Irony,* goes out the window in *Fragments*. Not so in *Postscript*. There, Climacus celebrates Socrates as the iconic subjective thinker, as one who embodies the project of reduplicating what he knows in how he lives.[23] In addition to offering a more appreciative take, the *Postscript* moves Socrates much more to the center of attention. Whereas the Socratic "A Hypothesis" (the view that truth is recollected rather than learned) is only briefly sketched out in *Fragments* as a foil to the real focus, the "B Hypothesis" (revealed Christian religion), *Postscript* reverses the ratio, expounding at comparatively greater length on Socrates and the ethical-religious subjectivity he represents. Ferreira writes, "Although it is true that there are references to Christianity throughout the *Postscript,* it is striking that any explicit discussion of Christianity proper is extremely short compared to the discussion of ethical subjectivity and ethical-religious subjectivity."[24]

Behind these qualitative and quantitative changes in the treatment of Socrates, Ferreira sees a fundamental shift in the way Climacus thinks about the relation between Christian and non-Christian modes of religious exis-

22. M. Jamie Ferreira, "The 'Socratic Secret': The Postscript to the *Philosophical Crumbs,*" in *Kierkegaard's "Concluding Unscientific Postscript": A Critical Guide,* ed. Rick Anthony Furtak (Cambridge: Cambridge University Press, 2010), pp. 6-7.

23. I discuss Socrates' significance for Kierkegaard in my contribution to *Why Kierkegaard Matters: A Festschrift for Robert L. Perkins,* ed. Marc A. Jolley and Edmon L. Rowell Jr. (Macon, GA: Mercer University Press, 2010), pp. 66-81.

24. Ferreira, "The 'Socratic Secret,'" p. 14.

tence. Ferreira concurs with Roberts in reading *Fragments* as fundamentally about contrast: there, Climacus sets up an "either/or" between immanent and transcendent religion, an opposition so stark that it becomes difficult to see the two even as species of the same genus. But Ferreira sees *Postscript* as presenting a "specific sort of 'both-and' " rooted in a positive relation between Socratic and non-Socratic religion.

> [T]he postscript tells us something new — namely, that the initial story presented the two elements [Religiousness A and Religiousness B] as if they were mutually exclusive, and that was misleading, because though they are qualitatively different, they are positively related to each other. . . . [W]hat makes . . . [*Postscript*] a genuine supplement to *Crumbs* is that it announces for the first time the indispensability of Socratic subjectivity and explores the positive relation between A and B.[25]

Ferreira makes a compelling case for a significant shift from *Fragments* to *Postscript,* but, as she notes herself, the exact character of the new "positive relation" between Socratic subjectivity and Christian faith remains ambiguous. On a minimalist reading, "Religiousness A could be just a jumping off point for B, something that is left behind when one moves to B."[26] As Ferreira notes, Climacus frequently uses language suggesting a relation of temporal sequence between the two modes of religious existence:

> Religiousness A must *first* be present in the individual before there can be any consideration of becoming aware of the dialectical B. (*CUP* 1:556; my emphasis)

> *Before* there can be any question at all of simply being in the situation of becoming aware of [the essentially Christian] one must *first* of all exist in Religiousness A. (*CUP* 1:557; my emphasis)

---

25. Ferreira, "The 'Socratic Secret,' " p. 16. Compare Stephen Evans: "[*Postscript*] is consistent with the message of *Fragments,* which is that genuine Christian faith must be a gift from God and is not a human achievement. However, the answer given in *Postscript* does considerably complicate the moral of *Fragments.* For we learn that although we cannot produce Christian faith, there are humanly achievable qualities that are necessary preconditions for such faith. *Postscript* is an extended series of reflections on those qualities and how they can be achieved." C. Stephen Evans, *Kierkegaard: An Introduction* (Cambridge: Cambridge University Press, 2009), p. 111.

26. Ferreira, "The 'Socratic Secret,' " p. 18.

When one puts this language of temporal sequence together with an understanding of the stages as developmentally ordered, it is easy to read Climacus as saying one must *go through* Religiousness A on the way to Religiousness B, in the manner that one must go through a particular way station on the way to one's final destination. Such a reading of *Postscript* suggests a classic supersessionist model for thinking about religious diversity: just as Christian theologians often viewed Judaism as a forerunner to Christianity, a necessary preparation for the new dispensation that decisively replaces it, so, on this reading, Religiousness A necessarily precedes but is definitively replaced by Religiousness B. Since Climacus (with Kierkegaard) sees Christianity as the one example of Religiousness B, this amounts to saying that all other religions are merely preparatory, like John the Baptist in relation to Jesus.

While acknowledging such an interpretive option, Ferreira points us toward a much more substantive reading of the "positive relation" between the two forms of religious existence:

> Religiousness A could be a continuing impetus within B, something that remains in play within one's Christianity; just as the aesthetic was claimed by Judge William in *Either/Or* to be preserved and transfigured in the ethical, so Religiousness A is preserved and transfigured in Religiousness B. At stake in the difference between the two interpretations is the possibility that within Religiousness B there is the lived co-presence of the Socratic in heightened subjectivity.[27]

Faced with the two possible readings, Ferreira argues vigorously for the latter reading. After all, Climacus spends most of *Postscript* trying to reawaken his forgetful readers to "what it is to exist humanly" by painstakingly, progressively developing the subjectivity of immanent religion (*CUP* 1:249). Is it plausible to suggest that Christian existence leaves all that behind? Ferreira asks rhetorically,

> Is Religiousness A a jumping off point that is left behind, superseded? If immanence means the locus for human subjectivity, then the break with immanence means a break with our humanity, our embodiedness, our concreteness — is this what is implied? Are the resignation, suffering, and guilt experienced in Religiousness A left behind with the transition to B?[28]

27. Ferreira, "The 'Socratic Secret,'" p. 18.
28. Ferreira, "The 'Socratic Secret,'" p. 21.

So framed, Ferreira's questions solicit a No, and with that a judgment that the "sharpened pathos [of Christianity] is an operation on Socratic pathos," an "accentuation" rather than a displacement.[29]

Ferreira's reading of *Postscript* carries profound implications for how we think about the relations between Christian and non-Christian religion. On Roberts's reading of *Fragments,* immanent and transcendent religion are two non-overlapping subsets of a rather toothless general category of religion. Such a reading invites an emphasis on difference, on maintaining clear boundaries. But on Ferreira's reading, Religiousness A *is* the general category of religion. Religiousness A designates the universal features of religious existence: an absolute relation to the absolute, suffering occasioned by resignation, guilt from failure to live out perfectly one's god-relationship. As such, all particular religious faiths, Christianity included, represent distinctive modulations of that underlying, shared, basic way of being. To hearken back to Kierkegaard's 1855 journal entry, this is to suggest that the "formula" for all religions is exactly the same. Rather than joining Roberts in insisting on sharp distinctions, Ferreira implicitly invites people of different faiths to explore the shared contours of their religious lives, to find common ground. As she reads it, the *Postscript*'s more appreciative picture of Socrates stands proxy for a more appreciative sense of the deep commonality of all religions.

"Preserved and Transfigured": Merold Westphal on Teleological Suspension

How is it that Roberts and Ferreira can find such discrepant, even contradictory, messages within the writings of Johannes Climacus? How is it that Climacus can shift from a relentless focus on Christian distinctiveness in *Fragments* to an emphasis on general features of religious existence in *Postscript*? Ferreira notes that a postscript, by definition, is a subsequent writing that modifies an original text, but the discrepant messages in Climacus's writings are not neatly separated in that manner.[30] Rather, we find Climacus's starkest exclusivist statement in *Postscript*:

> Religiousness B is isolating, separating, polemical. Only on this condition do I become blessed, and as I absolutely bind myself to it, I thereby

29. Ferreira, "The 'Socratic Secret,'" p. 19.
30. Ferreira, "The 'Socratic Secret,'" p. 6.

exclude everyone else. . . . The happiness linked to a historical condition excludes all who are outside the condition, and among those are the
countless ones who are excluded through no fault of their own but by the
accidental circumstance that Christianity has not yet been proclaimed to
them. (*CUP* 1:582-83)

How is it, then, that a hyper-exclusive particularism and an all-embracing
universalism can coexist not just within the same pseudonymous author
but within the same text? How are we able to reconcile Climacus's discor-
dant statements on the general category of religion and the specific religion,
Christianity?

In "Kierkegaard's Teleological Suspension of Religiousness B," Merold
Westphal argues that taking such conflicting statements as "dialectical contradictions" allows us to place them within the context of Kierkegaard's theory
of the stages and thereby to understand them as complementary, developmentally related insights.[31] The "stages on life's way" in Kierkegaard's writings
are "forms of life," and different texts within the authorship articulate those
different experiences from within. Since the experiences differ from each
other, we should expect variations in the articulations. Westphal focuses on
sharply contrasting assessments of Acts 5 between *Postscript* and later journal
entries, postulating "Religiousness C" as a further development of religious
consciousness beyond Climacus's Religiousness A and B. His characterization
of such a shift from one existential perspective to another as a "teleological
suspension" shines light on our immediate problem: Climacus's conflicting
statements on religion in general and Christianity in particular.

The term "teleological suspension" comes, of course, from *Fear and
Trembling,* where Johannes de Silentio uses it to explore Abraham's altered
relation to ethical norms when God commands that he offer Isaac as a sacrifice. Insofar as Abraham's obligation to obey God trumps his normal ethical
obligations (including the obligation not to harm his son), those normal
ethical obligations are said to be "teleologically suspended." As we have seen
in the previous chapter, all too many would-be interpreters of *Fear and Trembling* have read this suspension as a pure and simple cancellation, as ush-
ering Abraham into a terrifying amoral space beyond moral good and evil.
In contrast, the "refutation" Westphal has in view is not a simple rejection,

---

31. Merold Westphal, "The Teleological Suspension of Religiousness B," in *Foundations
of Kierkegaard's Vision of Community,* ed. George B. Connell and C. Stephen Evans (Atlantic
Highlands: Humanities, 1992), pp. 56-70.

a complete cancellation. Rather, in an unmistakably Hegelian manner, he uses "teleological suspension" to describe the way in which more limited truths are retained but recontextualized within a larger, more comprehensive perspective:

> The falsehood of the "refuted" moment is not the simple falseness of a binary logic but the relational falseness of the part that takes itself for the whole. Hence the "refuted" moment is not fixed, divorced, or executed, but reassigned, given a new, subordinate role to play. Hegel calls such refutation *Aufhebung,* in which the false moment is transcended and restored to its (limited) truth by being both negated (as putative whole, as absolute) and preserved (as designated part, as relative). Kierkegaard's name for this is teleological suspension. For example, the teleological suspension of the ethical does not mean that it is "relinquished" but "preserved in the higher, which is its *telos.*" If there is such a thing as an absolute duty to God, "then the ethical is reduced to the relative. From this it does not follow that the ethical should be invalidated [abolished; Lowrie]; rather, the ethical receives a completely new expression."[32]

While Kierkegaard uses "teleological suspension" only to describe the relativizing of ethical norms that goes along with a transition to religious existence, Westphal appropriates the term for more general use, employing it to describe the way the secure truths of any given existential perspective are "refuted" with a shift to another, more comprehensive existential perspective. Thus, the aesthetic is "teleologically suspended" within ethical existence: Judge William celebrates the "aesthetic validity" (i.e., enjoyable character) of marriage but subordinates it to the more comprehensive perspective of duty. The judge's self-satisfied focus on moral uprightness is, in turn, teleologically suspended in the move to decisively religious consciousness. Westphal's key suggestion is not only that we should speak of a teleological suspension in moving from ethical to religious existence but that we should understand relations between modes of religious existence, A, B, and (perhaps even) C, in those terms as well.

For Westphal, "the religious" as a general category emerges out of the experienced failure of the ethical project of "presiding over my own goodness" by following the dictates of socially defined moral codes.[33] Such codes,

---

32. Westphal, "The Teleological Suspension of Religiousness B," p. 112, citing *FT,* 70.
33. Westphal, "The Teleological Suspension of Religiousness B," p. 113.

by and large, set the bar pretty low — most bourgeois citizens can manage to stay out of trouble with the police — but as one becomes authentically conscious of God, the absoluteness of moral obligation brings ethical self-confidence crashing down:

> The other by whom this attempt [to preside over my own goodness] is overcome is, of course, the God who called upon Abraham to offer up Isaac. The teleological suspension of the ethical is the relativizing of social morality before the absolute claims of God. In this *Aufhebung* the self loses its moral life and identity, dying away from the immediacy of the ethical, and is regenerated or resurrected to the new life and identity of the religious.[34]

Within this general description of "the religious," Westphal locates Religiousness A and Religiousness B as distinctive forms. What distinguishes the two is *where* they each locate the "absolute claims of God." Religiousness A listens to the voice of God from within, identifying divine truth as entirely immanent. In contrast, Religiousness B experiences truth as coming to it from beyond itself when it confesses that "in humility [we] must accept as a gift the truth we cannot discover or even recognize apart from God's grace."[35]

In these two different modes of religious consciousness, we find the sources for Climacus's (and Kierkegaard's) discrepant judgments on religion in general and Christianity in particular. Religiousness A, because it experiences the divine as deep within every person at every time and place, affirms the universality of religion. The specific differences of the various faiths pale to insignificance beside the common god-relationship out of which all those faiths emerge. In contrast, Religiousness B experiences the truth as coming to it at a particular time and place. It experiences the coming of this truth as a rupture, as a fundamental break with its old self, which it retrospectively judges as divorced from truth. Insofar as that old self participated in general human religiousness, the new self's negative judgment on its old self involves a negative judgment on that religiousness. For this self, categorizing such a radically transformed god-relationship as just another species of the genus religion is misguided.

While they seem starkly different when juxtaposed in this way, Westphal's description of Religiousness B as a "teleological suspension" of Reli-

---

34. Westphal, "The Teleological Suspension of Religiousness B," p. 113.
35. Westphal, "The Teleological Suspension of Religiousness B," p. 116.

giousness A reminds us that the two are developmentally related: to talk of a *radically transformed* god-relationship is implicitly to acknowledge that such a god-relationship preexists whatever change the self undergoes in entering Religiousness B. That is, Religiousness A is at least as much the presupposition of Religiousness B as it is its logical opposite. As Ferreira also argues, Religiousness A lives on in Religiousness B, "preserved and transfigured."[36] The co-presence in *Postscript* of apparently contradictory statements on the universality of religion and the particularity of Christianity linguistically figures the way A endures within B, even as it reflects Climacus's ambiguous perspective as a "humorist" writing from a sort of no-man's-land between immanent and transcendent religion.

What are the implications of Westphal's reading of Kierkegaard's authorship as "informed by a religious teleology"?[37] What does Westphal's sketch of a broadly Hegelian dialectical progression moving first to and then through increasingly adequate modes of religious consciousness mean for the issue of religious diversity?

At first blush, Westphal's reading seems emphatically supersessionist. Given that Kierkegaard and his pseudonyms see Christianity as the one and only transcendent religion while viewing all other religions as immanent, to describe Religiousness B as "teleologically suspending" Religiousness A is to see Christianity as the fulfillment of the impotent aspirations of all other faiths. This impression seems underscored by Westphal's argument that we should read Kierkegaard's late, decisively Christian texts as articulating a "Religiousness C" that, in turn, teleologically suspends Religiousness B. Westphal writes,

> We know from Johannes Climacus that for Religiousness B Christ is the Paradox. From the works just mentioned [*Practice in Christianity, For Self-Examination,* and *Judge for Yourself!*] we learn that for Religiousness C Christ is the Pattern or the Paradigm. As Paradox Christ is to be believed; as Pattern or Paradigm he is to be imitated.[38]

Just as the self-reliance of immanent religion comes under question in an encounter with the paradoxical God-in-time, so the hidden inwardness of paradoxical faith is revealed as a compromise and evasion in light of a rad-

---

36. Ferreira, "The 'Socratic Secret,'" p. 18.
37. Westphal, "The Teleological Suspension of Religiousness B," p. 110.
38. Westphal, "The Teleological Suspension of Religiousness B," p. 115.

ical discipleship that expresses faith outwardly. And with this "teleological suspension of Religiousness B," Kierkegaard's existential dialectic arguably reaches its culmination. As Westphal describes it, the religion of suffering discipleship, the Christianity of Kierkegaard's "second authorship," sounds strikingly final and complete:

> It is only with the teleological suspension of Religiousness B in what I shall call Religiousness C that we get the answer to the question of what it means to become a Christian and with that answer the completion and unification of Kierkegaard's work as a religious author. . . . [I]t is only with Religiousness C that the teleological suspension of the ethical is accomplished. . . .
>
> At this point [suffering discipleship] the task is not to go beyond the stage one has reached, but simply to remain there. And this is the task of a lifetime.[39]

Westphal can be read in two ways here. At a minimum, he is saying that Religiousness C (suffering discipleship) is the final realization of Christian faith. But when we take into account Kierkegaard's sense of "religious teleology," Westphal can be read here as describing authentic Christianity as a final, accomplished mode of religious existence, one that does not stand in need of any further teleological suspension. On that reading, Christianity deserves to be described in Hegelian terms as an "absolute religion" in relation to which other modes of religious existence would suffer by comparison.

There is, however, another way to take Westphal's "teleological suspension of Religiousness B" that potentially carries very different implications for the issue of religious diversity. Religiousness B, after all, *is* Christianity — solid, orthodox, confessional Pauline Christianity that speaks with a distinctly Lutheran accent. So, what does it mean to show that a given expression of Christianity, be it ever so orthodox, is itself subject to "teleological suspension"? The obvious model of "teleological suspension" of a particular religion involves a recontextualization so profound that a new religion is seen to result, as with Paul's conversion from Judaism to Christianity or with the Buddha's departure from Vedic Hinduism.[40] But the transition from

---

39. Westphal, "The Teleological Suspension of Religiousness B," pp. 115, 124.

40. The judgment that a new religion has emerged may well be retrospective as what is self-understood as a reform movement within a religious tradition comes eventually to be seen as initiation of a new faith.

Religiousness B to Religiousness C that Westphal describes does not change a single Christian doctrine: "Kierkegaard wishes neither to deny such doctrines as incarnation and atonement nor to make them unimportant. He wishes only to see truth as doctrine teleologically suspended in the way and the life it is meant to inform."[41] Thus, what Westphal describes as "teleological suspension of Religiousness B" is a reframing, a re-envisioning, not a replacement. Specifically, by placing orthodox Christian affirmations in the context of the radical, costly discipleship recounted in the New Testament, Kierkegaard seeks to recover the authentic meanings of those doctrines. Here, "teleological suspension" names a project of retrieval.

If Westphal is willing to speak of "teleological suspension" whenever one fundamentally re-envisions prior convictions in light of either a new or a recovered context, then several significant implications follow.

First, "Religiousness C" loses any appearance of finality. If Religiousness C is Christianity *as Kierkegaard gave it expression in his final writings,* then assuredly it stands in need of a Religiousness D (and E and F and . . .) that will recontextualize, reappraise, and reorient it. That is, Christians will always need to find new articulations of Christianity to respond to changing circumstances as well as to reawaken classic articulations by recovering contexts lost from view. When Kierkegaard speaks of himself as "a corrective," he acknowledges his formulation of Christianity as specific to a situation. To generalize, we should acknowledge that each and every formulation not only of Christian faith but of all faiths is provisional, context-dependent, subject always to "teleological suspension." We can affirm that such suspensions are "teleological" — that we are ever striving to get closer to ultimate truth — without presuming that we will ever (this side of Jordan) achieve anything remotely resembling a final grasp of that truth. Climacus makes just this point when he recounts Lessing's parable of a choice between entire possession of the truth and a lifelong quest for the truth, saying that only the latter is appropriate to the human condition (*CUP* 1:106).

Second, Westphal's expansive conception of "teleological suspension" offers a striking model for thinking about interactions between faiths. He writes,

The "refutation" of any moment in a dialectical progression consists in overcoming its immediacy. A mode of experience or form of life is immediate just to the degree that it takes itself to be self-sufficient, complete,

41. Westphal, "The Teleological Suspension of Religiousness B," p. 119.

absolute. The necessity of passing beyond it is the experience of its other as such, as the other that reveals its insufficiency, incompleteness, and relativity.[42]

Westphal's characterization of immediacy as a form of life that "takes itself to be self-sufficient, complete, and absolute" applies perfectly not only to Kierkegaard's Christendom but to many situations of religious homogeneity. We have all heard the old saw that one only really learns one's own language when one learns another. In a parallel way, interaction between people of different faiths opens new possibilities for religious self-awareness. Unfortunately, that awareness can be oppositional, as when a religious "we" is forged in the heat of violent struggle with a religious "they." But Westphal's "teleological suspension" points toward a much more positive possibility: awareness of a religious Other not only can prompt a new level of religious self-consciousness and self-criticism but also allows for constructive reappraisal, re-envisioning, and recovery of one's own faith. Paul Knitter's *Without Buddha I Could Not Be a Christian* provides a vivid illustration of that possibility.

Knitter reports that as he entered middle age, he increasingly found core aspects of his Catholic Christianity — God's transcendence, personhood, and providence, among others — to be deeply problematic. Threatened with loss of meaning in his own faith, Knitter found in other faiths a resource to "review, reinterpret, and reaffirm" his Christianity.[43]

Like many of my theological colleagues, I have come to realize that I have to look *beyond* the traditional borderlines of Christianity to find something that is vitally, maybe even essentially, important for the job of understanding and living the Christian faith: *other religions*. That is, the Scriptures and traditions, the sacred texts, the past teachings, the living communities of other religious believers. It was only after I began to take seriously and to explore other religious Scriptures and traditions that I was able to more adequately understand my own. Stated more personally: my engagement with other ways of being religious — that is, with what I have studied, discovered, been excited about, or perplexed by in other religions — has turned out to be an unexpected but immense help

42. Westphal, "The Teleological Suspension of Religiousness B," p. 111.
43. Paul F. Knitter, *Without Buddha I Could Not Be a Christian* (London: One World, 2009), p. xiii.

in my job of trying to figure out what the message of Jesus means in the contemporary world.[44]

As his title indicates, Knitter confesses a particular debt to Buddhism, the non-Christian faith with which he has most deeply engaged (to the point that he calls himself a Buddhist Christian). Each chapter of Knitter's book follows a set pattern. He begins by identifying a core Christian belief that had become deeply problematic for him, then "passes over" into the Buddhist perspective on the issue in question, before "passing back" to "rediscover or retrieve" the Christian belief.[45] Engaging the fundamentally different Buddhist take on a variety of issues helps Knitter clarify why he continues to identify himself as Christian, but each reaffirmed conviction is reconfigured, reoriented, and reimagined through this process of retrieval. But isn't this what Westphal is talking about when he speaks of "teleological suspension"? In this case, Knitter recontextualizes what were all-too-familiar Christian doctrinal affirmations by placing them in dialog with a very different religious perspective. Through that process, Knitter is able to reaffirm his basic Catholic convictions but in a manner unmistakably different from his original — might we say immediate — affirmation of them. Admittedly, Knitter represents an extreme example of interfaith dialog, pursuing it to the point that his own religious identity becomes a bit blurry. That said, his experience of recovering and renewing his own faith through dialog with other religious perspectives is widely shared.[46]

And so Westphal's discussion of relations between Religiousness A, B, and C lends itself to two very different readings. To the extent that those relations are hierarchical and Religiousness C is final, his essay points us toward a supersessionist conception of Christianity in relation to other faiths. But insofar as "teleological suspension" is a constant possibility for any given

44. Knitter, *Without Buddha I Could Not Be a Christian,* pp. xi-xii.

45. Knitter, *Without Buddha I Could Not Be a Christian,* p. 14.

46. Westphal himself seems to aim at something along those lines in *God, Guilt, and Death: An Existential Phenomenology of Religion* (Indianapolis: Indiana University Press, 1987), which recovers the meaning of religious existence by comparing a wide range of different religious traditions. More recently, Westphal's *Levinas and Kierkegaard in Dialogue* demonstrates the value of bringing a Jewish and a Christian thinker into conversation. This text notes important similarities between the two, but it also highlights key differences. Westphal uses the distinctive emphases of the two thinkers — Kierkegaard stressing the transcendence of God and Levinas the immanence of the divine in the face of the other — to reframe each of their discussions. Here we find much of what Westphal associates with "teleological suspension" but without any suggestion of the precedence of one view over the other.

mode of religious life and thought, and insofar as conversation can be a route to mutual discovery and rediscovery for people of faith, Westphal's reading of Kierkegaard suggests great value in mutually respectful interreligious dialog.

Concluding Reflection

By traversing three different interpretations of Kierkegaard's discussions of religion and religions — that is, of religion as a general category and of specific religions — no simple, stable, univocal picture emerges. Clearly, Kierkegaard and his pseudonyms have no truck with a simplistic sense that all religions are ultimately alike. As Roberts shows, Climacus, like his creator, has a passion for distinctions. But as Ferreira shows, Climacus could not leave difference as the last word, returning in *Postscript* to affirm shared features of religious life. Westphal's discussion of "teleological suspension" offers us a way to see how Kierkegaard and his pseudonyms are able to hold in dialectical tension both a sense of religious faith as a universal human possibility and a robust affirmation of the uniqueness of Christianity.

CHAPTER 5

Kierkegaard and Confucius:
The Religious Dimensions of Ethical Selfhood

Søren Kierkegaard's pseudonymous text *Philosophical Fragments* opens with an admonitory epigram: "Better well hanged than ill wed" (*PF,* 3). Given his aversion to ill-conceived weddings, Kierkegaard may seem an unlikely candidate for comparative philosophy in general. To link him, as I propose, to Confucius may seem quite mad.[1] The popular conceptions of the two would have them as polar opposites with no common ground for fruitful comparison: one modern, one ancient; one Western, one Eastern; one theist, one not; one a poet of solitary individuality, one an aphorist of social connection.

The apparent gulf between Kierkegaard and Confucius has discouraged comparisons of the two, and the few extant attempts at juxtaposition identify elements of continuity only to make the differences stand out more clearly. Hwa Yol Jung finds a "common and sufficient denominator of comparison between existentialism and Confucianism" in their shared commitment to "a concrete analysis of the ordinary existence of man in the world."[2] Jung argues that while one wing of existentialism, represented especially by Buber and Jaspers, develops an idea of human reciprocity close to Confucius's key concept of *ren,* Kierkegaard's commitment to "theocentric subjectivity" leads him to advocate an individualism sharply at odds with Confucius. Jung writes, "For Kierkegaard, the attainment of man's inward subjectiv-

1. Henry Rosemont opens one of the few prior attempts at such comparison by admitting that his project "might appear silly, or perverse." Henry Rosemont, "Kierkegaard and Confucius: On Finding the Way," *Philosophy East and West* 36, no. 3 (1986): 201-12.

2. Hwa Yol Jung, "Confucianism and Existentialism: Intersubjectivity as the Way of Man," *Philosophy and Phenomenological Research* 30, no. 2 (December 1969): 189.

ity is, religiously and ethically, the *quantum satis* of every individual as his lifetime task, whereas for Confucius, in contrast, it is the fulfillment of *jen* or reciprocity as the lifetime task of every man."[3] In a similar vein, Henry Rosemont finds that Confucius and Kierkegaard "were both preoccupied with the philosophical question of *how we should live our lives*," but he argues not simply that the two thinkers answer that question differently but that they come at it on the basis of entirely different presuppositions.[4] Rosemont's goal in comparing the two is to highlight the gulf between Confucius's notion of selves as essentially relational and a Western conception of selves as individual, autonomous, rights-bearing atoms, of which Kierkegaard is purportedly a paradigmatic exemplar. In both Jung and Rosemont, Kierkegaard, the prophet of individualism, is set over against Confucius, the spokesperson for social relationship.

Undeniably, Kierkegaard celebrates the individual in ways that would seem alien to Confucius, but recent scholarship has promoted an enhanced sense of the social dimensions of Kierkegaard's thought and has challenged the stereotype of him as advocating isolated subjectivity.[5] In what follows, I will argue that if we look at Confucius and Kierkegaard anew, free from the standard labels, we find a surprising degree of common ground between the two, specifically on the issue of ethical selfhood.

Approaching the comparison with a focus on what is shared has several potential benefits. That two thinkers from such different times, social contexts, traditions, and languages would sound common themes in discussing the ethical dimension of life is significant in its own right, pointing toward broadly shared ethical experience. This comparison has further value in helping us get at the vexing question of the religious dimension of Confucius (or lack thereof). Many attempts to settle this issue approach it directly, looking closely at the rather limited group of passages in the *Analects* that mention Heaven *(Tian)*. The relative paucity and ambiguity of these passages have led to considerable disagreement. If, however, we seek to discern a religious dimension in Confucius by looking more broadly at his vision of ethical selfhood, we will be much better placed. Not only is there a much richer textual basis for investigation, but we are also attending to what is clearly the center of Confucius's concerns.

---

3. Jung, "Confucianism and Existentialism," pp. 195-96.

4. Rosemont, "Kierkegaard and Confucius," p. 201.

5. See, for example, M. Jamie Ferreira, *Love's Grateful Striving: A Commentary on Kierkegaard's "Works of Love"* (Oxford: Oxford University Press, 2001).

Other interpreters have pointed in this direction previously, notably Joel Kupperman in "Confucius and the Nature of Religious Ethics." Kupperman identifies two propositions characteristically asserted by religious ethics in contrast to secular ethics and then argues that both claims are implicit in Confucius's thought. He writes,

> We may begin by examining the following two propositions characteristic of much religious ethics: (A) The most important virtues are intimately connected with what someone prizes most or what gives that person most satisfaction. Broadly speaking, one has these virtues if one desires the right things, or avoids desiring the wrong things, or takes satisfaction in the right things, or avoids taking pleasure in the wrong things. (B) Someone's life will be unusually valuable (i.e., worth living), even at moments when he or she is not making or preparing for a moral decision, if, and only if, he or she possesses the most important virtues.[6]

While I think Kupperman is on the right track, his scheme is too binary. By classifying ethical visions as either religious or not, he fails to do justice to the protean characters of both religion and ethics.

This is where the comparison of Confucius and Kierkegaard proves useful. Kierkegaard relentlessly interrogates the relation between religious faith and ethical responsibility throughout his writings and shows that that relation takes a variety of forms. In *Kierkegaard's Ethic of Love,* C. Stephen Evans identifies four primary senses of the term "ethical" explored by Kierkegaard: (1) in *Fear and Trembling,* the ethical corresponds roughly to Hegel's notion of *Sittlichkeit,* the norms and mores of a concrete society; (2) in *Either/Or* and *Stages on Life's Way,* the ethical represents a distinct existence-sphere or stage, a way of being-in-the-world contrasted with both aesthetic and religious modes of existence; (3) in the Climacus literature, especially *Concluding Unscientific Postscript,* the ethical designates the self's appropriate concern with the absolute task of becoming itself; and (4) in *Works of Love,* the ethical represents the radical commandment of neighbor love.[7] As

---

6. Joel Kupperman, *Learning from Asian Philosophy* (Oxford: Oxford University Press, 1999), p. 165.

7. C. Stephen Evans, *Kierkegaard's Ethic of Love: Divine Commands and Moral Obligations* (Oxford: Oxford University Press, 2004). Merold Westphal also notes the variable significance of the term "ethical" in Kierkegaard's writings: "An advantage of pseudonymous writing for Kierkegaard is that he can let different authors mean different things by such terms as 'ethics' in order to explore a variety of different questions. But this means that the reader must be careful

we move through these four senses of the ethical, the religious dimension becomes progressively more emphatic, ranging from a bland civil religion that sanctions prevailing social codes in the first case to a shocking revealed commandment that overturns established notions of proper conduct in the last. Accordingly, the four senses together represent a sort of scale with the divine becoming progressively more transcendent and the ethical demand progressively more "counter-natural" as we shift our attention from one form of the ethical to the next. To the extent that we can place Confucius's understanding of ethical existence along that scale, we will have a suggestion as to the specific religious character of that understanding.[8]

But can we so place Confucius on this Kierkegaardian scale without doing violence to both thinkers? We can do so only if, as I have claimed, there are unexpectedly deep and rich resonances between the two visions of the human ethical condition. In what follows, I will argue that there are resonances between Confucius and all four Kierkegaardian senses of the ethical, limited and qualified in the first and the last senses of the ethical but substantive and significant in the two intermediate senses (the ethical as distinct stage as presented in *Either/Or* and the ethical as appropriate existential concern as presented in the *Postscript*). While these two intermediate senses do ultimately differ from each other, they share a common core conception of ethical existence. After describing this core conception, I will show that Confucius holds closely parallel notions. Once I establish this broad parallelism, I will turn to the more pointed question of which specific Kierkegaardian sense of the ethical corresponds more closely to Confucius. Since the two intermediate senses of the ethical differ from each other primarily in terms of their respective religious dimensions, the only way to align Confucius with one or the other is to ask which of the two more closely resembles Confucius's own religious sensibility. Because this questioning will be guided by the particular features and concerns of the two Kierkegaardian modes of ethico-religious existence, it will, I hope, cast the *Analects* in a new light, highlighting features of the text not typically noticed in discussions of Confucius's religious sensibility.

---

not to assume univocity." Merold Westphal, *On Becoming a Self: A Reading of Kierkegaard's "Concluding Unscientific Postscript"* (West Lafayette: Purdue University Press, 1996), p. 111n.

8. In an earlier draft of this chapter, I used the term "continuum" to describe the ordered series of Kierkegaard's use of "ethics." A reviewer helpfully noted the problematic connotations of "continuum" in discussing Kierkegaard. I have substituted "scale" to reflect the discontinuous character of the ordered series.

Qualified Parallels between Confucius and Ethics as *Sittlichkeit*

The weakest sense of the ethical, as Kierkegaard sees it, is that employed in *Fear and Trembling* where it designates Hegelian *Sittlichkeit,* the constellation of norms and mores of a concrete society. There is clearly a dimension of *Sittlichkeit* in Confucian ethics. A key element in Confucian ethical development is mastery of *li,* the complex array of rituals that guide proper human conduct and that constitute the medium of social interaction. These rituals, which range from grand public ceremonies to fine points of etiquette, are the norms and mores of a specific social order: that which prevailed in the early years of the Zhou Dynasty. But Confucian ethics cannot be assimilated to the model of *Sittlichkeit,* at least as Kierkegaard understands it. Kierkegaard views such a model of ethics negatively for at least two primary reasons. First, he sees it as a way in which a prevailing social order validates itself, insulates itself from criticism, and even divinizes itself by making its prevailing norms the unsurmountable standards of evaluation.[9] Second, when ethics is equated with prevailing social norms, ethical selfhood is reduced to conformism.

Neither of these charges is plausible in the case of Confucius (which is not to say that they have not been leveled). First, Confucius appeals not to prevailing social practices and standards but to those purportedly observed in the time of the early Zhou Dynasty, to his mind a golden age when the *Dao* (Way) had prevailed. Far from an endorsement of the status quo, Confucius's advocacy for reinstitution of proper ritual practice represents a sharp critique of current social arrangements.[10] Second, Confucius is no friend of unimaginative social conformity. Rather, he labels plodding ethical conformists as "village worthies" who are thieves of virtue (*Analects* 17.13).[11] In

9. Merold Westphal captures this Kierkegaardian theme nicely when he writes, "From the religious point of view, the ethical is the tendency of every society to absolutize itself, identifying as good those who meet its expectations and as evil those who are so irreverent as to defy them." Westphal, *On Becoming a Self,* p. 27.

10. While Confucius criticizes the present by holding it to the standards of an idealized past, he resists falling into reactionary conservatism. In *Analects* 9.3, we see that Confucius is quite willing to follow the majority in altering a ritual when the alteration preserves the real meaning of the ritual (substituting silk for hemp in ceremonial caps) but not when the alteration subverts the ritual's meaning (as when the majority cease to bow before ascending to the ruler's platform). For further discussion of the balance of innovation and conservatism in Confucius, see ch. 4 of Herbert Fingarette, *Confucius: The Secular as Sacred* (Prospect Heights, IL: Waveland, 1998).

11. All quotations from the *Analects* are taken from Edward Slingerland's translation, *Analects: With Selections from Traditional Commentaries* (Indianapolis: Hackett, 2003).

his personal life, he defied conventional moral judgment by giving his own daughter in marriage to a convicted criminal whom Confucius regarded as innocent but for whom the social stigma of conviction was nonetheless dire (*Analects* 5.1).[12]

Qualified Parallels between Confucius and Ethics as Obligatory Neighbor Love

There is also a resonance between Confucius and the fourth Kierkegaardian sense of the ethical: the ethic of neighbor love presented in *Works of Love*. Clearly, Confucius would want nothing to do with the nonpreferential love Kierkegaard describes since Confucian ethics is based on fine discriminations as to the particular sorts of actions and affections due to the various people in our lives based on our specific relations to each other. This is especially evident in the criticisms that later Confucian thinkers, such as Mengzi, direct against Moism's proposals of universal, nonpreferential love.[13] That said, *Works of Love* seconds Confucius's idea that appropriate feelings, not just actions, may be obligatory. Commenting grimly on the state of filial piety in his day, Confucius says, "Nowadays 'filial' means simply being able to provide one's parents with nourishment. But even dogs and horses are provided with nourishment. If you are not respectful, wherein lies the difference?" (*Analects* 2.7). While respect is not identical to love (though presumably the two are compatible), this passage does indicate that filiality involves an appropriate set of feelings and motives as well as specified actions, a point sympathetic to Kierkegaard's exegesis of the biblical passage, "You shall love."[14]

Substantive Parallels between Confucius and Kierkegaard's Two Intermediate Senses of the Ethical

The limited resonances between Confucius and Kierkegaard's first and fourth construals of the ethical are intriguing but do not justify drawing any conclu-

---

12. Slingerland comments, "In giving his daughter in marriage to a former criminal, Confucius is flouting conventional mores and making a powerful statement concerning the independence of true morality from conventional social judgments." Slingerland, in *Analects*, p. 39.

13. See Mengzi, Book 7A: 45.

14. For example, after discussing the duty to experience sorrow, Kierkegaard writes, "So it is with love. You do not have the right to become insensitive to this feeling" (*WL*, 43).

sions about the religious character of Confucius's ethical thought. Turning now to the intermediate senses of the ethical, I hope to show much deeper resonances that will underwrite suggestions on that issue. Though there are significant differences between these two Kierkegaardian senses, one designating a specific stage contrasted with the aesthetic and religious stages, the other designating generally a self's taking an infinite interest in its own actuality, the two senses share a common core. In this section, I will succinctly characterize this shared understanding of the ethical and then show that it is strikingly resonant with Confucius.

William's and Climacus's Shared Conception of Ethics

Pinning down what Kierkegaard means by "the ethical" in *Either/Or* and *Postscript* is no easy matter, in part because he careens between excessive specificity and excessive generality. In the first of the two long letters that make up Volume Two of *Either/Or,* Judge William, Kierkegaard's spokesperson for ethical existence, discourses at length on marriage as the paradigm of ethical existence. After such a narrow focus, the judge devotes his second letter to a highly generalized account of ethical existence in terms of the self's choice of itself. In *Postscript,* Climacus follows the lead of the second letter, describing the ethical primarily in generalized terms as subjectivity, infinite interest in one's own actuality, pathos, and appropriation.

Another reason it is difficult to pin down Kierkegaard's treatment of ethics is that it refuses to fit into the familiar categories of consequentialism and deontologism that have so dominated philosophical ethics. He is emphatically not a consequentialist; both William and Climacus define the ethical over against views that emphasize results, in the first case aesthetic existence and in the second a speculative fascination with world history. Climacus is especially forceful in his rejection of results: "True ethical enthusiasm consists in willing to the utmost of one's capability, but also, uplifted in divine jest, in never thinking whether or not one thereby achieves something" (*CUP* 1:135).[15] William similarly writes, "So I surrender all that importance

---

15. Another relevant passage on Climacus's disregard for results reads, "The ethical already establishes a kind of contrast relation between the outer and the inner, inasmuch as it places the outer in the sphere of indifference. The outer as material for action is a matter of indifference, because the purpose is what is ethically accentuated; the outcome as the externality of action is unimportant, because the purpose is what is ethically accentuated" (*CUP* 1:296-97n).

that often enough throws its weight around in life; I do my work and do not waste time calculating whether I am accomplishing anything. What I accomplish accompanies my work as my good fortune; I certainly dare to rejoice in it but do not dare attribute it entirely to myself" (*EO* 2:295). These dismissive comments about results point toward fundamental principles of the ethical for Kierkegaard and his pseudonyms: ethics concerns an inner realm of responsibility and equality. Results depend on factors beyond the agent's voluntary control, in terms of both talents and circumstances. The genuinely ethical is that which each of us is equally in a position to accomplish: to will to do what is right. For Kierkegaard, the concept of moral luck is an oxymoron.[16]

This rejection of results and celebration of inner resolve leads us to expect a deontological ethics, but these texts are strikingly free of references either to moral rules or to principles for selecting practical maxims. Rather, there is a robust emphasis on the way each individual's ethical task arises out of the concrete circumstances of his or her life.[17] Such context-dependency and particularity of obligation are more typical of consequentialism than of deontologism. Further, William and Climacus stress the "how" over the "what" of willing in a way that must disturb deontologists: paralleling Climacus's infamous remark that "truth is subjectivity," William writes, "what is important in choosing is not so much to choose the right thing as the energy, the earnestness, and the pathos with which one chooses" (*EO* 2:167). Clearly, neither William nor Climacus is a garden variety deontologist.[18]

What sort of ethics is this, then? As is widely recognized in recent scholarship, Kierkegaard and his pseudonyms stand in a broadly Aristotelian tradition of thinking of ethics as self-actualization or soul-making.[19] Both

---

16. See Evans, *Kierkegaard's Ethic of Love*, p. 93n.

17. "The ethical immediately embraces the single individual with its requirement that he shall exist ethically; it does not bluster about millions and generations; it does not take mankind at random, any more than the police arrest humankind in general. The ethical deals with human beings and, please note, with each individual" (*CUP* 1:320). It is significant here that Climacus uses the example of the police seeking a particular suspect rather than the standard imagery of a legislature passing laws that are generally binding. Similarly, William writes, "What every human being accomplishes and can accomplish is that he can do *his* task in life" (*EO* 2:295).

18. Evans argues for continuing to see Kierkegaard as a deontologist insofar as his focus is on duty over results, even though that duty cannot be defined in terms of a fixed set of ethical rules. Evans, *Kierkegaard's Ethic of Love*, pp. 99-103.

19. Evans writes, "Formally, the account of the ethical offered by Johannes Climacus seems Aristotelian, in that he sees the ethical task in terms of the actualization of a distinctively

William and Climacus state repeatedly that the key ethical task is becoming the self one is. Judge William writes,

> When around one everything has become silent, solemn as a clear, starlit night, when the soul comes to be alone in the whole world, then before one there appears, not an extraordinary human being, but the eternal power itself, then the heavens seem to open, and the *I* chooses itself or, more correctly, receives itself. . . . He does not become someone other than he was before, but he becomes himself. . . . [E]very human can be this if he so wills it. (*EO* 2:177)

Climacus writes,

> A truly great ethical individuality would consummate his life as follows: he would develop himself to the utmost of his capability. (*CUP* 1:135)

The developmental quality of this ethic gives it a teleological dimension: the self is progressively working toward a goal, namely, its self-development. But the unconditional character of this imperative and the ultimate indifference to external, non-moral results resembles deontologism. The focus on becoming the particular self one is — that is, the imperative to actualize the particular possibilities and answer the particular demands inherent in one's situation — explains the strangely formal quality of these discussions of ethics: since people's situations differ significantly, it is impossible to specify in generic terms what becoming oneself will involve. But several general points about this ethic of self-actualization can be made.

CHOICE

Both William and Climacus see choice as key to the development of moral selfhood. William writes, "'[T]o choose'; it is my watchword, the nerve in my life-view" (*EO* 2:211).[20] Other theories of moral development place emphasis on habituation, intellectual comprehension, and/or emotional attunement, but here the key to becoming oneself is to choose to do so. Such self-choice

---

human potentiality." Evans, *Kierkegaard's Ethic of Love*, p. 87. See also David Gouwens, *Kierkegaard as Religious Thinker* (Cambridge: Cambridge University Press, 1996), p. 11.

20. In his commentary on *Either/Or*, Johannes Climacus affirms this claim by William: "the ethical pathos in Part II [is transformed] into an embracing, with the quiet, incorruptible, and yet infinite passion of resolution, of the ethical's modest task" (*CUP* 1:254).

involves much more than vapid self-affirmation. Since being a moral self involves choosing by reference to moral criteria as opposed to one's immediate inclinations, to choose to be a self is to choose to choose in that distinctive way. It is to choose to view the world in terms of moral categories as opposed to aesthetic categories of preference and prudence. While William's talk of choosing to choose seems to threaten an infinite regression, he is making the crucial point that the ethical self differs from the immediate, aesthetic self in that it consciously and responsibly adopts its criteria for making choices rather than allowing accidents of nature and nurture to determine those criteria.[21] Such choice thus represents the self taking charge of itself and accepting responsibility for itself.

PERVASIVENESS

Such choice radically alters the self, reaching into every dimension of its existence. William and Climacus repeatedly speak of the self as transformed, transfigured, and even transubstantiated by choosing itself and entering into an absolute relation to the absolute good. Climacus writes, "[E]xistential pathos results from the transforming relation of the idea to the individual's existence. If the absolute τέλος [end, goal] does not absolutely transform the individual's existence, then the individual does not relate himself with existential pathos but with esthetic pathos" (*CUP* 1:387). Part of this change is negative in that the self's prior driving motivations are dethroned. But there is a positive dimension as well that comes out especially clearly in Judge William's account of marriage. The precondition of true marriage is immediate love, the spontaneous attraction of two people to each other. This spontaneous love undergoes a radical transformation when the two commit to each other in marriage. William speaks of their love as "lifted up into a higher concentricity" to express this qualitative transformation; he also expresses this change by saying that the wedding vow transforms the love as gift *(Gave)* into love as task *(Opgave)* (*EO* 2:47). What the judge says about the transformation of immediate love into marriage applies equally to the entire facticity of the self: as the self takes itself as it finds itself as its ethical assignment, its whole being is fundamentally transformed.

---

21. For an excellent discussion of this move from choices made on the basis of unchosen criteria to choices made in reference to chosen criteria, see Westphal, *On Becoming a Self,* pp. 101-2.

OPEN-ENDEDNESS

This task of transfiguring oneself into an ethical self is an open-ended, never-completed task. Judge William's selection of marriage as a paradigm of ethical existence makes the lifelong quality of moral commitment especially vivid. Climacus, in turn, describes the task of becoming subjective as "the highest task assigned to every human being, a task that can indeed be sufficient even for the longest life, since it has the singular quality that it is not over until life is over" (*CUP* 1:158).

BEATITUDE

Such ethical transformation of self is the unique route to genuine happiness, and the happiness it affords is secure against all the vicissitudes of life. For William, such happiness is available in the here and now, in the domestic bliss of hearth and home. Since erotic love is, for him, the unsurpassable mode of happiness (that is, the aesthetic at its highest pitch), and since such love is sustained securely only when it is transformed through marriage into duty, there is an essential link between duty and happiness.[22] Climacus speaks of a relation to eternal happiness as transforming this life, but this happiness is prospective; as he puts it, a relationship to eternal happiness manifests itself dialectically in this life as suffering.[23] Despite this difference, the shared conception of the two pseudonyms is that the ethical transformation of the self is the unique basis of genuine beatitude.[24]

Confucius's Parallel Conception of Ethical Selfhood

Now that we have laid out the core conceptions of the ethical shared by Kierkegaard's second and third senses of the ethical, many parallels to Confucius are immediately apparent. The first thing to note is that the basic

22. Though William warns against mysticism, he associates a quasi-mystical experience with the choice of oneself as an ethical self: "When the individual has grasped himself in his eternal validity, this overwhelms him with all its fullness. Temporality vanishes for him. At the first moment, this fills him with an indescribable bliss and gives him an absolute security" (*EO* 2:231).

23. "[B]y *the actuality of the suffering is understood its continuance as essential for the pathos-filled relation to an eternal happiness*" (*CUP* 1:443).

24. William writes, "[A] person's unhappiness never lies in his lack of control over external conditions, since this would only make him completely unhappy" (*EO* 2:188).

shape of Confucius's ethic parallels Kierkegaard's: Confucius espouses neither a consequentialist nor a deontological ethics but rather an ethic focused
on moral self-cultivation. When questions arise about the utility of ritual
practice or study, Confucius invokes the inherent value of these activities
apart from any question of results. For example, when disciples challenge the
traditional monthly lamb sacrifice (*Analects* 3.17) and three-year mourning
practice (*Analects* 14.40 and 17.21) as impractical and wasteful, Confucius
rejects their framing the question in terms of results. In opposition to a utilitarian mindset, he states, "The gentleman understands rightness, whereas
the petty person understands profits" (*Analects* 4.16). And, in a wonderfully
lapidary phrase, he states, "A gentleman is not a vessel" (*Analects* 2.12), that
is, is not a tool to perform some specific function. The issue of utilitarian
calculation becomes a great bone of contention between Confucianism and
Moism. Clearly, Confucius is not a consequentialist.[25]

While Confucius might appear to be a deontologist in that he values
adherence to ritual practice without direct reference to external benefits,
he does not really fit that mold. He rejects the idea of an ethics based on
fixed rules or laws as unduly rigid. In one striking passage, Confucius gives
contradictory guidance to two different disciples. When challenged about
his inconsistency, Confucius points out that one disciple is too cautious and
the other too impetuous, so one needed encouragement to act, the other
restraint (*Analects* 11.22). What matters to Confucius is not the abstract
rightness or wrongness of an action. Rather, actions matter as manifestations of and influences upon the characters of agents. Just as in Kierkegaard,
Confucius's ethic is first and foremost about character formation or, as it
is frequently termed, moral self-cultivation. Philip Ivanhoe discusses the
connection between the Confucian educational program and the goal of
character formation:

> The practice of the rites and the reading of the *Odes* were both pursuits
> with a moral dimension, integral parts of the larger project of self culti-
> vation. The person who successfully completed this process developed an
> enhanced sensitivity in understanding and explaining traditional patterns
> and applying them to actual affairs. Such a person could and would, on

---

25. This is not to say that he is indifferent to consequences. His deep concern for the well-
being of the people lies constantly in the background of his thought, but he is convinced that
what will actually improve the conditions of ordinary people is a non-utilitarian commitment
to ritual practice and moral self-cultivation on the part of the leaders of the state.

occasions when the situation warrants, depart from the traditional forms in order to realize the greater goal that these patterns were designed to achieve. The practices of Confucian moral self cultivation were not designed to blindly *habituate* people to virtue, and though their full realization would, under normal circumstances, result in a variety of both material and psychological goods, they could not be cultivated solely with the aim of acquiring such goods. The pursuit must be as an *expression* of who one is, a follower of the Way.[26]

The Confucian model of moral self-cultivation unquestionably parallels three of the four salient features of the Kierkegaardian model of ethical selfhood: pervasiveness, open-endedness, and beatitude.

PERVASIVENESS

The Confucian project of moral self-cultivation aims at a thoroughgoing reworking of the self, one that radically transforms every aspect of life. Joel Kupperman points out that whereas Western philosophical ethics tends to focus on life's "big moments" that present dramatic moral challenges, leaving the rest of life as an "ethical free-play zone," Confucianism cultivates a pervasive style: by thoroughly mastering ritual practice, all of one's actions become both correct and natural.[27] While Kupperman works to make Confucius's vision of pervasive self-cultivation invitingly plausible, Robert Eno highlights its strangeness to modern Western sensibilities:

> The varied syllabus of the Ruist school revolved around the theory and practice of *li,* and the end goal of self-cultivation was the complete ritualization of personal conduct.
>
> This call for complete self-stylization was the aspect of early Ruist thought and practice that most clearly distinguished Ruism from other philosophical schools. Ruists advocated a totally choreographed lifestyle,

26. Philip J. Ivanhoe, *Confucian Moral Self Cultivation,* 2nd ed. (Indianapolis: Hackett, 2000), pp. 7-8. Interestingly, in a book comparing Kierkegaard and Zhuangzi, Philip Ivanhoe and Karen Carr describe Kierkegaard's ethics in very similar terms, speaking of self-cultivation and personal development, but without noting a parallelism to Confucianism. Karen Carr and Philip Ivanhoe, *The Sense of Anti-Rationalism: The Religious Thought of Zhuangzi and Kierkegaard* (New York: Seven Bridges Press, 2000), pp. 78-79.

27. Joel Kupperman, "Naturalness Revisited," in *Confucius and the Analects: New Essays,* ed. Bryan van Norden (Oxford: Oxford University Press, 2002), p. 40.

where the formalities of ritual guided one's actions from one's first step outdoors in the morning to the time one lay down at night. The totality of the imperative cannot be underestimated [*sic*]. In the Analects, Confucius urges his disciple Yen Yuan not to see, hear, say, or do anything that is not *li*.[28]

While Eno's portrait of the Ruist community is perhaps extreme, a reading of Book 10 of the *Analects* confirms the pervasiveness of the ritual program of the Confucian community.

OPEN-ENDEDNESS

To take on the task of Confucian moral self-cultivation is to take on a strenuous, lifelong task. Even Yan Hui, Confucius's favorite disciple who learned the Way with a unique enthusiasm and ease, laments, "The more I look up at it, the higher it seems; the more I delve into it, the harder it becomes. Catching a glimpse of it before me, I then find it suddenly at my back" (*Analects* 9.11). Several passages later, the Master compares the task of self-cultivation to building a mountain with baskets of earth: "if I stop even one basketful of earth short of completion, then I have stopped completely" (*Analects* 9.19). In a famous autobiographical passage, Confucius does state that following the Way became easier and more spontaneous as he grew older (*Analects* 2.4), but there is no sense that he or anyone could possibly complete the task of moral self-cultivation.[29]

BEATITUDE

As Confucius sees it, Goodness *(ren)* is both the necessary and the sufficient condition of true happiness. It is necessary since, "Without Goodness, one cannot remain constant in adversity and cannot enjoy enduring happiness" (*Analects* 4.2). It is also sufficient: "Having in the morning heard that the Way was being put into practice, I could die that day without regret" (*Analects* 4.8).

28. Robert Eno, *The Confucian Creation of Heaven: Philosophy and the Defense of Ritual Mastery* (Albany: State University of New York Press, 1990), p. 31. Surely, Eno means to say either that the totality of the imperative cannot be *overestimated* or that it *should not* be underestimated.

29. One could argue that the sage represents for Confucius a person who has achieved complete moral development, but Confucius repeatedly denies either being or meeting such a sage. The sage represents either an unattainable present ideal or a mythic figure from the distant past.

Certainly, Confucius and his disciples express disappointment over lack of progress in achieving public office and grief over deaths, especially over the untimely death of Yan Hui, but there is a strong sense that one who has embarked seriously on the project of moral self-cultivation has an inner source of satisfaction that is both richer than any non-moral satisfactions and secure against misfortune. Yan Hui is the case in point: "What a worthy man was Yan Hui! Living in a narrow alley, subsisting on a basket of grain and a gourd full of water — other people could not have born[e] such hardship, yet it never spoiled Yan Hui's joy. What a worthy man was Hui!" (*Analects* 6.11).

CHOICE

While there is clear parallelism on three of the four highlighted points, there seems to be radical contrast on the fourth point, choice. Where Kierkegaard continually highlights the role of choice in both his titles *(Either/Or)* and his key concepts (choosing oneself, the leap of faith), Herbert Fingarette makes Confucius's silence about such fundamental choice a distinguishing feature of his ethics. Given that the dominant metaphor of the *Analects* is that of traveling a road, the Way *(Dao),* Fingarette takes it as significant that Confucius makes no use of the metaphor of a crossroads, a metaphor featured in Western ethical thought in general and Kierkegaard in particular. Fingarette opens his chapter, "A Way without a Crossroads," with a strong statement that the absence of this metaphor pervasively shapes Confucius's ethics, setting it in sharp contrast with Western ethics:

> Confucius in his teachings in the *Analects* does not elaborate on the language of choice or responsibility as these are intimately intertwined with the idea of the ontologically ultimate power of the individual to select from genuine alternatives to create his own spiritual destiny, and with the related ideas of spiritual guilt, repentance or retribution for such guilt.[30]

30. Fingarette, *Confucius,* p. 18. He reaffirms this judgment in a later response to Henry Rosemont, writing, "[C]hoice, that is, choice as crux, as a crucial reality or value determinant of what are in other respects equally real or equally valid alternatives, is simply absent in respect to the *li* in its entirety." Herbert Fingarette, "Response to Professor Rosemont," *Philosophy East and West* 28, no. 4 (1978): 511. A passage that seems to point toward Fingarette's reading is *Analects* 6.17, where the Master says, "Who is able to leave a room without going out through the door? How is it, then, that no one follows the way?" Under typical conditions, none of us debates whether to exit through the door or to climb out the window. The door is the obvious correct means of egress. Similarly, following the Way is the single correct manner of living, so

If Fingarette's reading stands, the gulf between Kierkegaard and Confucius on ethics is too great for parallels to be other than incidental, and my proposal to use Kierkegaard's various senses of the ethical as a means of assessing the religious dimension of Confucius's ethics is inappropriate.[31] On closer inspection, however, the gulf is much less wide than Fingarette makes it seem, and significant parallels between Confucius and Kierkegaard emerge even on this contested issue of choice.

First, there is more choice in Confucius than Fingarette makes out. Even if the Way provides unambiguous guidance for one who has adopted it as one's guide, to adopt it as one's guide is itself a choice. In his terse autobiography, Confucius states, "At fifteen, I set my mind upon learning" (*Analects* 2.4). Since learning *(xue)* designates not just intellectual assent but actual behavior, setting his mind upon learning is effectively resolving to shape his life by following the Way. Such a resolution is a fundamental choice: those who make it are on the road to becoming gentlemen; those who do not become small men. Though Henry Rosemont expresses substantial agreement with Fingarette on the issue of choice, he does qualify that agreement by noting this fundamental choice: "If it is our concern to give a description of Confucian ethics, of course, we will have to say that there is at least one basic choice which the follower of the Way must make, namely, the choice to have the *li* govern his or her actions."[32] Similarly, Lee Yearley writes,

> Fingarette does, I think, grasp a genuinely important aspect of Confucius' world view — an aspect that is alien to many contemporary understandings. I believe, however, that it is important to see that a kind of choice

---

there is no need for anguished, Hamlet-like choices. Henry Rosemont gives an admirably clear statement of this view in his review article of Fingarette's book: "[T]here can be no concept of moral choice or moral conflict [in Confucius], because in our terms any action A_1 will be moral if and only if it is in accordance with *li*. It follows that any action A_2 which is incompatible with A_1 cannot be in accordance the *li*, and hence A_2 must be, by definition, an immoral action. Thus the Confucian position does not allow for there being two or more morally viable options open in any given situation, and consequently there can be no situation which would involve genuine moral conflict or moral choice." Henry Rosemont, "Review Article: Confucius — The Secular as Sacred," *Philosophy East and West* 26, no. 4 (1976): 468.

31. After noting parallels between William and Confucius, Rosemont follows Fingarette in making choice the fundamental point of difference between the two. He writes, "[I]t begins to become clear how very far apart the Master is from Kierkegaard, for if there is only one Way, then there can be no freedom, in Kierkegaard's sense, to *choose* among a multiplicity of ways." Rosemont, "Kierkegaard and Confucius," pp. 204-5.

32. Rosemont, "Review Article: Confucius," p. 470.

does play a crucial role for Confucius. Even though the context for choice is presupposed and, more important, even though there is no "crossroads," one must nevertheless make a genuine *existentiell* choice or commitment to follow the Confucian Way. . . . For Confucius, then, we must make a reflexive commitment to the Way if we are genuinely to follow it.[33]

Just as recent Confucian scholarship has qualified Fingarette's radical denial of choice, recent Kierkegaard scholarship calls for a more moderate reading of Kierkegaard on choice. This rethinking is largely in response to Alasdair MacIntyre's interpretation of Kierkegaard as a proponent of criterionless choice in *After Virtue*.[34] Of these reappraisals, Edward Mooney's nuanced interpretation of Judge William on self-choice is especially relevant. Mooney argues that our tendency to think of choice as selection between available options blinds us to the relevant sense of choice for William: embrace.

In the milieu of industrial-bureaucratic society, the domain of free activities is modeled on selective choice. In politics, one chooses (or votes) for the one policy or candidate over another; in relationships, one "shops" for the right partner. Everything from recreational vehicles to lifestyles to religions can be presented as choice-options for autonomous agents. . . .

Yet clearly my self is not among several *items on display* awaiting my appropriation. . . . [T]he relevant volition seems more akin to willingness or readiness for embrace than to selective choice.[35]

William finds himself thrown into the world, given a complex but thoroughly contingent identity. His choice of himself is not an arbitrary selec-

---

33. Lee Yearly, "An Existentialist Reading of Book 4 of the Analects," in van Norden, ed., *Confucius and the Analects,* p. 253. In the same vein, Tu Wei-Ming writes, "Since being religious is tantamount to learning to be fully human, we are not religious by default but by choice. . . . We are by nature religious but we must make an existential decision to initiate our ultimate self-transformation." Tu Wei Ming, *Centrality and Commonality: An Essay in Confucian Religiousness* (Albany: State University of New York Press, 1989), p. 118. Roger Ames and David Hall go even further in locating genuine choice in Confucius by playing up the extent to which the exemplary person creatively and responsively adapts ritual practice to the particular situation. See especially ch. 2 in *Thinking through Confucius* (Albany: State University of New York Press, 1987).

34. See John J. Davenport and Anthony Rudd, eds., *Kierkegaard After MacIntyre: Essays on Freedom, Narrative, and Virtue* (Chicago: Open Court, 2001).

35. Edward Mooney, *Selves in Discord and Resolve: Kierkegaard's Moral-Religious Psychology from "Either/Or" to "Sickness unto Death"* (New York: Routledge, 1996), pp. 18-19.

tion between equivalent options so much as the taking up of this self in all its facticity as his ethical project. As such, the parallel to Confucius is striking. By sheer happenstance, Confucius was born in the state of Lu, the ancestral fiefdom of the Duke of Zhou. Like every other native of Lu, part of Confucius's given identity is this traditional tie to values and practices of the Zhou Dynasty. But Confucius does not passively receive the influence of that tradition; rather, he embraces it, immerses himself in it, regards it appreciatively, presents it attractively to others, and refashions it for new circumstances. This responsible embrace of his given circumstances is just what Judge William means by self-choice.

A final comment on the idea that choice is the point of fundamental disparity between Kierkegaard and Confucius: as noted, Fingarette makes much of the fact that, though Confucius thinks of ethical life in terms of traveling a road, he never invokes the metaphor of a crossroads, thinking of the Way as the single right way to move ahead. Though William does invoke the metaphor of a crossroads, he asserts that there is a single right way to go when one comes to it. Just after speaking of "moments . . . when I stood at a crossroads, when my soul was made ripe in the hour of decision," William writes that if one invests such moments with absolute significance, the way ahead is clear: "[T]here is only one situation in which these words [either/or] have absolute meaning — namely, every time truth, justice, and sanctity appear on one side and lust and natural inclinations, dark passions and perdition on the other side" (*EO* 2:157). This is crucial in William's project of bringing the aesthete (designated only as A) to whom he is writing over to ethical existence. If William can put A in the position of choosing between aesthetic and ethical existence, then, William believes, A will unavoidably choose ethical existence, just as a person who chooses ethically unavoidably chooses right over wrong. William, for all his talk of choice, does not attend to moral dilemmas, saying rather, "simplicity is the primary characteristic of everything ethical" (*EO* 2:219). For William, as for Confucius, there is a clear right way to live.

From Parallelism to Disagreement: William and Climacus on the Religious Dimension of Ethics

Having sketched the vision of ethical existence shared by William and Climacus and having shown significant parallelisms between that vision and Confucius, I turn now to the religious dimensions of these parallel visions.

While William and Climacus broadly agree in their understandings of ethical existence, that agreement breaks down when we turn to the question of the ethical self's relation to God. Some have misconstrued Kierkegaard's distinction between ethical and religious stages of existence as indicating that the former is purely secular.[36] But Judge William makes frequent reference to God, and that reference is essential to his distinctive ethical vision.[37] As discussed above, William's key idea is that the ethical self chooses itself, taking its particular circumstances as its ethical vocation. But what makes such self-choice obligatory rather than optional? For William, his givenness is a gift *(Gave)* from God that thereby becomes his task *(Opgave)*. While he highlights this complex of ideas in his discussion of marriage, it is especially clear in his reminiscences about his earliest encounters with duty. When William reached school age, his father enrolled him in school, gave him his books, and told him he was to be in the top three in his class at the end of the month (*EO* 2:267-69). The father then left it up to William to fulfill the assigned task. What emerges in this anecdote is an ultimate authority bringing an ethical self into existence, equipping it with the means to carry out its task, and then assigning the task. It is then up to the ethical self to perform the task. The underlying assumption here and in Judge William's entire discussion is that selves have the power to fulfill the ethical demands placed on them if they choose. Climacus puts this succinctly when he labels the ethical stage as "action-victory" in contrast to religious existence, which he labels "suffering" (*CUP* 1:294). Religious existence is defined by suffering because it is painfully aware of its ultimate inability to fulfill the demands of ethics; for the religious self, it is always already too late for the sort of moral self-satisfaction and confidence that drips from Judge William's letters.[38] Climacus writes,

36. For example, Henry Rosemont writes, "the ethical life is altogether secular, and therefore can offer us no clear path to the sacred." Rosemont, "Kierkegaard and Confucius," p. 203.

37. George B. Connell, "Judge William's Theonomous Ethics," in *Foundations of Kierkegaard's Vision of Community,* ed. George B. Connell and C. Stephen Evans (Atlantic Highlands: Humanities, 1991), pp. 110-29.

38. Evans writes, "The difference between the ethical and religious spheres . . . has little to do with belief or lack of belief in God. Rather, it has to do with the self-confidence of the persons who are seeking to become themselves, their conviction that the task is one that can be successfully carried off. The religious sphere begins when an individual acquires a sense that the demands of the ethical life are ones that cannot possibly be fulfilled." Evans, *Kierkegaard's Ethic of Love,* p. 49. See also Merold Westphal's discussion of the difference between William's and Climacus's understandings of repentance. Westphal, *On Becoming a Self,* p. 26.

Even at the moment the task is assigned, something is already wasted, because there is an "in the meantime" and the beginning is not promptly made. . . . And just as the beginning is about to be made here, it is discovered that, since meanwhile time has been passing, a bad beginning has been made and that the beginning must be made by becoming guilty, and from that moment the total guilt, which is decisive, practices usury with new guilt. (*CUP* 1:526)

These two versions of ethical existence parallel the two brothers in Jesus' parable of the prodigal son. Both relate to a divine father figure, but where Judge William stands before the father with the ethical self-assurance of the older brother, Climacus's religious self always knows itself as the wayward son, returning home after having squandered all. These two modes of ethical existence are, then, also two modes of religious consciousness.

Aligning Confucius: Does Confucius Parallel William or Climacus (or Neither)?

Having shown above that Confucius's understanding of ethical existence substantially parallels the understanding shared by William and Climacus, I turn in this final section to the question, Where does Confucius stand on the issue that separates William and Climacus, namely, the issue of the moral competence of human agents? Given his program of moral cultivation, the issue of the human moral capacity is unavoidable for Confucius, though, as we shall see, he sends mixed signals on this question in the *Analects*. For William and Climacus, the issue of moral capacity is as much a religious as an ethical question: two fundamentally different conceptions of human relation to the divine are implicit in the two different assessments of our moral competence. Can the same be said of Confucius? If we read Confucius as a nonreligious ethicist, then this aspect of the disagreement between William and Climacus drops out of the picture as irrelevant. But insofar as we regard Confucius as a religious thinker, insofar as we discern a religious dimension to his program of moral cultivation, placing him in reference to William and Climacus can help us discern *what sort* of religious thinker he is. That is, we can place him on Kierkegaard's scale of varying conceptions of the relation between religion and ethics identified above.

An obstacle to placing Confucius on this Kierkegaardian scale is that Kierkegaard works with a resolutely theistic conception of religion, while it is not at all settled that Confucius works within a theistic worldview. Luckily, I do not need to settle that issue for the purposes of this discussion. Since there is broad recognition that religious consciousness is a wider phenomenon than theistic belief, there is no a priori reason why Kierkegaard's scale cannot be applied beyond the scope of theistic religion. Robert Louden offers a useful characterization of Confucius that separates his status as a religious thinker from the issue of his theism and opens the way to placing him on the Kierkegaardian scale:

> Confucius' moral outlook is religious (though again not theistic) in the straightforward sense that he holds that moral standards are dependent on something outside of us, something bigger than human nature — or culture — that is much more than a human or even a rational construction. Additionally, to count as religious this source of value that is outside of us must be felt as holy or sacred. The sense of awe that Confucius experiences in contemplating *tiān* (compare [*Analects*] 16:8) meets this basic description of religious experience.[39]

If we accept Louden's encompassing view of what it is to be religious (whether we accept his denial of Confucius's theism or not), and if I have succeeded in showing that Confucius broadly shares an understanding of ethical selfhood with William and Climacus, then it makes sense to ask whether Confucius's religious consciousness more closely resembles that of William or that of Climacus. As Confucius experiences the ethical demand with a sense of numinous awe, does he hear a call to action to which he confidently responds or does he feel crushed by the infinitude of the claim placed upon him? Whether he shares their theism or not, does he share the moral self-confidence and corresponding religious sensibility of the former or the deep sense of inadequacy of the latter? Put in starkly Kierkegaardian terms, is Confucius a sort of Chinese Judge William (whose religious sensibility amounts to vesting the achievable goal of moral self-cultivation with a numinous aura), or should we see Confucius as an example of Religiousness A (whose awareness of the numinous humbles his sense of his own adequacy, even while inspiring him to strive unreservedly)?

In terms of both style and substance, there are a host of parallels between William and Confucius. Neither presents a theory of ethics; rather,

---

39. Robert B. Louden, "'What Does Heaven Say?': Christian Wolff and Western Interpretations of Confucian Ethics," in van Norden, ed., *Confucius and the Analects*, p. 81.

both speak as individuals to individuals, admonishing them to moral self-exertion. Both admonish by pointing to paradigmatic individuals who model the ethical life. Both strike a resolutely serious tone (that lends itself to ridicule by others who look at life with a more ironic eye). Both are, in some sense, state functionaries, Confucius more by aspiration than achievement, William by virtue of his position as a lower-level judge. And both conceive of moral self-cultivation in terms of specific roles and relationships, especially filiality in the case of Confucius and marriage in the case of the judge. Further, both see the ethically developed self as harmoniously uniting aesthetic, ethical, and religious dimensions of life. In contrast, Johannes Climacus is a sardonic social outsider who would want nothing to do with responsible official positions. His discussion of ethics is much more abstract, addressed to a generic reader, and prone to emphasize an ascetic break with one's desires. Undoubtedly, Judge William recalls Confucius much more than does Climacus. What is more, the judge cites with approval a Chinese proverb with clear Confucian themes: "There is profound meaning in the Chinese proverb: Raise your children well, and you will come to know what you owe your parents" (*EO* 2:76). The issue, however, is not broad similarity but the specific question of moral self-assurance. Does Confucius share William's confidence, or is he overwhelmed, as is Climacus, by the infinity of the ethical task?

Unfortunately, one finds many passages in the *Analects* that apparently confirm both of these conflicting sensibilities. A number of passages stress how close and available Goodness is for anyone ready to grasp it: "The Master said, 'Is Goodness really so far away? If I simply desire Goodness, I will find it is already here'" (*Analects* 7.30). But many other passages stress the elusiveness of the goal: "With a great sigh Yan Hui lamented, 'The more I look up at it the higher it seems, the more I delve into it, the harder it becomes. Catching a glimpse of it before me, I then find it suddenly at my back'" (*Analects* 9.11).[40] Especially striking are two pairs of passages in which Confucius sends diametrically opposed signals about moral success. In *Analects* 9.16, Confucius lists a variety of appropriate responses to ethical demands and then reports, "these sorts of things present me with no trouble." This reflects his sense that as one progresses in the project of moral self-cultivation, moral response becomes increasingly effortless and

---

40. Slingerland's comment on *Analects* 5.8 that Goodness appears to Confucius as a "dimly perceived and ever-receding goal" applies equally to Yan Hui's lament (Slingerland, in *Analects*, p. 42).

spontaneous.[41] But in *Analects* 9.17, he wistfully observes a river, noting that "it flows on like this, never stopping day or night." Commentary by Zhu Xi takes the steady flow of the river as a metaphor for the moral resolve of the ideal student, but Confucius laments in *Analects* 5.11, "I have yet to meet anyone who is genuinely resolute." There is a similar tension between *Analects* 12.3 and 12.4. In *Analects* 12.3, the Master explains that the Good person is hesitant to speak about Goodness because it is "so difficult," but in *Analects* 12.4 he describes the gentleman as free of anxiety and fear since when he looks within himself he finds no faults.

The tension between these passages reflects Confucius's project. He is not trying to state a theory of ethics but to prompt moral self-cultivation on the part of his disciples. As such, he needs to ward off both complacency and despair by stressing difficulty or feasibility as the case requires. So, it is not possible to align Confucius with either William or Climacus simply by producing "proof texts" from the *Analects*. Rather, such an alignment requires a more general sense of Confucius's moral vision. As I see it, while Confucius has a deep sense of the difficulty of a life committed to the Way, he never experiences the radical incapacity and guilt central to Climacus's account. Stated positively, the central article of faith in Confucian spirituality, the conviction that keeps Confucius going when he meets frustration after frustration, is that humans genuinely possess an aptitude for moral development. In discussing Confucian spirituality, Tu Wei-Ming writes,

> Implicit in this Confucian faith in the transformability of the human condition through individual and communal effort is the realization that we must rely upon our humanity to save us. Despite the human predicament of being earthbound and thus never totally liberated from a sense of unfulfillment, wastefulness and, indeed, self-destruction, human nature is intrinsically good.[42]

---

41. See Edward Slingerland, *Effortless Action: Wu-wei as Conceptual Metaphor and Spiritual Ideal in Early China* (Oxford: Oxford University Press, 2003).

42. Tu Wei-Ming, *Centrality and Commonality*, p. 101. Tu Wei-Ming's discussion is of *The Doctrine of the Mean* rather than of the *Analects* directly, but it is plausible to argue that the meaning of the *Analects* itself is determined as much by the ongoing tradition that develops from it as by any sort of authorial intent. Tu Wei-Ming's affirmation of the goodness of human nature places him clearly in the Mencian mainline of Confucianism. Mengzi's optimism about human predisposition to moral development is conventionally set over against Xunzi's pessimism. But even Xunzi's pessimism is not ultimately parallel to Climacus's notion of moral incapacity. Xunzi believes that humans can achieve moral development, but it will not happen

Tu Wei-Ming sets this Confucian understanding over against the Judeo-Christian tradition as described by Reinhold Niebuhr. The passage he quotes from Niebuhr parallels Climacus's sense of human moral incapacity:

> The order of human existence is too imperiled by chaos, the goodness of man too corrupted by sin, and the possibilities of man too obscured by natural handicaps to make human order and human possibilities solid bases of the moral imperative.[43]

If Tu Wei-Ming is correct to set Confucian moral self-confidence in contrast to an Augustinian sense of human moral incapacity, and I think he is, then plainly Confucius's vision of ethical existence is much more closely parallel to Judge William's than it is to Climacus's. By seeing this parallelism and thereby placing Confucius on Kierkegaard's scale of versions of the relationship between religious faith and moral duty, we can avoid falling into the trap of binary thinking. Rather than asking starkly whether Confucius is a religious ethicist or not, we can focus on the more illuminating question of what type of religious ethicist he is. If my placement of him on the Kierkegaardian scale is correct, then we can say broadly that he, with Judge William, encounters the divine fundamentally in the project of moral self-cultivation rather than as a transcendent other, and that he, like Judge William, experiences this encounter as a call to self-initiated action rather than as an unsettling question about the self's purported autonomy.

---

spontaneously. Rather, it is up to society coercively to impose *li* on its members. Needless to say, Climacus does not call for any such program of socially imposed moral formation.

43. Tu Wei-Ming, *Centrality and Commonality*, p. 68, quoting Reinhold Niebuhr, *An Interpretation of Christian Ethics* (New York: Harper and Brothers, 1935), p. 50.

Conclusion

The foregoing study of Kierkegaard and the question of religious diversity are, in a sense, anachronistic. From our perspective in a globalized, post-colonial, diasporic, multicultural world, the issue of the plurality of religious faiths looms large. In contrast, Kierkegaard's immediate context was the religious homogeneity of nineteenth-century Denmark. He targeted the smug complacency of that comfortably uniform religious culture, and so our question — how to think about and respond to a world of great religious diversity — is antipodean to his overt concern.

This study has been a test of the conviction that Kierkegaard's thought and writings represent a living legacy, not a fixed set of convictions but an adaptable set of tools, better, of lenses, that remain useful and relevant as we confront the dilemmas of our own time and circumstances. In the preceding chapters, I have worked through each of the four key philosophical issues that Philip Quinn identifies as implicated in religious diversity: conflicting truth-claims, religiously inspired and authorized violence, the relation between religion as a generic category and particular religions, and comparative study of religions and religious figures. When we put these questions to Kierkegaard, we find that he has much to say that is relevant and illuminating. So, in another sense, the issue of religious diversity, far from being an anachronism, is there right beneath the surface in Kierkegaard's texts even if it isn't explicitly presented as such. Often, I have gone beyond what the texts say explicitly on Quinn's four issues. Given the ambiguity and multivocality of Kierkegaard's texts, I feel sure that others could and, I hope, will draw forth other "Kierkegaardian" perspectives on religious diversity than I have in this study. There are already a number of published studies that manifest the wide range of ways Kierkegaard can be brought to bear on such issues, and I am quite aware that the suggestions I've drawn forth from Kierkegaard's texts reflect my own convictions and concerns. That said, there are a number of widely acknowledged key features of Kierkegaard's thought and writings that make them especially relevant to the issue of religious diversity.

First, Kierkegaard stresses that we live in a religiously ambiguous world. Against modernist impulses to find certainty, Kierkegaard insists that we all face key questions in life with incomplete and ambivalent evidence. Just as suffering is a fundamentally ambiguous feature of our world, calling some toward God and calling God into question for others, so religious diversity is a key part of the religious ambiguity of our world. For many, the coexistence of multiple faiths discredits religion, but for many others the ubiquity and rich variety of responses to the divine testify to its reality. As we wrestle with the ambiguous realities of religious diversity, Kierkegaard offers us a body of writings that accentuate life's ambiguity and offer suggestions about how we might come to terms with that ambiguity rather than futilely striving to escape it.

Second, Kierkegaard's thought and writings are resolutely perspectival. Against persistent philosophical aspirations to rise to a God's-eye view, to a "view from nowhere," Kierkegaard's texts, especially the pseudonymous texts, accentuate the particular existential placement of authors as they observe and comment on life. As people of different faiths engage each other, keeping in mind the significance of perspective is key. Kierkegaard's texts give us exercise in imaginatively identifying with a variety of perspectives. That capacity for empathetic understanding is crucial to healthy and respectful coexistence among people of diverse religious convictions. But even as his texts challenge us to empathize with other perspectives, they also insistently remind us that we all ultimately ask and answer questions from our own particular existential vantage points. Kierkegaard's "take" on religious diversity bears the unmistakable stamp of his own Lutheran Christianity. That usefully reminds all of us who take up this issue today to own our particular perspectives rather than pretending to some sort of neutral vantage point.

Third, Kierkegaard is unequalled as a thinker of paradox, and the issue of religious diversity is rife with paradox. The title of this study, *Kierkegaard and the Paradox of Religious Diversity,* points toward the pervasiveness of paradox as we apply Kierkegaard's thought and writings to the issues of religious diversity. Each of the chapters of this study, including the introduction, confronts a fundamental dialectical opposition, a pair of sharply contrasting affirmations, neither of which can be surrendered but both of which resist "mediation" (à la Hegel). In the introduction, I stressed strong universalist and particularist impulses in Kierkegaard. I traced the origins of this study back to 1983 when I listened to Gene Outka's analysis of those two impulses in *Postscript.* This study can be seen as extending Outka's insight beyond the one text to the whole of the authorship and applying it to the particular problem of religious diversity. What Outka identified as a deep tension between Kierkegaard's commitment to equal ethical and religious opportunity (a universalist motif) and insistence on the distinctive saving presence of the divine in the person of Jesus (a particularist motif) is not a contradiction to be reconciled but a paradox to be maintained. The overarching theme of this study is Kierkegaard's insistence on holding these two ideas in dynamic tension throughout his writings.

Each of the individual chapters has taken up one particular aspect of this root paradox. Chapter 1 focused on the historic Kierkegaard's views of and attitudes toward other religions. Here we find a dialectical tension between the indicative — what Kierkegaard actually thought and said — and the subjunctive — what, given the full context of his commitments, he could and should have said. There are plenty of passages that show a Kierkegaard who is condescending to other faiths, lumping them into just two categories (pagans and Jews) and regarding them as definitively superseded by Christianity. As Peter Tudvad has chronicled at length in *Stadier på Antisemitismens Vej: Søren Kierkegaard og Jøderne,* there are disturbing expressions of anti-Jewish sentiment and manifestations of invidious stereotyping both in Kierkegaard's writings and in his personal life. Whether Kierkegaard stands apart from his contemporaries in this and how deeply such attitudes are rooted in his thought remain topics of dispute. But these disturbing expressions are not the full picture. Alongside them, we find strong expressions of admiration for a number of pagan figures, notably Socrates, just as Abraham, the patriarch of the Jewish people, stands as the iconic "father of faith." Arguably, in his later writings, Kierkegaard retrieves the Jewish Christianity of the book of James, a book relegated to the periphery of the Protestant consciousness by Luther but celebrated by Kierkegaard for its focus on the practice of faith. So, paradoxically, despite his implication in the pervasive anti-Jewish sentiments of his day, Kierkegaard reasserts the deep roots of Christianity within Judaism.

Chapter 2 took up the issue of truth and religious diversity. Religious truth-claims are frequently seen as accentuating conflict between religions, leading many (e.g., John Hick) to argue for some sort of neutralization of such claims as the key to reconciliation among faiths. Kierkegaard, with his parallel concepts of objective and subjective truth, leaves us in a condition of unresolved paradox. On the one hand, and quite unlike Nietzsche, he continues to employ a traditional concept of objective truth as adequation between idea and thing. On this basis, he speaks of some religions, notably paganism, as worship of false and nonexistent gods. But on the other hand, he also famously develops his signature notion of subjective truth, in which the authenticity of one's belief is the locus of its truth. So, alongside an exclusivist, particularist commitment to an objective truth on religious questions, his developed thoughts on subjective truth invite a universalist appreciation of authentic religious commitment in a wide variety of forms. Again, Kierkegaard leaves us with an unresolved paradox.

Chapter 3 engaged the issue of religious violence by taking up the reading of *Fear and Trembling* in the aftermath of 9/11. Kierkegaard's resolve to confront the stark horror of the Akedah, of a divine command that Abraham kill his beloved son, Isaac, cannot but shake us as we read it post-9/11. But the key themes of *Fear and Trembling* — radical hope for restoration of loss and radical individuality before God — place it in a very different spiritual universe than that of today's religious terrorists. Kierkegaard, here and elsewhere, identifies religion with absolute commitment. But the pervasive message of Kierkegaard's authorship is that absolute commitment is manifest not in willingness to *kill* for one's faith but in willingness to *die* for it. His use of Genesis 22 — a text that does apparently valorize willingness to kill — as the center of his discussion of faith in *Fear and Trembling* leaves us, his readers, transfixed before unresolved paradoxes.

Chapter 4 took on the central paradox of universality and particularity by problematizing the category of religion as the genus into which particular religions fall as species. To employ the category of religion itself implicitly asserts the commonality of particular religions, sounding a universalist theme. By speaking of a "religious stage of existence," Kierkegaard acknowledges that commonality. But another particularist voice in Kierkegaard resolutely emphasizes the distinctiveness of Christianity and decries attempts to muddle differences between Christianity and other faiths. As he puts it in the epigram of *Philosophical Fragments*, "better well hanged than ill wed." Again, these two voices are left in paradoxical tension, unresolved.

The final chapter, with its comparison of Kierkegaard and Confucius, engaged a tension inherent in the project of comparative philosophy: the simultaneous recognition of similarity and difference. Such comparison is possible only if two different thinkers or two traditions of thought are sufficiently similar to allow for productive juxtaposition. But such comparison is useful and interesting only to the extent that differences emerge. So comparative philosophy, by its fundamental nature, involves making peace with paradox, thinking two contrasting thoughts at one and the same time.

For Kierkegaard, theory should always ultimately serve practice; thought should always serve life. And so, each of the paradoxes explored in this study finds its real import in the fundamental existential paradox posed by religious diversity: how to be authentically committed to one's own faith while simultaneously engaging respectfully, openly, cooperatively, and appreciatively with people who affirm different or no religious commitments. I opened this study by citing the dire either/or that William Butler Yeats describes in "The Second Coming": "the best lack all conviction while the worst are filled with insolent intensity." Do we face this Hobson's Choice between fervent commitment, which closes us off from real empathy and engagement with people of different faiths, and an openness to other views born of a tentativeness that never commits? Kierkegaard's significance for the issue of religious diversity, I want to argue, is his ability (ironically) to say both/and to the either/or of commitment versus respectful openness. In order to appreciate the ways in which Kierkegaard offers the prospect of holding commitment and openness together, we need first to acknowledge their apparent conflict.

For Kierkegaard, authentic religious faith is "an absolute relation to the absolute." In a manner seldom equaled and never exceeded, he thinks through the implications of God's qualitative difference, of God's utter otherness. A relation with such a God cannot be just one among many aspects of a diverse, balanced life. Rather, such a relationship relativizes everything else in one's life, claiming absolute, uncompromising devotion. It is the pearl of great price for which one sells all one has. Kierkegaard's critique of Christendom focuses precisely on its neutralization of the radical claim of religious faith. In Christendom, one's religious faith is just one among many elements in a rich and satisfying life. As Terry Eagleton puts it, "Societies become secular not when they dispense with religion altogether but when they are no longer especially agitated by it." Privatized and relativized, religion "dwindles to a kind of personal pastime, like breeding gerbils or collecting porcelain."[1] Kierkegaard has no use for that sort of religion. For him, religion is all or nothing, absolute.

But what room does such absolute commitment leave for peaceful, re-

---

1. Terry Eagleton, *Culture and the Death of God* (New Haven: Yale University Press, 2014), p. 1.

spectful, cooperative coexistence with people who don't share that commitment? As I write this conclusion in August of 2014, ISIS (The Islamic State in Iraq and Syria), having seized roughly a third of Iraq and having declared a new caliphate, is killing or driving out all religious minorities from the territory it controls. Ancient Christian communities have fled, and tens of thousands of Yezidis, a Zoroastrian religious minority, are surrounded and without supplies on a hot, arid mountain in northern Iraq. As we watch this horror unfold and think about many similar horrors, it is impossible not to ask whether the logic of absolute commitment leads to such atrocities. Many contemporary readers of Kierkegaard, convinced by his case for the absolute character of religious commitment, but appalled by the extremism such absolute commitment can lead to, draw back from religious faith as inherently dangerous. Others, such as Troels Nørager, call for a modernized, deabsolutized version of faith that domesticates it for life in a pluralistic, secular democracy.

But what if religious faith contains within itself key resources for encouraging respectful, cooperative engagement with others? What if religious faith offers unique disincentives to disrespectful, coercive, damaging interactions? In that case, to abandon or attenuate religious faith may leave us vulnerable to just the sort of horrors blamed on religion. In his authorship, Kierkegaard powerfully develops out of his Christian faith both positive and negative grounds for respectful coexistence with religious Others.

Positively, Kierkegaard's Christian ethics, developed most fully in *Works of Love,* identifies a divine mandate to care for the neighbor, not because that neighbor is like us in some way, but because we are commanded to see each and every neighbor as a beloved child of God. As Stephen Evans puts it, "The first person I see and people I will never meet are equally my neighbor. This means that it is always wrong to draw boundaries for moral concern, to regard the 'Other' who differs from me in family, sex, race, religion, ethnic group, or geographical region as outside the scope of my moral obligation."[2] For Kierkegaard, such nonpreferential love is radically counter-natural. It isn't at all what we are spontaneously inclined to do, and our natural reaction to the command to love the neighbor is scandal and offense. As he sees it, only as a divine command can this demanding, counterintuitive ethic speak to us.

Negatively, Kierkegaard identifies within the Christian faith powerful reasons to avoid the sort of religious imperialism that zealots all too often

---

2. C. Stephen Evans, *Kierkegaard's Ethic of Love: Divine Commands and Moral Theory* (Oxford: Oxford University Press, 2004), p. 301.

seek to impose on others. First, Kierkegaard insists that faith is essentially a relation between an individual and God. Any attempt by a third party to intrude into that relationship is a presumption doomed to failure. Kierkegaard explains his elaborate pseudonymous authorship as an attempt to step aside as any sort of authority. By disappearing as author and authority, leaving only a Cheshire Cat grin behind, Kierkegaard leaves his readers alone, before God. A thinker who went to such lengths to avoid intruding into anyone else's relation with God, a writer who spent his last year battling the religious establishment of his home country, is not someone who can be plausibly invoked in support of the sort of theocracy and religious monoculture that zealots so often desire. Rather, Kierkegaard shows why deep and serious religious faith motivates a deep and serious respect for each person's religious autonomy. Second, Kierkegaard finds both in the Christian faith and in its Jewish origins profound reasons to be humble about any and all purported human knowledge about God. God is utterly other, qualitatively different, and, as such, fundamentally beyond the capacity of human understanding. Religious zealots, who wish to dictate orthodoxy to others, implicitly or explicitly claim certainty on religious matters. For Kierkegaard, such smug self-certainty is radically incompatible with authentic faith.

As I read him, Kierkegaard shows that there are resources within the Christian faith, within authentic Christian commitment, that powerfully motivate respectful, humble, cooperative, and appreciative relations with others who don't share that faith. In contrast to a thinker such as John Hick, who argues for an attenuation of the distinctive features of Christian faith in order to move toward a more generic, less differentiated, and thus less contentious religious life, my sense is that a Kierkegaardian approach to healthy coexistence among the different faiths would call for all religious traditions to embrace their particular faiths in their full specificity. Marilyn McCord Adams argues that the generic theism most frequently debated in analytic philosophy of religion lacks the resources to confront the problem of evil; for her, only the thicker, richer symbolic and conceptual resources of the full Christian tradition can speak effectively to "horrendous evils." In a similar manner, I believe Kierkegaard points us toward seeing that healthy religious coexistence will require each tradition to look deeply into the full treasury of its specific resources to find effective motivations, symbolic vocabulary, and conceptual frameworks. Kierkegaard identifies key elements in Christianity that should motivate respectful coexistence with religious Others. While many of those reasons will have very close analogs in other faiths, especially in the other Western monotheisms, each particular faith will have its own sacred texts, its own traditions, its own sensibilities, its own ethical understandings. From what I know of the major religious traditions, I am convinced that all have rich resources to motivate and conceptualize constructive relations with people of other faiths. That said, each of these traditions clearly also has elements that motivate and validate assertive and oppressive relations with people who don't share its faith. Just as Kierkegaard contended for an authentic Christianity by invoking some elements of the Christian tradition against other elements that he saw as apostate, so people of good faith in each religious tradition will need to invoke the constructive, cooperative elements of those traditions against other elements that push toward conflict, intolerance, disrespect, and persecution.

Index of Names and Subjects

Index of Scripture References